W9-AZV-104

The Beat-Inflation Strategy

How to
Manage Your Money to Profit from the Inflation Cycles

by Roger Klein
and William Wolman

U.S.NEWS & WORLD REPORT BOOKS

How to Open a
SWISS BANK
ACCOUNT

by James Kelder

A division of U.S.News & World Report, Inc.   WASHINGTON, D.C.

U.S.NEWS & WORLD REPORT BOOKS

Directing Editor: Joseph Newman

Editors for this Dual Edition:
Roslyn Grant and Judith Gersten

Dual Edition Books, arranged with the original publishers and the authors,
are created and abridged especially for the U.S.News & World Report
Money Management Library

The Beat-Inflation Strategy
Simon and Schuster
Copyright © 1975 by Roger Klein and William Wolman

How to Open a Swiss Bank Account
Thomas Y. Crowell Company, Inc.
Copyright © 1976 by James Kelder

Copyright © 1976 by U.S.News & World Report, Inc.
2300 N Street, N.W., Washington, D.C. 20037

First Printing, 1976
Second Printing, 1978

All rights reserved, including the right to reproduce
this book or portions thereof in any form.

ISBN 0-89193-422-7

Library of Congress Catalog Card Number 76-14530

Printed in the United States of America

Contents

Contents

HOW TO OPEN A SWISS BANK ACCOUNT

Editor's Note

Inflation continues to afflict us, inspiring an ever-rising tide of books dealing with this national and international ailment. Most of them attempt to diagnose the phenomenon as a disease which can be cured by the particular remedy prescribed by the author. The trouble is that our economic experts, with or without doctorate degrees, seldom agree on the diagnosis and logically disagree on the remedy. This naturally creates uncertainty as to what should or should not be done to contain inflation and raises serious doubts whether anything, in fact, can be done to abolish inflation in our time—or any time.

Another approach to the subject is to accept inflation for what it is—whatever that may be—and to learn to live with it, and even profit by it in the process. Roger Klein and William Wolman, authors of *The Beat-Inflation Strategy*, have taken this approach. And they have developed it with sufficient authority to merit selection for this Dual Edition of the U.S.News & World Report Money Management Library.

The authors have their own theory of what causes inflation. Put simply, it is the cyclical policy of successive governments to pump paper money into the economy so as to stimulate activity and create more jobs. The result is rising prices and rising inflation which governments later attempt to curb by reversing their monetary policy at the risk of inducing a recession. But the real interest in this book lies not in its theory but in the "strategy" it proposes to enable the reader to successfully ride the waves of inflation. One type of investment is made when the money supply is increasing; an entirely different line is taken when the money supply is decreasing.

An altogether different technique for dealing with inflation is to run away from it and find a haven on some foreign shore. That's the course advocated by James Kelder, author of the second book of this volume, *How to Open a Swiss Bank Account*. The country he has chosen as a haven—Switzerland—has achieved such a reputation for monetary integrity that it has become the subject of a number of books extolling its virtues. We have selected Mr. Kelder's as one of the better researched and better written books about Switzerland as a refuge for frightened capital.

As in the case of other volumes in this Dual Edition series of abridged books, our editors have preserved the greater part of the original texts of both titles. Only less essential material has been trimmed to bring the essence of the books into sharper focus.

The Beat-Inflation Strategy

**How to
Manage Your Money to Profit from the Inflation Cycles**

Introduction

Promises, promises, promises, that's all that people will get from those who have the power to end inflation. Congress hasn't done it and is not likely to. Nor is the White House. Nor is the Federal Reserve.

There is only one way to stop inflation: a government policy that deliberately sends the economy into a tailspin and jacks up unemployment. Governments will continue to promise an end to inflation, but governments will not maintain mass unemployment long enough to end inflation. Nor is anyone certain that they should.

Citizens of the Western world have been reasonably sure that they could get a job during the past decade. And jobs are likely to continue to be fairly abundant, at least compared to the pre-World War II economy. What is new is high and volatile inflation. If you have a feeling that inflation has put you on a treadmill and kept you there, you have plenty of company.

The plight of the typical American in his attempt to keep up with rising prices is easy to document. In the United States inflation really took off in 1973. In just two years, 1973 and 1974, American families saw the purchasing power of their financial net worth—the value of their financial assets minus the value of their financial liabilities—drop by $538 billion. This pushed their financial wealth below where it was in 1965. The average man has been working hard for the past nine years and doesn't have much to show for it.

But it doesn't have to be that way. Inflation doesn't destroy the country's wealth. It doesn't change the number of cars the country can produce, the number of houses that can be built, or the amount of food that can be put on the family dinner table. It doesn't destroy the national parks, mountain lakes, or seashore. There is nothing about inflation that changes America's capacity for providing the good life for its citizens.

This means that those Americans who feel inflation is making them poorer and their lives more meager must be doing something wrong. With net worth down $538 billion, millions of families are obviously in this position. There is a feeling of economic hopelessness abroad in the land.

But there is no reason why you have to number yourself among the victims of inflation. Inflation is just another economic force. You are perfectly capable of making it work to your advantage.

This book will tell you how to do it. Inflation does not destroy wealth. Rather, like Robin Hood, rising prices take from some and give to others. Get out of your head the idea that you must be an inflation loser. It is just as easy to be an inflation winner. The book gives simple directions on how to conduct every aspect of your economic life in a way that will allow you to keep ahead of rising prices; how to protect the income and pension benefits you get from your job; and more importantly, how to invest to beat inflation.

When you know how to win, the inflationary investment game is exciting and can be enjoyed. When inflation is perpetual and volatile—and that is the way it is going to be—the investment game will provide much bigger rewards than when there is no inflation. But if you don't understand what inflation does, you are fated to be a bigger loser than when prices are stable.

If you are like most Americans, you have been one of inflation's losers. For most American families, in personal finance, the rules for responsible behavior derive from the "Puritan ethic" classically embodied for the United States in Ben Franklin's *Poor Richard's Almanack:* Work hard, be thrifty, don't borrow.

Poor Richard's rules are fine when prices are stable or falling. But they are a primrose path in a world of permanent inflation. The first thing you've got to do is to break all the habits you've learned from Poor Richard.

Poor Richard's shadow will be hard to cast off, because it falls almost everywhere. He still blares at you from all sides: payroll deductions for series E bonds, automatic plans to transfer money from your checking account to a savings account that "pays the highest interest that the law will allow" (5½ percent or so), the New York Stock Exchange's Monthly Investment Plan, which allows you to buy shares in inflation-devastated companies at high brokerage commissions. All this is embodied in the slogan of the obscure, although important, Clyde Savings and Loan Association of Berwin, Illinois: "Put a little aside at Clyde." And what goes on in the chic upper East Side of Manhattan is not much better, even though George Plimpton may be telling television viewers that the "in thing" to do is to save at the Drydock Savings Bank.

Don't imagine that the so-called pros have done any better. The table on page 14 shows how the 1973-74 inflation wrecked the pros of the investment management business. They're probably managing a good part of your pension fund if you're working for a big company, and include the major New York banks. When it comes to managing money when inflation is rampant, David Rockefeller, chairman of Chase Manhattan, is in the same boat as most other people.

In fact, despite their radical chic, most American economists have been and are likely to continue to be Poor Richard's high priests. Their attitude toward inflation has been to sternly condemn it and to tell policy makers how to stop it. In our weaker moments we still do this. We abhor inflation and would like to see it end. But we now recognize that this moralistic attitude has caused us to fail in our most important job: advising people how best to cope in a difficult world.

Looking back at the inflationary years since the Vietnam War began, most economists would have to confess plenty of failures. First, their moralistic advice made the wish father to

COMMINGLED EQUITY FUNDS
FOR EMPLOYEE BENEFIT ACCOUNTS

Total Rates of Return—With Income Reinvested
(Years Ended 12/31)

	1972	1973	1974
Bank of New York	+19.7	−11.2	−23.3
Bankers Trust	+20.5	−28.4	−30.5
Chemical Bank	+11.4	−16.3	−20.6
Chase Manhattan	+ 6.5	−17.9	−27.3
First National City	+22.4	−18.3	−27.6
Irving Trust	+22.5	−18.4	−29.6
Manufacturers Hanover	+25.1	−20.2	−32.8
Marine Midland N.Y.	+11.8	−21.0	−11.9
Morgan Guaranty*	+25.9	−20.8	−36.1
U.S. Trust	+21.9	−22.9	−34.1
Standard & Poors 500	+18.9	−14.8	−26.5
Dow Jones Industrials	+18.4	−13.6	−23.8

*Morgan's 1974 figure is not from its commingled equity fund. It is the result for a $200-million General Electric Savings and Security Program. It is not necessarily typical of all Morgan pension trust and profit-sharing funds.

Source: *New York Times*, February 20, 1975

the thought. Because they wanted inflation to end, and kept telling the government how to end it, they began to base their practical advice and forecasts on the notion that inflation would end. But prices kept soaring.

The fault does not lie with economics but with the moralistic approach that economists have followed. Practical economics has a lot to say about developing strategies for beating inflation, and we now know that we can best do our job by stating strategies as clearly as possible for all to see. We have cast out the window the inhibitions placed on us by the moralistic tradition of economics. We advise you to do the same thing. Stop worrying and learn to love inflation. You *can* beat inflation.

Although we believe we have cast off the moralistic biases that warp the work of many economists, we also believe we bring to the development of a beat-inflation strategy the best that economic analysis and research have to offer. The reader can rest assured that what we have to say about a practical strategy to beat inflation will also find acceptance in the most rarefied of academic circles. We do not apologize for this; we think it is a plus. Whatever the failures of its practitioners, economic theory has much to say about what to do to beat inflation.

Although we agree that many economists with good credentials have fallen down, some investment advisers with a wide following counsel everyone to place their faith in something hard, such as gold, regardless of its price. They and their followers have had some successes in recent years. But the world of high and volatile inflation is no place for the simpleminded or the inflexible.

Beating inflation requires some study and effort and a subtle touch. But the payoff will be big.

1

Perpetual Inflation— Many Causes, No Cures

Everyone hates inflation. But elected governments cause inflation. They cause it not by giving people what they hate but by trying to give them what they want most: jobs, higher income, and big increases in government benefits.

If governments weren't reflecting the strongest desires of voters, there would be some hope that inflation would end someday. But in almost every world capital, governments are responding to the deepest desires of the public. This is why inflation will continue to be high and volatile. It is also why you will have to learn to live with it, beat it, and even enjoy it.

Although high officials claim their hands are tied, they always have choices open to them. But if you put yourself in their position you would make the same decisions. Suppose Mr. Gallup were to present you with the following: Choose between more inflation next year and one million more people on the unemployment rolls.

Unless you feel more secure than most people do, the odds are that you would gamble on inflation. Citizens don't have this conscious choice open to them. But some people in high places do. And when they make the choice they are only reflecting what the public wants them to do. The public dislikes both inflation and unemployment. But it dislikes unemployment even more than it dislikes inflation.

It was not always so. Prior to World War II almost no one believed that he had an inherent right to a job. Prices went up but they also went down, so, on average, prices were essentially stable. Now everyone believes in his right to job security, and inflation is rampant around the world.

The impact of the change in attitude is illustrated in Figure 1, demonstrating the difference between the behavior of prices in the period before World War II and their behavior since World War II. Charts drawn for other major industrialized countries such as Germany, France, Japan and Great Britain would look very much the same. Before 1945, wartime inflation was inevitably followed by postwar deflation. After World War II, however, prices still rose during wartime, but didn't come down afterward. And after the United States pulled out of Vietnam, prices really exploded.

The reason for this difference is not complicated. The year after World War II, the U.S. Congress passed the "full employment" act, stating that the government would vigorously promote two essentially inconsistent goals—price stability and full employment. Under the prodding of the United Nations virtually every other country adopted similar legislation.

In practice, the goal of full employment has taken precedence over the goal of price stability most of the time. There have, however, been brief periods in which price stability has temporarily moved to the fore. These periods are crucial to the beat-inflation strategy.

The balancing feat envisioned by the Employment Act of 1946 and similar legislation in other countries has been enshrined by economists in a concept known as the trade-off. Policy makers operate in the belief that they can generate higher employment rates by accepting somewhat higher inflation rates. The problem is that the higher employment that results from inflationary policies lasts only for a while. In order to keep the unemployment rate permanently low, inflation must accelerate.

Fig. 1. Inflation and Deflation: The Historical Experience

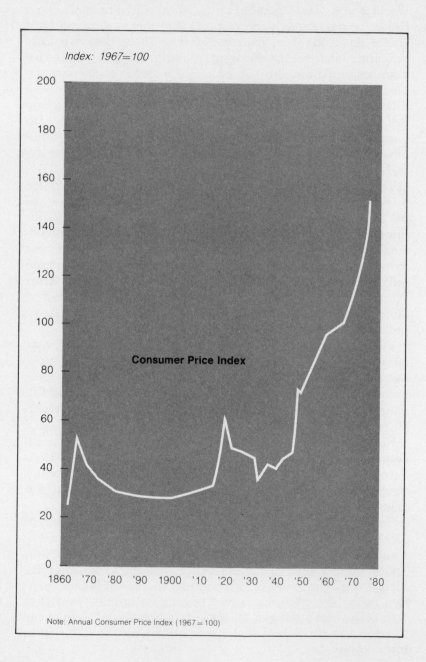

Index: 1967=100

Consumer Price Index

Note: Annual Consumer Price Index (1967 = 100)

This is what has been happening in the U.S. economy since World War II. The U.S. inflation rate averaged 2 percent in the 1950s, 2.3 percent in the 1960s, and 6.1 percent thus far in the 1970s. The primacy of the full employment goal has similarly led other Western governments into accepting gradually accelerating inflation.

Although the inflation rate will move up and down, none of this will fundamentally change. Finance ministers and central bankers will continue to respond to what the public really wants.

The public wants inflation for more than one reason. They think they get more than just job security from it. Inflation has other attributes that make life easier if only temporarily.

If prices are stable, the workers and their union leaders can get a bigger share of the pie only if business gets less. When prices are rising the situation is more confused, and it can seem for long periods of time that the economy is generating much more for everybody. It seems to matter little that it really can't. It takes more output of goods and services to make the pie bigger. But it takes a lot less skill for union leaders and management to hang onto their jobs when prices are shooting up.

Inflation makes it easier to weather so-called liquidity crises, such as the Penn Central failure in 1970 or the difficulties of Franklin National Bank in 1974. The Federal Reserve has two choices: either more inflation or more bankruptcies. In the good old days, it was thought that bankruptcies, like unemployment, were natural and inevitable, indeed, healthy. Today they are abhorrent. As a consequence, Washington lends money to Lockheed, rescues the commercial-paper market when Penn Central bites the dust, and becomes Franklin National Bank's chief supplier of funds—low-cost funds at that. The frequency of these rescue operations will increase. Society always chooses inflation; people like it better than bankrupt companies that have few employees.

Inflation is more palatable than gunboat diplomacy. When Teddy Roosevelt was speaking softly but carrying a big stick, a move by the Arab states to quadruple the price of oil would have been inconceivable. King Faisal would have been exiled to a modern-day Saint Helena. And the U.S. Army Corps of Engineers would be pumping oil in the Persian Gulf.

But there is more than one way to get the oil. In today's

world the creation of paper money can accomplish what gun-boats used to. And what was true of oil in late 1973 can be just as true in future years for other raw materials whose supplies are controlled by the so-called less-developed countries. Just as inflation can be used to mask domestic conflict between labor and management over the distribution of income, so can it be used to mask international conflicts over the distribution of income and wealth.

Inflation makes the welfare state more palatable to those who aren't on the dole. A famous Italian economist of the early twentieth century, Vilfredo Pareto, observed a tendency for the distribution of income to be the same in all epochs of history and in all societies in the same epoch of history. Some dents have been put into the kind of income distribution curves that he drew—Pareto curves. In general, however, attempts to re-distribute income from the rich to the poor have failed, for one reason or another, no matter where they have been tried.

Pareto's observations are relevant to the modern welfare state. When the New York taxi driver sees jobless people re-ceiving bigger checks from welfare without working, he fights to get more and succeeds, at least as far as the number of dollars in his paycheck is concerned. The fight to maintain relative status in the face of rising welfare payments has been a force making for inflation.

Inflation seems to solve a lot of problems. It is little wonder that governments choose policies that are inflationary. But it isn't quite that simple. When governments try to solve prob-lems with inflation, it dooms society to accelerating inflation.

The "money illusion" explains why. To beat inflation you've got to understand the money illusion. Suppose that the govern-ment "solves" high unemployment. The classic way is to pump more money into the economy. Money is created by the ac-tions of the Federal Reserve. When the Federal Reserve wants to increase the supply of money it orders its New York branch to purchase government securities. These securities are usually purchased from government security dealers, banks, insurance companies and other major financial institutions. What hap-pens is simple but crucial. When some institution sells securi-ties to the Federal Reserve it gets in return a check drawn on the Federal Reserve. When the Federal Reserve honors that check, the supply of money is increased. And Federal Reserve checks are honored immediately.

The process of money creation doesn't stop here. When the initial transaction is completed the financial institutions have more money and fewer securities than they had before. The money has to be put into use before it can earn interest, so the financial institutions will use it to buy other securities and to increase loans. When they do this the money supply rises by a multiple of the original Federal Reserve security purchase. Given the nature of the financial system right now, a Federal Reserve purchase of $1 billion in securities will increase the money supply by approximately $2.6 billion.

The effect of a surge in money is to jack up business sales volume. Companies hire more workers. But as business gets better, prices rise, usually faster than wages, which are pegged by longer-term union contracts. When prices rise faster than wages, the unions demand and get bigger wage increases. The source of their ire is a declining real wage, a situation where prices are rising faster than the number of dollars in the pay envelope, and purchasing power is declining. Workers won't stand for this. Either they get big wage increases right away or go on strike and get them afterward. After that happens, the extra company profits that resulted from more money being pumped into the system vanish. Everyone's purchasing power is left about where it was before, but the price level is higher and the unemployment rate is back to where it was before the money supply was pumped up.

This is an example of the birth, life, and death of the money illusion, and how government uses it to solve a problem in the short run. The whole process depends on a money illusion because at each stage of the process by which employment is raised somebody has to be fooled: the businessman into believing he will get permanently higher unit volume, the worker into believing that he will get permanently higher real wages. But the illusion dies, first as the worker realizes his purchasing power isn't rising, then as the businessman watches his unit profits eroded by higher unit wage costs.

The moral of this story—however immoral it may be—is that once a government gets hooked on inflation to solve problems, it can't kick the monkey without causing extreme pain. Initially the government made people feel better by pushing the unemployment rate down with inflationary policies, but the effect of a given dosage of inflation wore off. So to prevent things from going back to the miserable state at which they started, the government again has to jack up the inflation rate. Those who want to beat inflation will therefore find it prudent to count on accelerating inflation as their working rule. For just as the average inflation rate was higher in the 1960s than in the 1950s and higher in the 1970s than in the 1960s, it will be higher in the 1980s than it was in the 1970s. The beat-inflation strategy is geared to the reality of accelerating inflation. The questions are: How much inflation; how steady an inflation?

2

The
Inflation
Cycle

Inflation will accelerate. But the path to higher and higher rates of inflation will be anything but smooth. The inflation rates will move ahead in fits and starts. There will be years when inflation accelerates and years when it slows down.

These gyrations in the inflation rate will create tremendous investment opportunities for those investors who have the right strategy for coping with inflation. A world in which inflation moves up and down will contain more and easier money-making opportunities than a world where inflation is steady or nonexistent.

Since governments create inflation, those investors who watch government policy closely will get ample advance warning of the amount of inflation that government will be creating. Whether its practitioners are willing to admit it or not, conventional investment strategy is based on the idea that prices will remain stable.

The beat-inflation investment strategy, by contrast, is based on the idea that inflation will occur in predictable cycles.

The investor must learn to understand these cycles and anticipate them. The major reason most American families have been on a treadmill since 1965 is that they didn't see inflation coming and therefore did little to guard themselves against its effects. You need never be caught unaware again.

The problem here is to separate those things that are ephemeral from those that will have lasting effects. Daily experience provides no clear-cut guide to the future of prices. And what it does tell you is often misleading. It is dangerous to form impressions about the future inflation rate from what happens on your job, from your visit to the supermarket or even from what you found out from Walter Cronkite. In fact, the successful investor will shut these impressions out. He will keep his eye on government policy. But in order to do this in an effective and efficient way the investor needs a framework.

The framework is provided by our concept of the inflation cycle. An understanding of this cycle is fundamental to investment success over the next decade. Ups and downs in the inflation rate will affect the prices of everything you own and can buy: stocks, bonds, commodities, gold, currencies and real estate. Some of these assets—such as commodities, gold and real estate—are superstars when the inflation rate is rising. Others, such as stocks and bonds, light the sky when the inflation rate is falling. The investor will make money by shifting his investments from accelerating inflation superstars to decelerating inflation superstars depending on what stage of the inflation cycle the economy is in.

The government policy cycle is rooted in the inflation/unemployment trade-off that was described in the preceding chapter. It occurs because policy makers shift with predictable regularity between measures primarily designed to reduce unemployment and measures designed to curb inflation.

Although inflation and unemployment both menace the politician, they never menace him equally. Looking at economic policy since World War II, it is easy to break up the period into alternating subperiods when inflation or unemployment was the number one enemy. Concentrating on the years since 1965, in Figure 2, when the Vietnam War heated up, an analysis will show you that Washington was fighting unemployment from early 1965 to early 1966, inflation from

Fig. 2. **Money Supply**

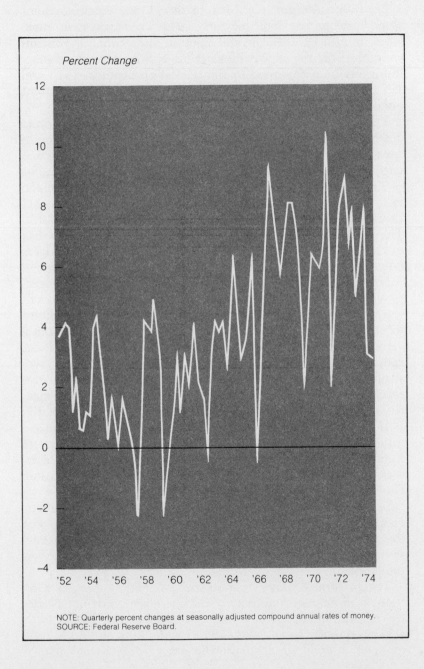

Percent Change

NOTE: Quarterly percent changes at seasonally adjusted compound annual rates of money.
SOURCE: Federal Reserve Board.

early 1966 to late 1966, unemployment from late 1966 to early 1968, inflation from late 1968 to late 1969, unemployment again between late 1969 and early 1971. There was some vacillation in mid-1971. But in the election and economic-controls year of 1972, the government tried to slaughter unemployment, creating the need to fight inflation again in 1973 and 1974. In 1975 the focus of policy was clearly unemployment once again.

The first "fight unemployment" phase of the inflation cycle occurred in 1965, when the cost of a war was piled on top of spending for the Great Society. In late 1965 the escalating war costs were visible everywhere except in the official statements of President Johnson and his chief economic advisers. Yet the official working hypothesis of the administration was that there was ample room for both more guns and more butter. The Federal Reserve let the quantity of money grow fast enough to accommodate the rise in spending, and employers began to scrape the bottom of the labor-market barrel.

By mid-1966 inflation started making headlines and unemployment was pushed to the back pages. Government responded in its typical way; it started to fight inflation. President Johnson proposed an income-tax surcharge but it took about a year for Congress to pass it. The Federal Reserve, however, moved more quickly and swung hard toward monetary restraint. These were the days when the money illusion was still something policy makers could count on. As a consequence, the inflation rate moderated rather quickly in response to the Federal Reserve's restrictive policy. The economy developed some symptoms of recession although the National Bureau of Economic Research, keeper of the seal in business-cycle matters, never officially labeled the period a full-blown recession. Unemployment, however, did rise.

Since Congress finally passed President Johnson's tax surcharge in early 1967 many Washington economists felt that this would lead to fiscal "overkill." Therefore, policy makers switched to the other side of the trade-off—combating unemployment.

The Federal Reserve opened the monetary spigot so wide that the deflationary impact of higher taxes could not be detected. And inflation again began to accelerate.

Consequently and predictably, President Nixon shifted policy goals to combating inflation in early 1969. It took over a year for these restrictive policies to begin to impact the inflation rate. The more often a country goes through policy cycles, the harder it is to fool people.

This time it took a prolonged period of anti-inflation policy and a real recession to get the inflation rate down. In fact, progress was so slow that on August 15, 1971, President Nixon pushed the panic button and slapped on controls to get the inflation rate down. But it wasn't too long before policy turned expansive once again. Since policy makers fear unemployment more than they fear inflation, the controls served as a veil under which economic policy again turned superexpansive.

Watergate was not the only thing that was done to influence the outcome of the 1972 election. Mr. Nixon and his administration were taking no chances that high unemployment would cost him the election as it did in 1960. They pursued one of the most expansive monetary and fiscal policies in history throughout 1972.

This policy more than anything else was responsible for the accelerating inflation in 1973 and 1974. And freed of electoral concerns, Washington again turned its policy in a restrictive direction and remained generally restrictive for almost two years. It was only when unemployment really shot up in late 1974 that policy again shifted toward expansion. By the spring of 1975 policy was highly expansive.

The investor can tell whether policy is expansive or restrictive because the policy cycle is embodied in a monetary growth cycle. Anybody who is somewhat familiar with the work of economists knows that some stress monetary policy as the prime mover of the economy while others stress fiscal policy. The decibel level of the debate on this question has fortunately dropped. We have a preference for analyzing the investment outlook in terms of monetary policy. Specifically, we focus on the steps that the Federal Reserve takes to increase or decrease the monetary growth rate. The way we look at the world, tight money means a slowdown in the rate of growth in the money supply as occurred, for example, between late 1968 and late 1969. Easy money means a speed-up in the rate of growth of the money supply, as in 1972.

We believe that economic research indicates that changes in monetary policy have quicker and more easily discernible effects on asset prices than does fiscal policy—changes in government spending and taxes. However, almost all of the time, monetary and fiscal policy move together. This should not be surprising; when government turns expansive all policy wheels turn in the same direction. And when the brakes go on, all the engines go into reverse.

There is another, more esoteric reason why monetary and fiscal policy move together. When fiscal policy turns expansive, governments incur bigger deficits, which means they have to borrow more. Mechanically, there is no reason why higher borrowing by the Treasury must lead to a faster rate of money creation by the Federal Reserve. But in practice it does. Research by the Federal Reserve Bank of Saint Louis shows that monetary and fiscal policy have moved in the same direction in 90 percent of all the quarters since World War II. One reason why we prefer to work in terms of monetary policy rather than fiscal policy is what happens the other 10 percent of the time. When monetary and fiscal policy move in different directions, monetary policy swamps fiscal policy and determines the direction of economic activity and asset prices.

A major technique, perhaps *the* major technique, in putting the beat-inflation strategy to work is to spot changes in monetary policy. Figure 2 shows how monetary policy has swung during the post-World War II period. These policy swings are measured by changes in the rate of growth of the money supply. As we apply the beat-inflation strategy in detail we will frequently talk about monetary *acceleration* and monetary *deceleration.* Acceleration of the monetary growth rate means that the money supply is growing faster than it was. For example, in December 1971, the money supply was 6.3 percent above the money supply in December 1970. By December 1972, it was 8.7 percent above that of December 1971. Clearly the monetary growth rate had accelerated during 1972. All that the deceleration of the monetary growth rate means is that the money supply is growing slower than it was. For example, as contrasted to the 8.7-percent growth in the money supply between December 1972 and December 1971, the monetary growth rate was only 6.1 percent between December 1973 and December 1972. Clearly the monetary growth rate had decelerated during 1973.

The monetary growth cycle, periods of accelerating monetary growth followed by periods of decelerating monetary growth, produces a cycle in output and an inflation cycle. Everybody knows about the alternation between prosperity and

Fig. 3. **Consumer Price Index — All Items**

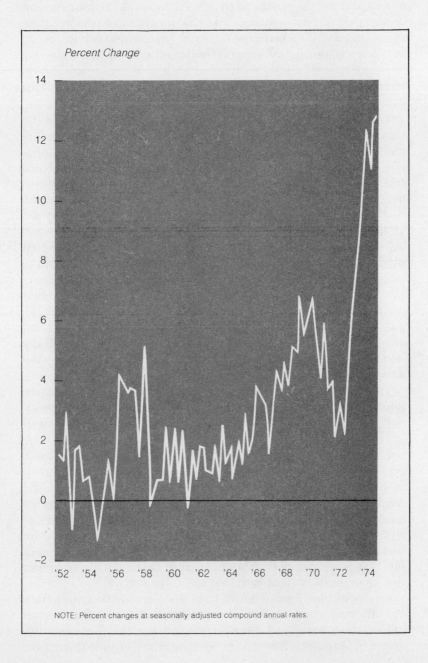

Percent Change

NOTE: Percent changes at seasonally adjusted compound annual rates.

recession. Economists have been writing about it for over a century. A decisive cycle in prices, however, is a phenomenon of the post-Vietnam years. It is the newness of this inflation cycle that has knocked conventional investment advice on its ear. As long as inflation remains high and volatile, the only way to increase your family's wealth is to follow the beat-inflation strategy and play the inflation cycle rather than the output cycle.

The behavior of inflation over the last ten years provides the investor with a framework for understanding the inflation cycle. As Figure 3 indicates, there have been three distinct inflation cycles since mid-1965. The first one lasted from the third quarter of 1965 to the end of 1966. Its accelerating phase was very brief, covering the last quarter of 1965 and peaking in the first quarter of 1966. Its decelerating phase ran from the end of the first quarter of 1966 to the end of 1966. The second inflation cycle lasted from the end of 1966 through the first quarter of 1972. Its accelerating phase took three full years to work itself out, 1967 through 1969. The decelerating phase also lasted a long time, from the end of 1969 through the first quarter of 1972. The accelerating phase of the third cycle began in 1972, reached the double-digit figures in mid-1973 and only peaked out in the fourth quarter of 1974. The economy was still in this decelerating phase of the inflation cycle in the first half of 1975.

The three inflation cycles over the past ten years illustrate four outstanding characteristics that will persist into the future and can therefore serve as the basis for the beat-inflation strategy.

1. The inflation cycle is preceded by the monetary growth cycle. Figure 4 brings together the money growth cycle shown in Figure 2 and the inflation cycle shown in Figure 3. The dotted line shows the rate of change for the consumer price index since 1952. The solid black line shows that the rate of change of the money supply lagged two years behind. The two-year lag simply means that the figure for the money supply that is plotted for 1974 is the rate that actually occurred two years earlier—that is to say, 1972. And so on.

The resulting figure shows that accelerations in monetary growth lead accelerations in prices and that decelerations in monetary growth lead decelerations in prices. The monetary growth cycle therefore serves as an early warning system for

Fig. 4. **Money and Prices**

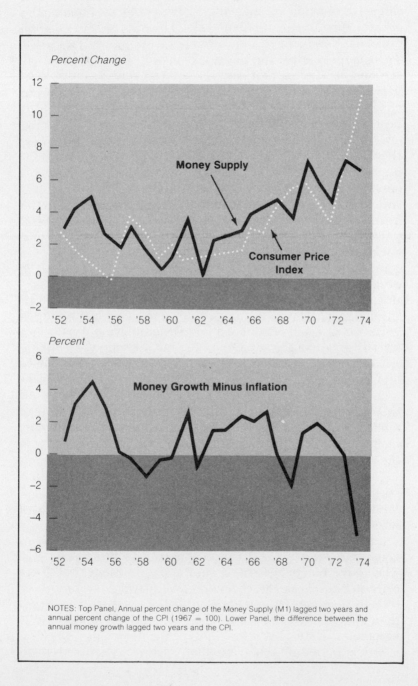

NOTES: Top Panel, Annual percent change of the Money Supply (M1) lagged two years and annual percent change of the CPI (1967 = 100). Lower Panel, the difference between the annual money growth lagged two years and the CPI.

spotting turns in the inflation cycle. When an investor detects a decisive swing in the monetary growth cycle he can expect a definite turn in the inflation cycle. The turn in the inflation cycle will usher in a sequence of opportunity-creating events. Their consequences for the stock market, the bond market, the commodities market, and the interest rates obtainable on your short-term investments are described in subsequent chapters of this book. Taking advantage of them is what the beat-inflation game is all about.

2. The longer inflation lasts, the bigger the ups and possibly the downs in the inflation cycle. Figure 4 shows that the inflation cycle has already become more volatile and this is likely to continue.

Remember that the inflation cycle is rooted in the economic policy cycle. The government is always fighting either unemployment or inflation. In the early days of the inflation cycle, back in the mid-1960s, it was easy for Washington to get quick results when it swung from one goal to the other. This was because the inflation cycle started after decades of relative price stability. The experience with stable prices meant that the money illusion was strong. And this in turn meant that the government could eliminate a lot of unemployment with only a relatively small acceleration in the money supply.

When the money illusion is strong, people are easily fooled into believing that a change in their money incomes will make them much better off. But after inflation has lasted for a while they learn to be suspicious of a rise in their money wages or money profits because they know that when there is more money in their pay envelopes or their cash register, a rise in the prices of the things they buy is not too far off.

Therefore, the longer inflation lasts, the more stimulus it will take for government to reduce the unemployment rate. And this in turn means bigger and bigger doses of money in periods when government is bent on economic expansion.

It also means that an expansionary policy will be followed by bigger accelerations in inflation. And this in turn means that when government switches from the employment goal to the price-stability goal, the change in policy will have drastic effects, first on output and then on prices. In short, the longer the inflation cycle continues, the more volatile it is likely to become.

3. The periods in which inflation accelerates will be longer

than the periods in which inflation decelerates. Policy makers hate both unemployment and inflation, but they hate unemployment even more than inflation. As a consequence, policy makers are likely to panic more quickly when unemployment rises than when inflation gets out of hand. Furthermore, the longer inflation lasts, the quicker unemployment will shoot up when restrictive policies are adopted. This means that governments will lose their nerve soon after restrictive policies are put into effect, and they will switch to an expansionary policy. Expansionary policies will be in place longer than restrictive policies.

4. Although inflation will be going through periods of acceleration and deceleration the inflation rate will trend upward on average. As the money illusion weakens, the government must increase the money dosage just to keep the unemployment rate steady on the average. And since a higher money growth rate on average will always bring a higher inflation rate on average, the rate of inflation will trend upward. This is illustrated in Figure 4.

Figures 2, 3, and 4 all show rates of change. Although these charts show cycles very well, they don't show trends very well. Trends show up well in charts like Figure 5. This chart shows the level of the consumer price index drawn on a scale where equal percent changes show up as equal vertical distances, so that a constant percentage rate of change shows up as a straight line. Since 1965 the line has been generally getting steeper. This means that the trend of the inflation rate has been rising.

However, it is almost certain that the extremely steep rise in the price line in Figure 5 that occurred in 1973-74 gives a misleading impression of the speed with which the trend of inflation is accelerating.

As we have described it, the inflation cycle is frightening, bringing as it does a volatile price level in the short run, coupled with accelerating inflation rates in the long run. But some perspective is required. It would turn out to be a grave mistake to identify the double-digit inflation of 1973-1974 as the rate that was being produced by the monetary acceleration that occurred in the 1971-1972 period.

If you are going to be one of inflation's winners, you must be able to determine what the trend rate of inflation is, because your investment decisions are going to depend on your esti-

Fig. 5. **The Consumer Price Index**

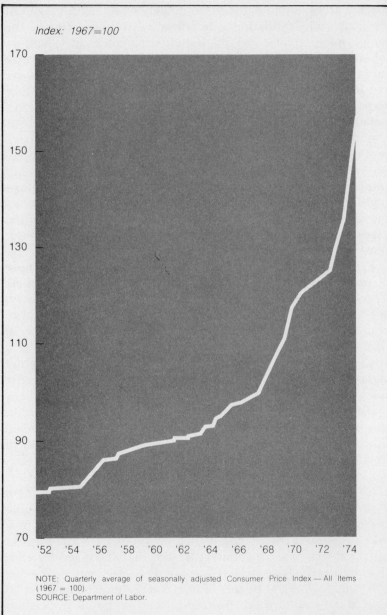

Index: 1967=100

NOTE: Quarterly average of seasonally adjusted Consumer Price Index — All Items
(1967 = 100).
SOURCE: Department of Labor.

mate. The biggest money-making opportunities will occur when there is a large difference between the current inflation rate and the trend rate.

As we have seen, the best way to get a grip on the trend of inflation is to keep your eye on what governments are up to as evidenced by the amount of money they are creating. Those who will beat inflation will keep their eye on the money supply.

Figure 6 shows the trend of money supply and the trend of prices. Two things stand out: (1) The trend rate of money-supply growth does not change very often, and (2) the money-supply growth rate is directly related to the rate of inflation. For example, in the 1950s the average money-supply growth was 2.6 percent while the average inflation rate was 2.0 percent. In the 1960s the money supply growth was 3.7 percent while inflation averaged 2.3 percent. Thus far in the 1970s the money-growth rate has averaged 6.2 percent and inflation has averaged 6.1 percent.

This kind of relationship holds up very well no matter what country you look at. Most of the Western countries keep honest track of their price levels and money supplies. And the money-inflation equation works well.

For the United States, the trend rate of inflation is generally about 1 to 2 percentage points below the average rate of growth in money supply. This does not mean that it is 1 to 2 percentage points below the money-supply growth rate in any given month, but rather 1 to 2 percentage points less than the money-supply growth averaged over a three-year period. Using this rule, the trend rate of inflation is currently 4½ to 5½ percent because the money-supply growth rate has averaged about 6½ percent over the past three years. Since the inflation rate lags behind the monetary growth rate, the 4½ to 5½ percent trend rate of inflation will persist for some time.

All this talk of inflation rates of 4 percent, 5 percent, or 6 percent may seem like an overoptimistic prediction for a society that suffered double-digit inflation in late 1973 and 1974. But it illustrates that the trend rate of inflation can differ substantially from the actual rate and differ from it by a lot for quite a while. These are the times when those who put the beat-inflation strategy to use can make the most money.

The actual rate of inflation can differ from the trend rate of inflation for several reasons. The first is the existence of the

Fig. 6. **Money and Prices**

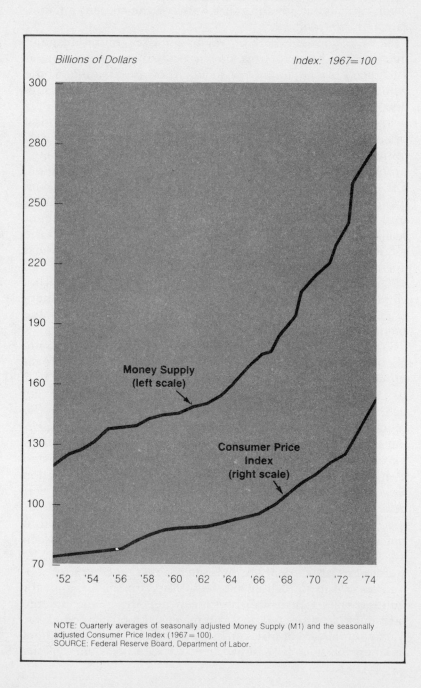

Billions of Dollars   Index: 1967=100

Money Supply
(left scale)

Consumer Price
Index
(right scale)

'52 '54 '56 '58 '60 '62 '64 '66 '68 '70 '72 '74

NOTE: Quarterly averages of seasonally adjusted Money Supply (M1) and the seasonally adjusted Consumer Price Index (1967 = 100).
SOURCE: Federal Reserve Board, Department of Labor.

inflation cycle—which means that at any given moment, the actual inflation rate reported monthly will be moving above or below the trend line that describes the long-term inflation rate. The second is the existence of a phenomenon that has been recognized by statisticians for a long time: random events cluster. It was this kind of cluster that boosted the inflation rate into the double-digit zone in 1973-1974. It took an incredible number of negative events to make it.

It started with the dollar devaluation in 1971 and 1972, a move that wrecked the U.S. price level by boosting the cost of foreign imports.

In a pre-election move to boost farm-product prices, the Nixon Administration sold wheat to the Russians at prices that even they couldn't refuse, draining U.S. farm surpluses and making the country vulnerable to an enormous surge in grain prices.

Off the coast of Peru a thriving anchovy-fishing business had developed. These fish swill hogs and feed cattle. They were a critical source of high-protein animal feed. Their disappearance from South American waters boosted the price of other high-protein feeds, mainly soybeans, and the price of meat soared throughout the world.

Then came the Arab-Israeli conflagration that gave the Arabs the opportunity to quadruple the price of oil and make the higher price stick.

The negative cluster of random events, combined with a worldwide boom in money-supply growth—mainly the result of the final futile attempt to prop up the dollar—blew the lid off the U.S. controls program, and double-digit inflation was on.

It took the painful monetary restraint of 1973 and 1974 to end it. By mid-1975 the inflation rate had subsided. But it had taken a steep rise in unemployment and a jump in excess capacity to do the job. But the signs of the next accelerating phase of the monetary growth cycle were present, since the aim of policy had turned to combating unemployment.

In a world of high and volatile inflation the investor who understands the anatomy of inflation is the one who will beat it rather than be victimized by it. Figure 7 is a schematic depiction of the anatomy of the inflation cycle. At each critical point in that cycle the asset mix that will beat inflation will be different, as subsequent chapters will show. The investor must

Fig. 7. **Phases of the Inflation Cycle**

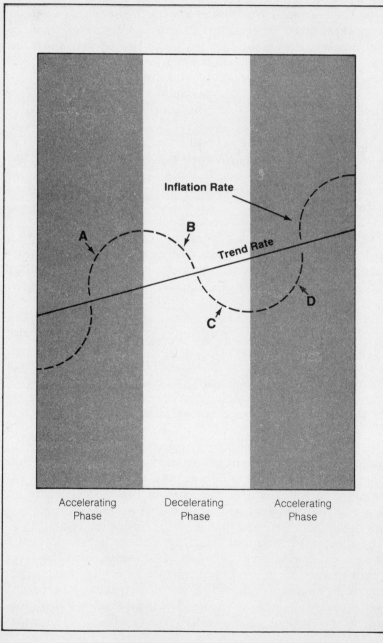

therefore always know where he is in the inflation cycle. He can do this at any time simply by getting the Federal Reserve Bank of Saint Louis publications described in chapter 12. These publications will provide him with the data to construct a real-life inflation-cycle chart which will quickly tell him where the economy is in the inflation cycle. The remainder of this book will tell him what investment moves to be making at each point in the inflation cycle.

For illustrative purposes we have picked four points in the inflation cycle. Inflation is going on at all times but each of the points requires a different strategy to benefit from inflation.

At point A, the actual inflation rate is still accelerating, but it is near its peak and well above the trend rate. At this stage of the inflation cycle, the investor knows that the time has come to dump hard assets such as gold and commodities, get into short-term money-market instruments and get ready to buy paper assets such as stocks and bonds.

At point B, the actual rate of inflation is decelerating but it is still above the trend rate. By this time the investor is completely out of hard assets and is converting short-term money instruments into a portfolio of stocks and bonds ideally suited to take advantage of decelerating inflation.

At point C the inflation rate is below the trend rate and is in the process of bottoming out. The investor is on the telephone to his broker, getting rid of his stocks and bonds, getting into liquid assets and thinking about the commodity and gold plays that will permit him to ride the accelerating phase.

At point D the inflation rate is below the trend rate but is in the initial phases of accelerating. The investor is already out of stocks and bonds and converting his liquid assets to hard assets such as commodities and gold.

Poor Richard and the Protestant ethic have led the average American to draw a distinction between speculation (bad) and investment (good). One characteristic of Poor Richard's concept of an investment is that it is purchased and held for a very long time. Buying and holding was considered both ethically superior and more financially rewarding than in-and-out speculative trading. This may still be true with respect to any single asset. Trading in and out of stocks, for example, will probably make the broker rich but you poor.

However, Poor Richard's way to invest is the wrong way to invest in a world of high and volatile inflation. Over the entire inflation cycle no asset is ethically superior or more rewarding than any other asset. If you are going to make money over the inflation cycle, you must change the asset mix of your portfolio. The assets that will beat inflation at point A in Figure 7 will lose you money at points B, C, and D. There is no investment for all seasons, but there is a season for all investments.

3

How Inflation Transfers Income and Wealth

Anyone who has ever played Monopoly knows that sometimes you win and sometimes you lose. But the way you would play would be different if you knew that all the prices—rents, the cost of the property, the fines you have to pay, and the rewards you get—double after every five times around the board.

Playing Monopoly in an inflationary environment would not change any of the physical aspects of the game. But you would play the game differently. Because you would know the inevitability of inflation you would want to hold little in the way of cash, and borrow to the hilt in order to buy property and build houses and hotels. Moreover, your incentive to do these things would be greatest on the turn around the board just before the prices went up. Eventually you and your fellow players would develop a whole new set of rules for playing the game, and those who caught on fastest to the effects of inflation would be the biggest winners.

As with Monopoly, so it is with life. Inflation does not destroy the physical aspects of the game. But it does change the rules. Inflation does not necessarily produce disaster, but it does change who are the winners and who are losers. It does not destroy wealth or income, it redistributes it.

There are many views of inflation and its consequences that are contrary to our view. Predictions that inflation will destroy the game and the players are common; that society cannot develop tactics, rules, and strategies to allow members to live with inflation and still prosper. We believe, by contrast, that just as in Monopoly, the players in the economy will develop new ways of coping that will allow them to be comfortable when prices are rising. Indeed, there is plenty of evidence that help in adapting to inflation is on the way—cost-of-living clauses in wage contracts, Social Security benefits tied to changes in consumer prices, and variable-rate debt securities issued by bank holding companies and corporations.

The view that society will adapt to inflation is at the opposite pole from the one held by the gold bugs and the silver bugs, who see disaster behind every uptick in the price indexes.

It is true that the advice emanating from this intellectual underworld in 1974 was far better than conventional investment advice. The trouble, of course, is that the intellectual and factual underpinnings of their arguments simply don't hold water. The most obvious case is gold. Gold bugs, in general, counsel a strategy of either holding gold or the stocks of gold-mining companies regardless of their current price.

The reader should be wary. Under circumstances that could easily be foreseen (for example, a decelerating period of inflation like the one between points B and C in Figure 7), nothing could be more disastrous than the buy-and-hold strategy recommended by gold bugs or any other one-asset bugs. Like any commodity, gold is an asset that will fare best in the accelerating phase of the inflation cycle. The key to profiting from permanent inflation is a flexible investment policy that plays no favorites among assets. Each asset will have its season. And the investor will move in and out of each asset based on his assessment of its merits for each stage in the inflation cycle.

Real income, real wealth

Inflation will do no systematic damage to your chances to enjoy the good things in life, just as it didn't destroy the Monopoly board. This means that you can have more of everything as you progress in your chosen career path.

In order to always understand how well off you are, you must be aware of the distinction between the changes in the number of dollars you report to the IRS every year and what those dollars can actually buy.

Adam Smith, in *An Inquiry Into the Nature and Causes of the Wealth of Nations,* published in 1776, clarified this distinction once and for all. The "real" wealth of nations or individuals, he said, must be measured by the quantities of goods and services that they can command. Modern economists describe changes in these quantities as changes in "real" magnitudes, "real" income, "real" wealth, "real" wages and so on. The characteristic of these real magnitudes is that they do not necessarily go down when prices rise. This is why inflation can be enjoyed rather than feared.

To improve your standard of living, you must increase your money income faster than prices are going up. What is true for the individual is also true for the country as a whole. The government spends a great deal of money providing the tools for drawing a distinction between changes in money values and changes in real values. Indeed, all the price indexes that the government puts out and you read about can be used for this purpose. For example, suppose the amount of money spent on automobiles rose by 10 percent in one year. At the same time, the Bureau of Labor Statistics reports that auto prices jumped by 10 percent over the same period. This means that the number of cars sold was unchanged. Or, in other words, there was no "real" growth in auto sales. And what is true of autos is true of everything else; when you adjust changes in money values for changes in prices—economists call this process deflating—the number you come up with is a "real" number: personal income divided by a measure of consumer prices is called "real" income, and wealth divided by an index of asset prices is called "real" wealth.

The basic finding of economic research spanning many centuries and many countries is that there is no fixed relationship between the rate of inflation and the growth in real income. In general, some countries have had high inflation and high real growth (Japan and Brazil are conspicuous examples) while others have had high inflation and low real growth (Italy and the United Kingdom are examples). Cases can also be cited for

countries with low inflation and low real growth and low inflation and high real growth.

Given all the uncertainties in the world and the large errors
made by forecasts, the prospects for the United States seem to
be for high and permanent inflation and somewhat slower real
growth than was chalked up in the 1960s. Looking at the years
through 1979, we foresee a real growth rate of 3.5 percent,
somewhat slower than the 4.3 percent that existed in the
1960s. For what comfort it provides, our forecast is not too
different from the other forecasts included in a recent survey
of long-term forecasts conducted by the economics department at RCA. Of the twelve forecasts included, the median
growth rate forecast was 3.9 percent, the high 4.6 percent, and
the low 2.9 percent. Remembering the wonderful world of
compounding, this leaves plenty of room in which you can
increase your standard of living.

Many readers may find the idea that inflation need not interfere with your chances of enjoying the good life somewhat
hard to digest, yet a little bit of introspection and observation
shows that indeed it doesn't interfere.

First consider how you yourself responded to the 1973-74
double-digit inflation. Economists have known, since Adam
Smith's time, that a nation's growth rate is determined mainly
by the character of its people and the quality of their education and by the increase in the number of hours worked by its
labor force.

If you are like most other people, the odds are that you
worked just as hard and maybe even harder in the face of
accelerating inflation. A survey of psychologists conducted by
The New York Times in the summer of 1974, a period of double-digit inflation in the United States, showed that inflation
per se was having little impact on people's actual behavior
although it was obviously high on the list of personal gripes.
And when it comes to growth, it is not what people gripe
about, but how they act, that counts.

The United States is not unique in this respect. The Japanese
have had a high inflation rate for some time now but have not
abandoned the work ethic. By the same token the Germans
and the Swiss have combined hard work with relatively low
inflation rates. Even internationally, it is not the rate of price
increase but other more fundamental characteristics, such as
population growth, the rate of technological advance, and the

level of education, that decide how fast the country's standard of living improves.

There is an important exception to this rule of the nonimportance of inflation. Many people's perceptions of the horrors of inflation are based on a small sample of highly unusual cases of hyperinflation: the great inflation in the Confederate states during the Civil War, the inflation in the twenties, particularly in the Weimar Republic in Germany and Austria and Hungary, and the inflation in continental Europe after World War II. In each of these cases prices rose so rapidly and economic activity became so disorganized that real output tumbled. The common characteristic of these inflations is that they were enormously high by any standard.

As long as inflation falls far short of multi-digit figures (twenty-eight digits in the case of the Hungarian inflation in 1946), high real growth is possible even though inflation is extremely high by the standards of U.S. history. Brazil, for example, where inflation is running between 15 and 20 percent, has a real growth rate that is among the highest in the world. Japan, another fast-growth economy, has had much higher inflation rates than the United States.

Inflation should not be taken as a cause for despair, since income will continue to grow in any situation that falls short of hyperinflation for the United States or the world. Therefore, the practical question for the reader is how to position himself for the kind of inflation that is to come. To do this the reader must understand how inflation transfers income and wealth. From this will flow the strategy that will enable him to be one of inflation's big winners.

Income transfers

Irrelevant to real growth as it usually is, inflation does have enormous impact on the distribution of income and wealth. Like the inflation cycle, the process by which inflation transfers income and wealth is a key element. Some people will be winners and others will be losers. What happens to you will be determined by your actions or inactions.

The rule for ending up in the winner's circle is to be on the right side of four kinds of transfers:

1. *The transfer of wealth from creditors to debtors.* Here it is your net position that is crucial. If your assets valued in dollars, such as cash, savings deposits, and bonds, exceed your liabil-

ities valued in dollars, such as bank loans and mortgages, you are a net monetary creditor. You are hurt by inflation. If your assets valued in dollars are less than your liabilities valued in dollars you are a net monetary debtor. You gain by inflation.

You have to be a borrower. The funds must be invested in the right portfolio, one that is designed to take advantage of inflation.

2. *A transfer of income from those who work in industries and professions where prices and wages are rising slowly to those who work in areas where prices and wages are rising more rapidly.* Early in this century the U.S. Department of Agriculture invented the idea of a parity index. This index measures the prices received by farmers and compares it to the prices paid by farmers. Those who will beat inflation must have a good subjective notion of their own parity position. They then must take the kinds of action that will at least prevent their parity index from declining, and, ideally, make it rise.

This point is important. It is the only way to avoid getting trapped by the money illusion. In your own personal life the money illusion is the failure to recognize that while your wages and income from investments may be rising, so are the prices that you are paying to stay alive. Purchasing power is what matters.

3. *A transfer of wealth to those who invest in assets whose prices go up faster than the general price level from those whose assets go up less rapidly than the general price level.* In the inflation that occurred in 1973 and early 1974, commodity prices in general were clearly the star price performers; common stocks laid the biggest egg.

4. *A transfer of wealth and income to those who correctly foresee the future inflation rate and take advantage of their foresight.* Those who can foresee what the inflation rate will be are in a position to benefit from the transfers. They will buy the right assets, be in the right industries, and arrange their balance sheets correctly.

There are two basic approaches to this wealth-and-income transfer. One approach is defensive-conservative, while the other is risky-aggressive but also potentially the most rewarding. The conservative hinges on what has come to be known as indexing. Under this approach, the idea is to neutralize inflation (i.e., to merely keep up with inflation). The strategy is to tie all income receipts and payments to some measure of the change in the general price level—the consumer price index, for example. But if you want to make inflation work in your favor, the risky-aggressive approach is your cup of tea. It means that you must form your own ideas about the speed of increase of the general price level, as well as determine what specific prices will rise the fastest.

The basic idea is that money is a veil. What really counts is real income and real wealth: what your income and wealth can buy in physical goods and services. Money, by contrast, is a medium of exchange which facilitates an efficient transfer of real income and real wealth. It does not become any more productive when prices go up; indeed, in some sense its productivity declines because each existing dollar represents a smaller fraction of total real income and total real wealth.

When inflation occurs, physical wealth is worth more in terms of money. For example, as inflation has accelerated, the value of your home has gone up with it, because it is more expensive in terms of dollars. But the claim against this physical, or hard, asset, probably a mortgage, does not change in value. You still owe the same number of dollars, but those dollars purchase less. Thus the homeowner's net worth—the difference between assets and liabilities—has increased. This is the way that inflation works to transfer wealth from net monetary creditors—in this case the owner of the mortgage—to net monetary debtors—in this case the owner of the house. All wealth transfers occur in this manner.

Income transfers are much simpler to see. Again, keep the parity index in mind. It is not hard to see that those who are sellers in markets where prices are rising most rapidly because of inflation will come out ahead.

Finally, those who are able to guess correctly about the future path of inflation will benefit at the expense of those whose guesses are not as good, because those who are correct are simply going to be able to choose the right industries, write favorable contracts, and bunch their borrowing and lending decisions in periods when the terms are most favorable. Above all, they will make the right investments.

The arithmetic of wealth transfers

Readers who would like to nail down the lesson about how inflation transfers wealth should take a look at the following example showing why it pays to be a net monetary debtor when inflation is rife. Let's look at the balance sheets of three people: one a net monetary creditor, one neutral (monetary assets equal monetary liabilities), and one a net monetary debtor.

Mr. Net Creditor's balance sheet looks like this before inflation starts. He is a net creditor because his monetary assets, cash in this example, exceed his monetary liabilities, a mortgage in this case. In all examples, the house is a "real" asset.

Mr. Net Creditor

| Cash | 10 | Mortgage | 5 |
| House | 10 | Net Worth | 15 |

Net worth is the difference between the dollar value of your assets and the dollar value of your liabilities and is a measure of how rich you are.

Mr. Net Creditor's net worth is 15: his assets (Cash, 10, and House, 10, for a total of 20) minus his liabilities (Mortgage, 5). If prices, including prices of physical, or hard, assets—houses—double, Mr. Net Creditor's balance sheet looks like this:

Mr. Net Creditor

| Cash | 10 | Mortgage | 5 |
| House | 20 | Net Worth | 25 |

This man's net worth has increased from 15 to 25. So far so good. But net worth has not doubled as prices did. This man has fallen behind in the inflation race. The purchasing power of his net worth (wealth) has been reduced by inflation.

Mr. Neutral's balance sheet looks like this, before inflation starts. He is neutral because his monetary assets equal his monetary liabilities.

Mr. Neutral

| Cash | 5 | Mortgage | 5 |
| House | 10 | Net Worth | 10 |

A doubling of prices has this effect on his balance sheet:

Mr. Neutral

Cash	5	Mortgage	5
House	20	Net Worth	20

This man's net worth has increased from 10 to 20. He has exactly kept pace with inflation. The purchasing power of his net worth (wealth) has stayed the same.

Mr. Net Debtor's balance sheet looks like this. He is a net debtor because his monetary assets are less than his monetary liabilities.

Mr. Net Debtor

Cash	3	Mortgage	10
House	12	Net Worth	5

When prices double, his balance sheet looks like this:

Mr. Net Debtor

Cash	3	Mortgage	10
House	24	Net Worth	17

This man's net worth has increased from 5 to 17. When net worth more than triples while prices only double, inflation has been beaten. The purchasing power of his net worth (wealth) has risen. He has been on the right side of the inflation-induced wealth transfer.

Notice that you don't have to be on the verge of bankruptcy to be a net monetary debtor. You can have cash, but you want a large portion of your assets to be physical, or hard, assets. As a matter of fact, you can get tremendously rich and still be a net monetary debtor. In our example, Mr. Net Debtor's net worth has tripled, but he is still a net monetary debtor, still positioned to benefit from more inflation. Most people who get and stay rich in the years ahead will have balance sheets that are leveraged this way. Their assets will primarily be composed of investments whose prices rise at least as fast as the general price levels at each stage of the inflation cycle. Cash does not fit into this group of inflation-benefiting assets because the purchasing power of a dollar shrinks with inflation. On the liability side you take the opposite tactic. Liabilities should be fixed in terms of the number of dollars owed so that they do not increase when the general price level rises. Mortgages or other IOUs generally fit this bill. The purchasing power you must surrender to honor them shrinks with inflation.

The principles that apply in our simple examples also apply in the real world. No matter how complex their balance sheets, net monetary debtors are the ones who will win. There are, of course, more complex effects of inflation on balance sheets that have entries for depreciation and inventories. These have important implications for your investment decisions and your common stock choices. They are covered in chapter 6.

CHAPTER 4

Investing to Beat Inflation

Those who will beat inflation will put their chips on those investments that are on the right side of the wealth and income transfers that come as a result of inflation. They will be on the right side of the transfer of wealth from net creditors to net monetary debtors: of the transfer from those who do not anticipate the inflation rate correctly to those who do; of the transfer from those industries where prices rise slowly to those industries where prices rise more rapidly.

We have looked at a large number of portfolios ranging from those held by people with normal income and wealth to the ones held by the very rich. Very few are structured to take advantage of inflation.

Nor does it matter much whether your portfolio was created on your own or by some institution that has a big name, a fancy office and a lot of professional money managers.

This is not to say that the kind of conventional wisdom that guides the work of the professional portfolio managers should be thrown out the window. In fact, many of the principles that they talk about, such as diversification and efficient portfolios, cannot be ignored. But the standard rules of investment must be applied differently in an inflationary environment. They must be adapted to take advantage both of the inflation cycle and of the wealth and income transfers that it brings.

The primary focus of investment analysis has been to find undervalued assets to buy and overvalued assets to sell. We agree with this approach. Indeed, the search for undervalued and overvalued situations is not the reason for the poor investment performance since the inflation cycle started. Instead, the problem has been failure to recognize that the inflation cycle has changed the criteria for spotting overvalued and undervalued situations. Conventional investment analysis has simply not taken account of the inflation cycle and its impact on asset prices. When looking at an asset, the fundamental consideration of the investor should be what the inflation cycle does to the potential return from investing in that asset. The investor concentrates on the impact of the inflation rate on asset prices more than anything else.

An efficient portfolio

To take advantage of inflation's transfers, you must begin by thinking in terms of your total portfolio and balance sheet. Then you have to arrange them so that they efficiently serve the beat-inflation goal.

Most of the hundreds of millions of dollars that have been spent on investment research over the years have been thrown down the drain. A major exception is the money that has been spent to develop the concept of an efficient portfolio. The real credit goes to two men whose names are hardly household words: Harry Markowitz and William Sharpe. According to Markowitz and Sharpe, an efficient portfolio is a collection of assets that maximize the return or income for a given level of risk. Therefore there are many efficient portfolios, depending on the investor's goal and the amount of risk he is willing to accept.

The fact that you know the concept of an efficient portfolio is no guarantee of your investment results. In professional money management it is only a little exaggeration to say that the goal of each portfolio manager has been to design a portfolio to be like that of every other portfolio manager. Portfolio managers have a strong desire to play it safe in the sense of not doing much worse than anyone else. These problems show up most vividly in what has come to be known as a lack of liquidity in the stock market. Clearly you don't want a portfolio that is faddist, but one that is efficiently designed to meet the goal of beating inflation.

Once you get one of these portfolios in hand, you can afford to feel comfortable, but only for a while. Because, as inflation begins to push the price of your assets up, the faddists will start jumping in. At this point asset prices will begin to overdiscount inflation. It will be time to design a new portfolio to beat inflation. One will be available because you will be buying what the faddists are selling after the price drops.

Safety in diversification

Not everybody who wants to beat inflation will buy the same portfolio. People have different tastes, preferences, likes and dislikes. They have different feelings on the amount of risk they are willing to accept. Here is where diversification comes in. Although professional money managers have used this idea to justify portfolios that do not serve any goal efficiently, it does have some meaning to the beat-inflation strategy.

During the course of designing your portfolio, you will decide that there is one investment at a given moment that is better than any other investment. There is some chance that you will be wrong. Therefore, the portion of your money that you will invest in that asset will depend on your attitude toward the possibility of losing everything. You will feel you must hedge against that possibility; most people will want to diversify among several assets with beat-inflation possibilities. Some of these will promise smaller returns but will be safer than others.

Good diversification also means that the particular assets in your portfolio will complement each other. Suppose that you start with the asset you like best, say cocoa commodity contracts whose chances of benefiting from inflation are grossly underestimated by the market. Like any single asset it carries with it some risks that could not have been foreseen. Suppose further that someone suddenly discovers that cocoa causes cancer in mice. You obviously wouldn't want all your assets in contracts that benefit from higher cocoa prices. Indeed, you would want some of them in assets that will benefit from inflation almost as much as cocoa contracts, but which can't be hurt by bad news. This is what economists call minimizing the risk to obtain the highest possible return, and it is what Markowitz and Sharpe mean by efficient portfolios.

You don't get the safety of diversification by buying such close substitutes as gold, silver, platinum, and diamonds. The efficient strategy for beating inflation requires that you not put all your eggs in one basket, or even in a number of extremely similar baskets.

A beat-inflation portfolio could easily include, say, some U.S. stocks, some Swiss time deposits, and maybe some forward marks. A futures market for foreign exchange exists at the Chicago Mercantile Exchange. There, contracts are traded which allow the investor to speculate that the mark will rise in price.

Investment timing

The general investment-timing rule to beat inflation is: *Buy those assets whose prices do not fully reflect the benefits that inflation will bring. Sell those assets whose prices already overdiscount inflation.* There are special factors surrounding any particular asset, which means that inflation will have special effects on its price. However, the way to begin the exercise of judgment required to select the right vehicles is to compare the change that has occurred in its price to the change in the general price level over an appropriate period.

Take gold as an example. During most of the post-World War II period, gold was an extremely poor vehicle to beat inflation because its price, even in the free market, went up more slowly than prices in general. This should not be surprising. Gold is essentially useless and yields a negative return. That is to say, a gold bar or a certificate indicating you own one yields no interest. In fact, holding gold costs you money for insurance and storage and also interest payments if bought partly with borrowed money. The price of gold limped along through the 1950s and 1960s, since that period was not characterized by great fears of rapid inflation, while talk of collapse of world monetary systems was sporadic and lacked credibility.

By the year 1970, the price of gold had been carried to a 100-year low relative to prices in general. This kind of situation must be watched because it contains possibilities for rapid appreciation, if conditions change even slightly.

In 1971 they changed more than slightly. Governments all around the world adopted highly proinflationary policies, and the overvalued dollar, which had become the pivot of the world monetary system, began to tremble.

The environmental conditions for gold became perfect as inflation shot up and the dollar shot down. Between the middle of 1971 and the end of 1973, the price of gold almost tripled. In fact, between those dates, the price of gold went up by almost twenty times the rise in the consumer price index. Early in 1974 it shot up even higher to a point where it was clearly no longer cheap on a historical basis. This kind of movement should make those who want to beat inflation wary. On April 15, 1974, gold was at $173.50 per fine ounce; then the price dropped 21 percent in three months.

The risk level

We have expressed a great deal of skepticism about the advice offered by the conventional money managers; but what they have been saying for years about the amount of risk that a person should be willing to take holds good in a world of perpetual and cyclical inflation. Generally, you should be willing to accept a high level risk if you are young, have good income prospects from your job, and have considerable wealth. You should settle for lower-risk investments if you are older, have poor prospects of increasing your job income, and have little wealth.

Your psychological makeup also plays a role which often dominates. Some people are simply nervous. Others love to gamble. In short, when it comes to the risk level you are willing to accept, follow the advice of Socrates: "Know thyself."

However, those willing to take the biggest risks are the ones who will stand to benefit from the most powerful of inflation transfers—that from net monetary creditors to net monetary debtors.

The right currency

You should buy assets that are denominated in currencies of countries that will have the lowest inflation rates. When the fixed-exchange system prevailed, the exchange rate of a given country would stay constant for long periods of time even though the country was undergoing rapid domestic inflation compared to its trading partners. But when the currency values changed under this system, they changed by massive amounts.

Under the flexible-exchange-rate system that currently exists, however, you can be relatively certain that a country's exchange rate will quickly reflect its inflation prospects. Countries with low inflation rates will boost their exports relative to their imports. They experience trade surpluses. Countries with high inflation rates will boost their imports relative to their exports. They experience trade deficits.

The currencies of the trade-surplus nations tend to rise in value relative to the currencies of the trade-deficit nations. Therefore, hold as much of your wealth as you can in countries that you expect to experience low inflation rates. But watch out. Make sure that the faddists haven't been there first. It could be true, for example, that Switzerland will experience a very low future inflation rate. But those who have been recommending Swiss francs may have driven the price of the Swiss franc way up—so high, in fact, that assets denominated in this currency are bad investments as compared to those denominated in other currencies that also have relatively good inflation outlooks.

There are, in summary, five conventional investment imperatives:

1. Design an efficient portfolio.
2. Diversify your portfolio.
3. Time your buy and sell decisions correctly.
4. Choose the risk level you feel comfortable with.
5. Choose the right currency in which to denominate both your assets and your liabilities.

These are imperatives no matter what your investment goals may be. Portfolios will differ for different individuals. Each, however, will be based on the same premise: Assets will be bought whenever their prices do not reflect the benefits that inflation will bring. Assets will be sold as soon as they show signs of overanticipating the impact of the future inflation rate on their price.

CHAPTER 5

The
Case
of Bonds

The investor who beats inflation will always be holding the right combination of stocks, bonds, cash, commodities and currencies. No one of these investment vehicles is for all seasons. But there is a season when each of them will be the right thing to hold.

The inflation trend will be high and the inflation cycle will be volatile. This means that nothing can be put away in your safe-deposit box and forgotten, not even your jewelry. The investor must be nimble, flexible, and always alert. Moreover, if he lets other people manage his money for him, he'd better be aware of what they are up to. If money managers are to beat inflation for you, they are going to have to adopt policies that will work within the context of a high trend rate of inflation and a volatile inflation cycle.

Successful investing in inflation requires certain automatic responses to signals of changes in the inflation rate. Fortunately, these responses will not be hard to learn. As you read the subsequent chapters of this book that deal with specific investment vehicles, you will discover that the response mechanism that will guide you in investing in stocks, bonds, cash, commodities, and currencies will always be the same. Therefore, the remainder of the book is a series of variations on three novel investment themes. To find the right portfolio for now—any particular moment in time—the investor must take three steps:

1. *Classify all investment vehicles by their appropriateness for accelerating and decelerating inflation.* Commodities, short-term cash-equivalent instruments such as commercial paper, large ninety-day certificates of deposit or variable rate notes will benefit from accelerating inflation. Stocks and bonds will benefit from decelerating inflation. Currencies require a separate but related set of rules.

2. *Decide whether inflation is about to accelerate or decelerate.* The basic rule here is to keep your eye on the money supply. Accelerations in the monetary growth rate lead to accelerations in the inflation rate. Sustained decelerations in the monetary growth rate lead to decelerations in the inflation rate.

3. *See if the prices of particular assets incorporate your view of the inflation outlook.* Once you have decided whether inflation is about to accelerate or decelerate, see if the prices of stocks, bonds, commodities, short-term money-market instruments and currencies agree with your estimate. You know, for example, that stocks benefit from decelerating inflation. If you are in fact expecting inflation to decelerate over the next six months, you will have one more decision to make before you conclude that stocks are the investment for the upcoming season. That decision will depend on whether the price of stocks *already reflects* a major deceleration in the inflation rate. If they don't, stocks are clearly right. If they do, there may be better alternatives available.

We are now ready to apply the beat-inflation strategy to the case of bonds. Bonds, in certain circumstances, can be the perfect vehicle. Certainly they provide the clearest example of how inflation creates and destroys wealth.

Unfortunately bondholders have had a lot more experience with the destruction of asset values than with their creation. Chances are that those investors who have bonds in their portfolios right now have observed at first hand how destructive inflation can be.

When inflation starts, it begins the process of transferring income and wealth from the lender to the borrower. A bond is a commitment to pay a fixed number of dollars in interest per year. When inflation starts to accelerate, the number of dollars in interest on newly issued bonds will be higher to compensate for the rise in the inflation rate. When this happens, bonds already outstanding must fall in price to put their income stream in line with newly issued bonds. The lender is hurt in two ways. He is receiving less in terms of interest than he could on newly issued securities. Moreover, since the value of his security has fallen, he has suffered a decline in wealth. Thus there has been a transfer of both income and wealth from lender to borrower.

Before inflation got started, the world of bonds was correctly geared to an economic environment in which the long-term inflation rate was close to zero and was expected to stay there. In that kind of world nothing mattered but whether the interest on that bond reflected the inherent risk of lending to a particular company.

Today, inflation dominates the bond market. Inflation rates are incorporated into bond yields in the simplest and purest way possible. A bond is normally issued for twenty or thirty years. The interest that will be paid each year is decided—in a marketplace where lenders and borrowers are continuously interacting—at the time the bond is issued. The interest rate carried at the time of issue incorporates borrowers' and lenders' expectations of what the inflation rate will be during the period that the bond is in existence.

The lender obviously wants to be compensated for giving up his purchasing power now. The interest rate does this. But if prices in general are expected to rise during the period that the bond is outstanding, he needs a bigger incentive in the form of higher interest rates. He demands protection from the adverse wealth transfer—from borrowers to lenders—that inflation brings. Indeed, economists now look at the market rate of interest, which in economic jargon is referred to as the "nominal" rate of interest, as the sum of two components—a "real" rate and an inflation premium.

The nominal rate is the rate that the market puts on newly issued bonds. When you hear people talk about the current cost of long-term money, that is what they are talking about.

The real rate of interest is the rate that would prevail if prices were stable. Even if there were no inflation, lenders would demand compensation for giving up purchasing power now. Borrowers are willing to pay for credit because they figure they can use the money productively. In a world of stable prices the long-term interest rate is determined by the interaction of productivity and thrift. History suggests that the real rate of interest in the United States is approximately 3 percent.

The inflation premium is the extra compensation that lenders demand because they expect the dollars they give up today to buy less tomorrow. If prices are expected to rise at 2 percent per year, only the unsophisticated would be willing to lend without demanding an extra 2 percent in interest. For this reason an inflation premium over and above the return to productivity and thrift gets incorporated into interest rates during a period in which inflation is expected to exist.

Because the real rate of interest has been relatively constant over long periods of time, almost all the movement in long-term bond rates comes from changes in expectations about inflation—the inflation premium. Economic research also indicates that investors and borrowers tend to look at past rates of inflation when trying to guess at future rates of inflation. Bond yields and past inflation rates are related. Bond rates moved up when the inflation rate moved up and bond rates moved down when the inflation rate moved down.

Followers of the beat-inflation strategy can make money in bonds because there will be times when the inflation premium that is built into the market yields of bonds represents an incorrect estimate of the future inflation rate. Throw away the notion that bonds must be held to maturity. Only in a world of no inflation, or one in which the inflation rate is constant and fully reflected in the interest rate, does a buy-and-hold-to-maturity strategy make sense.

Bonds are pure debt; therefore the inflation-induced wealth transfer tends to occur quickly and with a vengeance in the bond market. The investor can reap rich rewards from being on the right side of this transfer at the right time. Bonds, in a world where the inflation rate is likely to be variable, are anything but dull.

To make money by getting on the right side of the wealth transfer, the investor must follow several basic rules.

Bond rule number 1

The right time to buy bonds is when the inflation rate incorporated into their yield exceeds your best judgment of the future rate of inflation. This is most likely to occur just before the inflation cycle moves into its decelerating phase.

With many rules, the decision to buy or sell turns on whether the market price or yield of the asset correctly incorporates the trend rate of inflation.

The investor has two problems. First, he must determine the inflation rate built into the yield on newly issued long-term bonds. Second, he must determine what inflation rate ought to be built into the yield on long-term bonds, for once he does this he can easily form his best-judgment yield on long-term securities.

The best-judgment long-term bond yield is an important concept. It is by comparing the current market yield with the best-judgment yield that the investor can decide whether long-term bonds are a buy or a sell.

Figure 8 shows you how to form your best-judgment yield for long-term bonds. This yield is the yield that is consistent with your estimate of the trend rate of inflation. When yields on newly issued bonds rise above your best-judgment yield you buy bonds; when yields on newly issued securities fall below your best-judgment yield you sell bonds.

The best-judgment rate is the simple sum of the real rate of interest plus the inflation premium that is consistent with the trend rate of growth of the money supply. The inflation premium that you use to get your best-judgment interest rate reflects the trend rate of inflation implied by the monetary growth rate on a one-to-one basis. If the trend rate of inflation is 5 percent (money has been growing at 6 percent for the preceding two years), then the best-judgment inflation premium is 5 percent; if money has been growing at 7 percent, the best-judgment inflation premium is 6 percent, and so on.

To find out what inflation rate is being incorporated into current-market bond yields, subtract about 3 percent from the current market yield on new issues. For example, if the stated interest rate on new bonds is 9 percent, it means that borrowers and lenders believe the inflation over the life of the bonds will average about 6 percent. To formulate your best judgment about the future inflation rate you must keep your eye on the money supply. If money growth has been a steady 7 percent,

Fig. 8. **Bond Investing
and the Inflation Cycle**

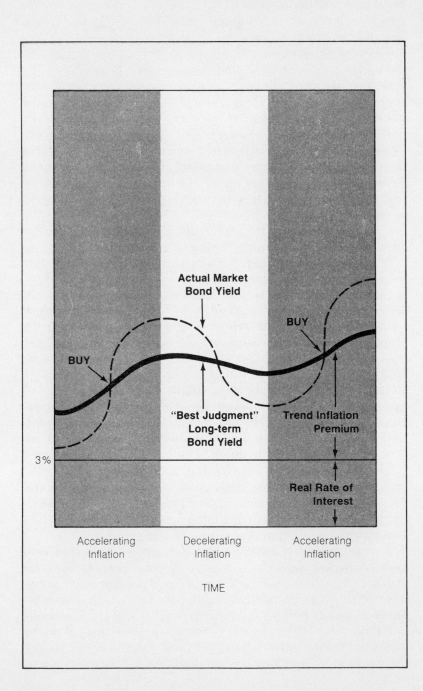

the trend rate of inflation will be 6 percent. Therefore, in our example, bonds are a buy when yields rise over 9 percent; the higher the better for you.

To see how your ability to form a best-judgment yield on long-term bonds would have made you money, compare the movement of the best-judgment rate with that of the actual market long-term rate in figure 8. The chart shows that the actual market yield exceeds the best-judgment yield late in the accelerating phase of the inflation cycle and early in the decelerating phase. The difference is widest around the turning point in the inflation cycle. Therefore, the best money-making opportunities occur just when the inflation rate is about to decelerate. Remember that when bond yields on newly issued bonds fall, the prices on older bonds rise.

Bond rule number 2

Move into lower-quality or lower-rated bonds when you believe the market is incorrectly reflecting the risk premium. The biggest opportunities are likely to occur in lower-rated bonds. Plays on AT&T or U.S. Government bonds are tame as compared to some lower-rated bonds, such as those issued by the airlines. AT&T always pays a lower rate of interest than Pan American World Airways. The difference between the interest rate paid by AT&T and Pan Am is an example of a risk premium. Just like the inflation cycle, there is a cycle in risk premiums too. Most of the time the inflation cycle and the risk-premium cycle move together. When inflation is accelerating, people will be talking about tight money and liquidity crises, and the risk premium will be going up. The risk premiums are likely to be the biggest in the final spasms of accelerating inflation. Figure 9 schematically demonstrates the widening and narrowing of the risk premium over the inflation cycle.

Remember though, the lower the bond ratings, the more risk you incur. Ordinarily, when you dip below B-rated, the risk of default goes way up. The final spasm of accelerating inflation is not hard to spot. When business and economic news moves onto the front page of your newspaper, you are right in the middle of one. In the wake of the Penn Central debacle in June of 1970, risk premiums widened. They also widened when Con Edison omitted its dividend. For example, after Con Edison's board of directors announced their dividend omission on April 23, 1974, the interest-rate spread between AAA-rated

Fig. 9. **Yield Spreads and the Inflation Cycle**

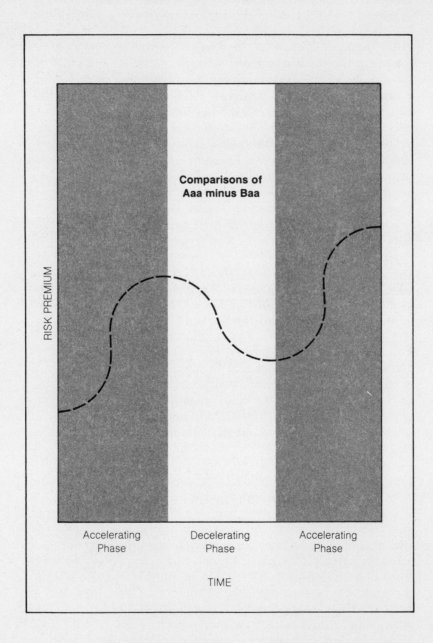

corporate bonds and AA utilities widened from 87 basis points to 136 basis points in a few months. A basis point is one one-hundredth of a percentage point.

This fact has been documented with data going back to 1900. In a study, *Corporate Bond Quality and Investor Experience*, published by the National Bureau of Economic Research, W. Braddock Hickman found that when low-grade corporate bonds were purchased near the trough of an investment cycle (these correspond to peaks in our inflation cycle) the investor fared better than with similar purchases and sales of high-grade corporate bonds. He concluded that when low-grade bonds have been knocked way down in price, the market usually overestimates the risk of default. In fact, virtually all the economic research that has been done on the behavior of the risk premium shows that the risk premium has been more than enough to compensate the bondholder for additional risk. But be careful and remember the principle of diversification.

Penn Central bonds did default. But many other issues were tarnished by Penn Central, Con Edison, and Franklin National Bank. After the Penn Central crisis evaporated, the risk premium narrowed again: the same was true after the Con Edison crisis and the Franklin National Bank crisis. For example, after Con Edison cut its dividend, the market overreacted and risk premiums on *all* issues rose.

This overreaction represented a beat-inflation opportunity. With inflation on the verge of decelerating, risk premiums were bound to narrow. In fact, between July and November of 1974, the risk premium between AAA corporate bonds and AA utility bonds fell by 75 basis points. AA utility bonds normally yield more than AAA corporate bonds. This yield differential is generally regarded as a measure of the risk premium between the two rating classifications. When the dividend omission at Con Edison was announced, the risk premium widened. However, when investors had time to think about what happened, the risk premium began to fall. Consequently, the investor who bought AA utilities made an even greater killing than the one who played it safer.

Bond rule number 3

The right time to incur long-term debt is when you expect the inflation rate to accelerate. It is the right time for the individual investor to become a net monetary debtor.

The correct time to take on debt is during those brief periods when interest rates fall. These periods will occur during the decelerating phase of the inflation cycle. And the bottom in interest rates is likely to occur toward the end of the decelerating phase and just prior to reacceleration.

This is an extremely critical period for the investor. The strategy will require him to rearrange his portfolio. One step that he certainly ought to take is to increase the degree to which he is a net monetary debtor. This means that he should increase his holdings of real assets (commodities, real estate) and finance his buying spree with the profits that he is likely to have made in the stock market and, most importantly, with long-term debt.

How you go about increasing your long-term debt depends on who you are and how rich you are. No matter what your position, though, you should start thinking like the big corporate treasurer and see what avenues are really open to you so that you can borrow money at favorable rates that will be available just prior to the upswing in the inflation cycle. When you do this you will find a surprising number of options available.

The key is to try to borrow at fixed rates which will be relatively low at the bottom of the inflation cycle. One possibility would be to borrow the cash value of your life insurance. Also possible, but much more risky, is to arrange a second mortgage on your home and put the money to work in real estate or commodities. Don't forget your friendly neighborhood banker. Banks are apt to be flush with money toward the end of the decelerating phase of the inflation cycle. And most investors simply do not exploit the possibilities of using personal credit from their banks. Remember, your banker makes his money by lending to you, not by accepting your deposits.

Bond rule number 4

When the beat-inflation strategy tells you bonds are a buy, you can maximize your profits at no additional risk by buying a portfolio of discount bonds. A discount bond is simply a bond that was issued some time in the past. For example, the AT&T 2⅝% of 1986 are deep discount bonds. They are selling way below their par value because their coupon interest rate is far below the coupon on newly issued bonds. Studies by Salomon Brothers indicate that during bull markets in bonds, discount bonds give the investor a higher total return than a similar amount of newly issued bonds. During the bond bull market in the third quarter of 1970, for example, the total return to holding discount bonds was 36 percent at an annual rate compared to only 25 percent for newly issued bonds. Similarly, when bond prices are falling a portfolio of discount bonds performs worse than a portfolio of newly issued bonds or premium bonds.

Bond rule number 5

Those investors who want to play the interest-rate swings ought to take advantage of the rotation in the yield curve. The yield curve is a shorthand expression that bond-market people use to describe the relationship between interest rates on short maturity and longer maturity debt instruments. A positively sloped yield curve exists when short rates are lower than long rates. Figure 10 shows the positively sloped yield curve that existed in the spring of 1971. A negatively sloped yield curve exists when short-term rates are higher than long-term rates. Figure 11 shows the negatively sloped yield curve that existed in July 1974. In the preinflation-cycle days, the yield curve had a positive slope most of the time. But now that high and variable inflation is here to stay, the yield curve will show wide and relatively frequent fluctuations. Short-term rates will be higher than long-term rates toward the peak in the inflation cycle; short-term rates will be lower than long-term rates toward the bottom of the inflation cycle. This means that short-term rates swing more than long-term rates over the inflation cycle, and herein lies an opportunity for financing your investments in a most profitable way.

Why does the yield curve swing from positively sloped to negatively sloped? When interest rates are extremely high by historic standards, investors expect them to come down. They are therefore willing to lend for long periods of time at lower rates. When rates are low by historic standards, investors expect them to rise. They therefore demand a higher interest rate for long-term money than for short-term money and borrowers with similar views of the outlook are willing to pay it.

The yield curve will be steeper for a negatively sloped yield curve if everybody is looking for a big decline in interest rates over the near term. When it is upward-sloping it will be steeper in an upward direction if everybody is looking for a big rise

Fig. 10. **Positive Yield Curve**

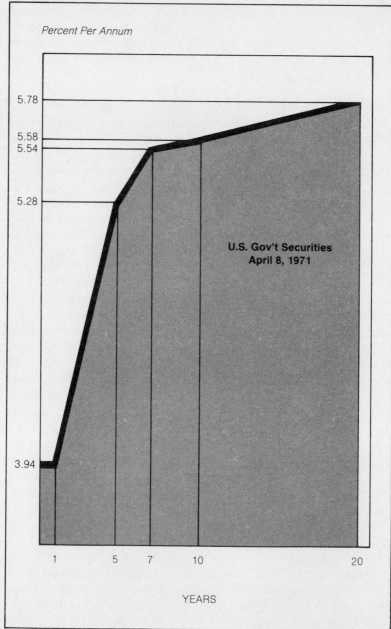

Percent Per Annum

5.78
5.58
5.54

5.28

**U.S. Gov't Securities
April 8, 1971**

3.94

1   5   7   10   20

YEARS

Fig. 11. **Negative Yield Curve**

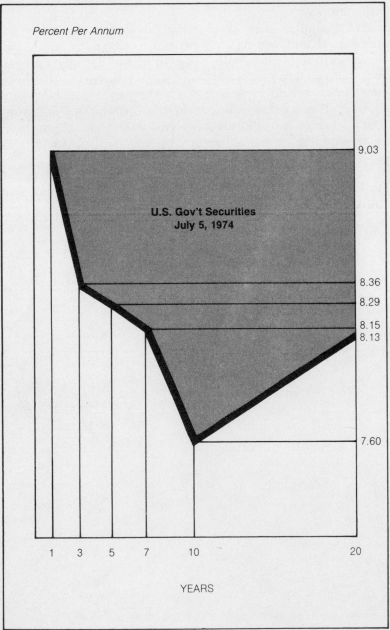

in interest rates over the near future. If your expectation of inflation and hence interest rates is markedly different from that embodied in market interest rates, there may be a beat-inflation play.

For example, if the yield curve has only a slight upward slope to it and you believe inflation is about to surge, and hence interest rates will move dramatically upward, you would do well to keep your financial investments in the short-term area and do what borrowing you can in the long-term market. This is because long-term interest rates will not incorporate a large enough inflation premium to warrant purchase. You would get a higher return by constantly turning over short-term financial assets.

Similarly you should borrow short and lend long when the yield curve is not steep enough in the downward direction and inflation is about to decelerate sharply.

CHAPTER 6

Inflation and Common Stocks

In the 1950s and most of the 1960s, stocks were a super investment vehicle, outperforming everything else.

This was so even though stocks were being sold on what proved to be a false premise. Everyone then selling stocks advertised equities as the ideal hedge against inflation. The investor was told that equity investment—a share of ownership—was the only way to keep ahead of rising prices. The only alternative that investment advisers and brokers thought was suitable for the prudent man—bonds—yielded only a fixed number of dollars per year. Stocks, by contrast, could be expected to provide an ever-growing stream of dividends.

The 1950s and the first half of the 1960s was a period when everybody turned to Wall Street for protection against inflation. And, in fact, the day in 1958 when AT&T decided to invest employees' pension money in common stocks rather than in the traditional bonds, the "cult of equities" was born.

The cult of equities is dead now, killed by the very thing that was supposed to be giving it life—inflation. As long as inflation remained only a sales argument, it could be used to justify the cult of equities, and stocks sold well. But, ironically, when inflation actually began in earnest, it played hob with the fundamental determinants of stock prices.

The reason inflation has undermined the stock market is essentially simple. It can be found in *Security Analysis,* a book written in 1934 by two professors at the Columbia University Business School, Benjamin Graham and David L. Dodd. The book is the security analyst's bible.

It suggests a simple equation that accurately portrays the fundamental determinants of the value of a stock. The equation has three elements: expected profits and dividend growth, expected interest rates, and some measure of risk. When expected profits go up, stock prices go up; when expected interest rates go down, stock prices go up; when investors feel more certain about future profits and interest rates, stock prices go up. When inflation actually came, it dumped the market. Inflation fouled up corporate earnings; inflation jacked up interest rates; inflation made people far more uncertain about the outlook for interest rates and profits.

Inflation makes real profits hard to come by, hard to understand and therefore hard to trust. From 1966 to the bottom of the 1970 recession, corporations were on the wrong side of inflation-induced income transfers. Inflation was concentrated in wages, services, construction, and borrowing charges. This meant that the cost of staying in business went up and profits were small. Profits actually declined, even though prices went up. So instead of being a hedge against inflation, stocks bore the brunt of inflation. After-tax profits fell by 26.3 percent in current dollars over the period. Adjusted for inflation they fell even more—39.9 percent. In the battle for who gets what out of the economic pie, the profits share of gross national product plummeted, while the wage and salary share rose.

Beginning in late 1970 things started to look up for profits. Wages had more than caught up with past inflation, and inflation itself began to decelerate and brought interest rates down with it. In 1970, the inflation rate was running 5.9 percent; in 1971, 4.3 percent; in 1972, 3.3 percent. At the same time that the inflation rate was coming down, corporate profits started up, pulling stock prices with them. Hence, as the economy

moved from a more inflationary environment to a less inflationary environment, profits did better, stocks did better and
the old saw that stocks were a hedge against inflation was
turned on its head.,

The irony became total in 1973 and 1974. Inflation really
headed into the double-digit range, and this time profits really
responded. Commodity prices led the advance, and the wholesale prices rose much faster than wages. But, even though
profits were rising, again the accelerating phase of the inflation cycle killed the market. This time the problem wasn't
sluggish profits; it was that nobody trusted the profits numbers.

Rising prices create two big problems in the arithmetic of
profits reporting. Both problems make the profits numbers
larger than they should be, and larger than they can be expected to be if the inflation rate slows down.

One problem is the big gains that companies make on the
products and materials that they already have on hand when
inflation accelerates. These gains are reported in the profits
figures and are taxed. But people know that any ongoing business has to replace the stock in its inventory. The profits gener-
ated by inventories can't be used in any other way. They are
not available to pay stockholders dividends or to buy new
plants and equipment or to pay for the research needed to
develop new products. Therefore, profits coming from inventory windfalls are not the basis to build stock market dreams
on.

Depreciation raises a second problem that is even more obvious. As part of the cost of doing business, companies charge
off the cost of replacing their equipment, so that when it wears
out they will have funds available to replace it. The guidelines
for how big these expenses can be are laid out by the Internal
Revenue Service—hence, the bigger they are, the slimmer
corporate tax collections will be. When prices rise, so does the
cost of replacing equipment. It's universally accepted that inflation renders depreciation charges inadequate to replace the
equipment. As a consequence, profits are overstated. And, to
add insult to injury, these overstated profits are taxed.

Inflation also pumps up interest rates, making other financial assets relatively attractive compared to common stocks.

Inflation increases uncertainty, raising doubts about the future profitability of American industry. When inflation strikes,
people have more legitimate reasons to worry than when

prices are stable. Inflation brings with it three big worries:

Fear of recession. Although government policy has become far more permissive on inflation than it used to be, rampant price increases will meet with some response from Washington—a throttling back of the rate of monetary expansion. This in turn leads to recession, dumping corporate profits and increasing business failures.

Fear of financial collapse. Inflation brings sky-high interest rates. And since interest rates and financial asset prices move in different directions, this could spell trouble for banks, other financial institutions and even ordinary companies. These institutions are on the wrong side of the wealth transfer. They are stocked with IOUs that they can't sell for their face value. When interest rates shoot up, any bank that has to liquidate will be insolvent. This is what happened to the Franklin National Bank in early 1974. The market value of Franklin's liabilities exceeded the market value of its assets.

Fear of worldwide depression. Countries are much more interdependent than they used to be so liquidity crises in one country can spill over to other countries. Many strange new international financial markets, such as the Eurodollar market, have come into being. Together with the system of floating exchange rates, these markets increase the risk inherent in financial transactions, particularly for banks and other financial institutions. When rapid inflation brings sharply escalating interest rates around the world, worries over a world financial crisis intensify.

But the investor who obeys the following six rules can find stocks that have the potential of doubling at some points in the inflation cycle.

Stock market rule number 1

Buy stocks when your best judgment of the future rate of inflation is markedly less than the rate of inflation that the public expects. Sell stocks (or sell them short) when the trend rate of inflation that the public (and the stock market) expects is less than your best-judgment rate.

As in the case of bonds, the investor needs to know two things in order to make stock market decisions. First of all, he must establish his own best estimate of the future inflation rate and the implication of this inflation rate for stock prices. Second, he must determine the future inflation rate that is built into current stock prices. Your buy and sell decisions are importantly, but not solely, based on a comparison of your best judgment of the inflation rate with the future inflation rate that is built into current stock prices.

Calculating the inflation rate that is built into stock prices requires a small dose of mathematics. Enormous amounts of money have been lost in the stock market since 1965, primarily because of a failure to recognize how the inflation cycle impacts stock prices.

The equation we use is a variant of the Graham and Dodd equation. It says $P = D/(k-g)$. In the equation:

P = stock prices; in our example we will use the Dow Jones Industrial Average.

D = current dividends; in our example we will use a measure of the current dividends on the thirty stocks in the Dow Jones average.

k = the expected rate of return. That means it is the total return that investors expect to get from investing in stocks at current prices.

g = the expected rate of growth in dividends. This simply is the rate at which investors believe dividends will grow in the future.

This equation allows you to determine what inflation rate is built into stock prices. To illustrate this, let's see what the equation would have shown at the end of 1974. P, or the Dow Jones average, was around 600. D, or dividends on the Dow Jones stocks, were $38. You can't determine what k and g are by looking at the financial pages.

In order to determine what values to use for g and k you must make some assumptions. To estimate g, simply take the trend rate of inflation and add 3 percent to it. The 3-percent figure is our estimate of the real growth dividends. The trend rate of inflation is an old friend. At the end of 1974, it was 5 percent, the trend rate of inflation consistent with a money-supply growth rate of 6 percent.

In our formulation of a beat-inflation strategy for stocks, k swings with the inflation cycle. Stocks are alternatives to other investments. In order to buy stocks an investor must be persuaded that his purchase will pay off as well as an investment in short-term liquid assets, long-term bonds, and commodities. Because the return from other assets, such as short-term liquid assets and commodities, moves up during the accelerating phase of the inflation cycle, so must k. Similarly, when rates of return on alternative investments fall in the decelerating phase of the cycle, so does k.

The key to stock investing is to remember that whatever pushes k up is bad for stocks and whatever pushes it down is good for stocks. When k goes up, the market applies a higher rate of discount to the current level of dividends, and thus P (stock prices) falls.

Like bond yields, k is composed of a real rate component and an inflation premium. And since the real rate doesn't vary much over time, the movements up and down in k occur because of changes in inflation expectations in the stock market.

We are now ready to figure out whether stocks are a buy or a sell at various stages of the inflation cycle and various levels of the stock market. Our basic example is drawn from the situation that prevailed at the end of 1974 when the Dow Jones Industrial stocks were paying $38 in dividends and the market was around 600. Remembering that we estimate g to be 8 percent, based on previous trends in the monetary growth rate, solving the equation for k shows that the expected rate of return was 14.3 percent at the end of 1974. The question for the investor is what estimate of the inflation rate does this expected rate of return contain. The answer is 8.3 percent because our research indicates that the real rate of return to stocks in a world that has adjusted to the inflation cycle is around 6 percent. Therefore, at the end of 1974, 8.3 percent was the inflation rate built into stock prices.

The investor should have compared this to his own best-judgment estimate of the future inflation rate. At the end of 1974 the economy was in the initial stages of decelerating inflation and our estimate of the trend rate of inflation was 5 percent. Plugging a 5-percent inflation premium into k gives you a value for k of 11 percent. And solving the equation this time for P gives you your best-judgment value for the Dow Jones for 5-percent inflation—a value of 1266 for the Dow Jones. Clearly the market was a buy at the end of 1974; our formula indicated that stock prices could double as inflation expectations were receding during the decelerating phase of the inflation cycle. The table on page 77 solves the equation for various inflation premiums using the $38 dividend figure for 1974. The table illustrates how dramatically stock prices respond to changes in the inflation premium. This exercise also

The Inflation Premium and Stock Prices

Inflation Premium in Stock Prices	Value of Dow Index
4%	1,900
5%	1,266
6%	950
7%	760
8%	633
9%	542
10%	475

Note: Stock prices calculated by assuming g = 8 percent, the real component of k = 6 percent, and D = $38.

tells you how well a bet on stocks is covered. For example, if the trend rate of inflation turns out to be 7 percent instead of 5 percent, stock prices should be 26.6 percent higher than they were at the end of 1974.

The calculations are based on trend rates of inflation and take no account of the way the inflation cycle influences expectations in the stock market. When inflation is accelerating, the stock market is apt to be far more nervous than when it is decelerating. And although the equation may indicate that stocks are a buy, remember all of the problems that accelerating inflation raises for stock prices and corporate profits. Therefore, the equation should only lead you to buying decisions when the economy is in the decelerating phase of the inflation cycle.

Unless inflation is decelerating or about to decelerate, you don't want stocks—any stocks. Get rid of them. When money managers tell *Wall Street Journal* reporters that they are in cash, they generally mean that they have changed their portfolios from 10 percent cash and 90 percent stocks to 15 percent cash and 85 percent stocks. Do not emulate them. When you expect inflation to be worse than the market expects it to be, get out of stocks. Under these circumstances there will be other good places to be: commodities—including gold—and short-term money instruments.

By the same token, when you expect the rate of inflation to be materially less than the market expects, stocks will be an ideal vehicle; so will some bonds.

Stock market rule number 2

The richest stock market rewards will occur just before the inflation rate begins to decline. A declining inflation rate will change the elements in Graham and Dodd's equation in such a way as to jack up equity values on a fundamental basis. Stocks become a good play when the inflation cycle is in the declining phase. For a fleeting moment stocks will regain the glow that made them stars in the 1950s and early 1960s.

The ideal time to be in stocks is just before the decline in inflation occurs, and certainly before the fact that it is occurring becomes widely recognized. The beat-inflation strategist will have advance warning of the impending turnaround in the inflation rate because he will have been tracking the money supply. Moreover, commodity prices already will have weakened, and short-term interest rates will be above long-term interest rates. Everyone will be pessimistic; there will be more bearish recommendations about stocks than bullish recommendations; fund managers will be telling *The Wall Street Journal* that they are moving into cash. In short, conditions will be ideal to buy.

Stock market rule number 3

Beta is more than the second letter in the Greek alphabet. It is the symbol that statisticians and econometricians use to measure the volatility of a given stock relative to the overall stock market. Suppose that an econometrician calculates the *beta* for the XYZ Corporation to be 1.5. This means that in the past the price of this stock has on the average increased 50 percent more than stocks in general when the market was rising, and decreased 50 percent faster than stocks in general when the market was falling. In short, XYZ Corporation is a high-*beta* stock—one that is more volatile than stocks in general. A stock with a *beta* of 1.0 would on the average be about as volatile as stocks in general, while stocks with a *beta* of less than 1.0 would be on the average less volatile than most stocks.

When he expects the stock market to go up, an investor who is willing to take some risk will do much better than the market if he constructs his portfolio by buying stocks with *betas* significantly greater than 1.0.

A simple way to do this is to buy a no-load mutual fund whose *beta* is significantly greater than 1.0. You have to pay a sales commission of up to 8½ percent on most mutual funds, particularly those that are sold by brokers. This means that for every $100 you put in you only have $91.50 working for you when you start. With a no-load there is no sales charge, so $100 out of every $100 put in is at work and it doesn't have to rise by 8.5 per cent just to get even. Moreover, the evidence indicates that no-load funds perform just as well and just as badly as funds that charge sales commissions.

The beat-inflation investor, however, need not always use high *betas* for leverage. A portfolio with a *beta* of 1.0 (say the thirty stocks in the Dow Jones Industrial Average) bought on margin will ordinarily serve you just as well as a high-*beta* portfolio. If you buy stocks that do no better than the market as a whole with 50 percent borrowed money, you will do just as well as if you had bought a portfolio of stocks whose average *beta* was 1.5.

Stock market rule number 4

Be sure you know the impact that inflation is having on the companies whose stocks you are planning to buy. Remember that inflation distorts income statements and balance sheets. Accelerating inflation gives a false glow to corporate profits because it leads to large inventory profits and inadequate depreciation reserves. When Arab oil ministers quadrupled oil prices, oil companies benefited because their oil inventories immediately became much more valuable. They reported enormous profits gains in late 1973 and early 1974, but their stockholders saw little benefit. The value of their shares basically went nowhere.

One reason was fear that the government would grab a big share of the windfall profits. Another was recognition that the surge in profits was temporary and would dwindle once oil companies used up their lower-priced oil inventories. This is a classic example of inflation's effect on reported profits and why

Betas For 25 Well-Known Stocks

Company	Beta
American Telephone & Telegraph	.75
Avon Products	1.20
Black & Decker Manufacturing	1.20
Burroughs Corp.	1.40
Citicorp	1.25
Eastman Kodak	1.05
Eli Lilly & Co.	1.00
Emerson Electric Co.	1.00
Exxon Corp.	.95
General Reinsurance Corp.	1.00
Halliburton Co.	1.10
Imperial Oil Ltd.	.85
International Business Machines	1.05
Merck & Co.	1.05
Mobil Oil	.95
Pepsico Inc.	1.05
Polaroid	1.45
Schlumberger Ltd.	1.10
Sears Roebuck & Co.	1.00
Sony Corp. ADR	1.05
Standard Oil of California	1.05
Syntex Co.	1.30
Walt Disney Productions	1.40
Weyerhaeuser & Co.	1.05
Xerox Corp.	1.20

Source: Value Line Investment Service

Betas For 25 Selected No-Load Funds

Fund	Objective	Beta
Afuture Fund	Maximum Capital Gains	1.55
American Investors	Maximum Capital Gains	1.26
Babson	Growth	1.06
Beacon Hill	Growth	0.92
Colonial Growth Shares	Growth	1.11
Columbia Growth	Maximum Capital Gains	1.06
Dodge & Cox Stock Fund	Growth and Current Income	0.98
Drexel Equity	Growth	0.95
Edie Special Growth	Maximum Capital Gains	1.16
Energy Fund	Growth	0.92
Foursquare Fund	Growth	1.13
Growth Industry Shares	Growth	1.11
Guardian Mutual Fund	Growth, Income & Stability	0.96
Johnston Mutual Fund	Growth	1.08
Mathers Fund	Maximum Capital Gains	1.07
National Industries Fund	Growth, Income & Stability	1.08
Neuwirth Fund	Maximum Capital Gains	1.12
Nicholas Fund	Maximum Capital Gains	1.54
Northeast Investors Trust	Income	0.23
One William Street	Growth and Current Income	1.05
Price Growth Fund	Growth	1.17
Rowe Price New Era	Growth	0.89
Rowe Price New Horizons	Maximum Capital Gains	1.24
Scudder International Investment	Growth	0.60
Selected American Shares	Growth and Current Income	0.97

Source: Wiesenberger Services, Inc.

profits attributed to inflation should be examined carefully.

The steel industry contains many companies that reported excellent profits during the inflationary surge in late 1973 and 1974. Inventory profits were important here too, but the inadequacy of depreciation allowances also played a critical role. These companies' stock prices did not respond to higher profits in the usual way. The inventory profits in the steel industry were heavily discounted, as they were in the oil industry. But recognition that depreciation allowances would be inadequate to replace worn-out equipment created skepticism that the high profits could be maintained without massive additional financing. This shows up most clearly in the difference between the book value—the value assigned to the company by the accountants on the basis of the historical or purchase price of its net assets—and its market value. For most steel companies this gap was very large. For example, Wheeling Steel had a book value of $79.38 per share on December 31, 1973, and on the same day its market price was $13. Jones and Laughlin was worth $44.99 per share, according to the accountants, but the stock was selling for $18.88.

A big difference between book value and market value has never been a good reason to buy stock.

Stock market rule number 5

Seek opportunities in interest-rate-sensitive stocks when inflation begins to decelerate.

All stocks tend to move in the opposite direction from the interest rate. But some stocks respond particularly to changes in short-term interest rates—rates on treasury bills, commercial paper and bank certificates of deposit. Among the stocks most sensitive to interest rates are those of finance companies, real estate investment trusts, and savings and loan associations. In general these companies borrow short term and lend longer term. Short-term rates move up and down with changes in the inflation rates more quickly than long-term rates. Hence, when inflation decelerates, short-term rates come down more than long-term rates, and the profits of these companies rise. When inflation accelerates, just the opposite happens.

Stock market rule number 6

Recognize that most companies deal in a world market. And, in a world of volatile and permanent inflation, recognize that those companies with major exposure in countries with relatively low inflation rates will do best. Chapter 9 will show that profits can be made from holding the currencies of countries with the lowest trend rates of inflation. Because the value of their currencies will rise, profits earned in these countries will become higher when valued in terms of dollars.

Like bonds, stocks should never be put in your safe-deposit box and forgotten. The beat-inflation investment race will be won by the nimble.

CHAPTER 7

Cash: How Much You Should Keep and Where You Should Keep It

In a world of high inflation, how you manage your cash, that ready-access portion of wealth that people used to keep in their pockets, or checking account or savings account when inflation did not matter, is extremely important. When interest rates are sky high, cash management can make a major difference in how well you beat inflation.

A few years ago, investment advisers had no need to write about cash management. The reason was simple. In general, the rules to follow came right out of Poor Richard: Keep enough in your checking account for monthly expenses, plus a little for emergencies, and what's left over keep in a savings account.

Everybody, including the tight-fisted treasurer of a giant corporation, followed these rules until the early 1960s. But then some of the nation's corporations, helped by some of the nation's giant banks, began to play an exciting new game called "intensive cash management." What is good for General Motors is good for you, too. And the financial world is changing in a way that allows the individual investor some of the cash plays that were available only to the giant corporations a few years ago.

The new routes available for intensive cash management will sometimes play a critical role in the beat-inflation strategy. There will be times when you will want most of your investable funds in them. For example, between the beginning of April and the end of September in 1974, short-term money-market instruments, such as U.S. Government treasury bills and prime commercial paper, were the only place to be. For, while everything else from gold to soybeans to Polaroid was on the skids, yields on short-term money-market instruments zoomed. So the smart investor could earn 12 percent or more with little risk in money-market instruments and wait for other opportunities to arise.

High inflation and high interest rates have meant a growing public awareness that it is easy to put out money for extremely short periods of time at high rates. Banks, for example, lend money to each other quite literally overnight for use during one working day in the Federal Funds market. Almost the same option is available to the smaller investor in the new money-market funds that are being announced each day. So there is no reason not to lend your money out at high rates, even if you know you are going to need it soon—perhaps tomorrow.

The game of intensive cash management is safe and simple. The treasurer of the giant corporation follows certain simple rules in playing it. To beat inflation you should follow them too.

Cash rule number 1

Keep that portion of your portfolio which yields zero interest at a minimum. When asked how much noninterest-bearing cash they think it advisable to hold, some corporate treasurers answer, "None." Their reasoning is straightforward. As long as they can see at least some interest on their money elsewhere, they ought to keep no cash. Theoretically, the correct amount of currency to keep in cash and in checking accounts is zero.

This should be your goal, but it is an ideal goal no one can attain. The difference between you and the corporate treasurer, of course, is that he is dealing with millions, and thus the interest return is worth somebody's time.

Although it is impossible, or, at least, impractical to emulate the corporate treasurer, the individual investor could probably get by with less cash if he put some effort into it.

Cash rule number 2

Keep no excess funds in your checking account. There is no reason to keep emergency funds there. Bad as it may be as a beat-inflation play, a day-of-deposit—day-of-withdrawal account in a savings bank is a better place for emergency funds. If you are afraid of running your checking account down too low and having a check bounce, get an overdraft privilege.

When interest rates are sky high, as in mid-1974, the overdraft privilege can be a cheap source of funds. Take advantage of the government pressure on banks to keep the rates of interest on consumer borrowing low. In mid-1974, rates on consumer overdraft loans were the same as the prime rate—the rate that the banks charge their best corporate customers. When the beat-inflation strategy suggests that the time to move is now, don't hesitate to leverage your bank for every cent you can get. The beat-inflation strategy frequently turns up investment opportunities with high reward-risk ratios when interest rates are very high and money is hard to come by. To make sure that he can get his hands on plenty of money in periods like this, a corporate treasurer arranges for lines of credit well in advance. He does not have access to these funds for nothing. There is a charge to a corporation for a guaranteed line of credit. The individual investor can get the same privilege for nothing.

The right time to arrange for your line of credit is not when credit is scarce but when there is plenty of it around. You will be able to get a bigger credit line if you tap your bank when credit is plentiful. And banks are honorable; once they give you a credit line, they rarely take it away.

Cash rule number 3

Obtain the highest return possible consistent with safety for your funds. Consider the rich variety of alternative places to put cash you have available now:

• Savings banks are offering a choice of maturities as well as the day-of-deposit—day-of-withdrawal account. We consider funds placed for ninety days or less liquid enough to serve as an emergency fund or as a haven for investment funds when other alternatives don't offer beat-inflation opportunities. Savings deposits are riskless—they are FDIC-insured up to $40,000 per account.

• Money-market instruments are offered for sale by the U.S. Treasury, and by large and very creditworthy corporations and banks. The safest of these instruments are U.S. Treasury bills. These are issued in minimum denominations of $10,000 and auctioned every Monday. The large corporation's equivalent of the Treasury bill is high-grade commerical paper, which is usually issued in denominations of $25,000, and may be purchased through dealers or brokers. Negotiable certificates of deposit are the bank's Treasury bill equivalent. They carry a maturity of at least thirty days and the investor must make a minimum purchase of $100,000.

You may find it difficult to get your hands on these instruments. Obviously, you must have plenty of money to buy them. The organizations issuing them don't like to sell them to individual investors. And many brokers won't knock themselves out to get them for you because commissions are low and they can't make a living that way. Therefore the individual investor would do well to consider the excellent alternative presented by money-market funds.

Money-market funds are simply portfolios of money-market instruments put together by an investment manager and made available to individual investors. When the individual investor buys one of these funds he enjoys almost all the benefits of owning the money-market instruments himself. In addition, he avoids almost all their disadvantages.

Money-market funds are highly liquid. They can be bought and sold daily. In general they can be bought in increments of as little as $1,000. Interest accrues daily—seven days a week.

In some cases you can actually write checks on the money in your account. Fidelity Management & Research Company of Boston, Massachusetts, has set up such a fund. Your invested funds are easily accessible through a check-writing redemption system administered by National Shawmut Bank. Any time you like, you may write a check for $1,000 or more on your funds, just as if they were in a regular checking account. Investors who put money into this fund seem to have found the best of all possible worlds: they are getting a high current interest rate on something that is very close to a checking account. At the same time they are participating in a diversified portfolio of money-market instruments. And no matter how low the risks of default may be for any single issuer of certificates of deposit or commercial paper, the investor should always seek diversification if it comes at low, or no cost.

Cash rule number 4

Avoid paying your bills for as long as possible. Corporate treasurers have learned that there can be big payoffs to the imaginative procrastinator. Become systematic as you receive your bills. There are some bills with no explicitly stated interest penalty. These go in the far-future payment file. Never pay cash. The cost of credit is already figured in the price of the item.

8

When Commodities Beat Inflation

The great inflation of 1973-74 brought on an age of commodities. People who didn't know soybeans from sorghum began to realize that there was a good chance to make money if the difference could be learned. It is already history that commodities were a super investment play during 1973-74. The reasons for the extraordinary performance of commodities are not so well known nor do they imply that a golden age of perpetually rising commodity prices is upon us. In fact, an analog of forces that pushed commodity prices up in 1973-74 could just as easily push them down. Most of the newspaper talk about rising commodity prices focused on limitations of supply—sometimes assumed to be perpetual—that would keep commodities permanently in the shortage category in the face of rising demand.

Supply constraints did play something of a role in 1973-74 commodity inflation. But more important, even though less publicized, was the ballooning of the world money supply in 1971 and 1972. Together with the several devaluations of the U.S. dollar, which made U.S. exports more attractive to foreigners, the surge in the world's money supply caused a surge in world output, which in turn led to an increase in the rate at which commodities were chewed up and to a surge in their prices.

Similarly, the decline in commodity prices which occurred in the first half of 1975 was the result of the drop in the world money-growth rate that occurred in 1973 and 1974. As with every other investment, the investor will time his commodity purchases to swings in the money supply.

The time to buy commodities is in the accelerating phase of the inflation cycle; it is the only time to buy commodities. And even if you expect inflation to accelerate, you still have to be very careful. This is so even though the accelerating inflation of 1973-74 gave commodities a bright new look—and as a consequence made many brokerage houses, which normally push their stock business, attempt to get investors to consider commodities as an alternative. Like other companies, brokerage houses try to push business in one line when they are losing it in other lines.

The kinds of stories that salesmen tell are going to be breathtaking. The price of soybeans rose from $4.21 per bushel to $8.30 between January 4, 1973, and August 23, 1973; the price of wheat from $2.71 per bushel to $4.99 per bushel; cotton from 34.18 cents per pound to 76.35 cents per pound.

Commodity contracts, moreover, are almost always bought on margin—thin margin. With a 10-percent margin requirement, the right timing on investment decisions would have turned $10,000 into $197,150 in soybeans, $184,133 in wheat, and $223,376 in cotton. (This is somewhat of an oversimplification. Every futures contract is for a specific quantity determined by the Commodity Exchange.) These heady examples could be duplicated in almost every commodity.

What happened over the next seven months is also worth knowing. Soybeans skidded by 27.1 percent between August 23, 1973, and March 28, 1974; wheat by 12.3 percent; cotton by 15.7 percent. Investors who put in their $10,000 around the time the peaks were reached would have been wiped out quickly.

Low margin requirements and wide price swings make commodity investment the next thing to shooting craps in Las Vegas. Those who want to beat the commodities game must be supersensitive to the very first indication of a change in the inflation rate. To capitalize on commodity price changes, the investor must be certain that he understands the inflation early warning system completely. He must receive a clear and certain signal that the inflation rate is about to change. If he has any doubts, the best advice we can give is to stay away.

The commodity market in which the ordinary investor trades is a futures market; it exists primarily because the real pros, the baking companies that need wheat, the feedlot operators who need soybeans, do not want to take the risk that wide fluctuations in price will drive them out of business. The commodity-futures markets exist because the companies that use commodities do not wish to take the risk of price fluctuations. So it should not be suprising that the average investor loses on commodity futures far more often than he gains according to authoritative studies.

To avoid sharing the fate of the multitude, investors must proceed warily. But there may nevertheless be times when those who like to gamble will have the odds stacked in their favor. Those investors guided by the following six rules will have a fighting chance of making a triple play: finding the right commodity, finding the right period, and finding the right transaction—a buy or a sell.

Commodity rule number 1

Buy commodities only in the accelerating phase of the inflation cycle. The purchase should be timed so that it occurs early in this phase. Commodity prices are the first place that accelerating inflation shows itself, well before the newspapers tell you that a rise in the cost of living is making housewives unhappy or unions restless. It is just as easy to sell commodities for future delivery as it is to buy them. Those investors who can spot an early deceleration in the inflation rate have a chance to sell commodities and make big profits. For example, on August 7, 1974, you could have sold soybeans for future delivery on January 9, 1975, at $8.47 per bushel. When January 9 rolled around you could have honored your contract by buying soybeans in the spot market for $6.70 and pocketed the difference. This kind of play should only be made early in the decelerating phase of the inflation cycle, the earlier in the phase the better.

Commodity rule number 2

Only make a commitment to commodities when the change in the inflation rate that you expect will be major and largely unanticipated by the general public.

When the commodities salesman calls you, the first thing he will do is to ask you if you would like to receive booklets detailing all the factors that influence the price of each commodity. These booklets will also tell you what clues to watch for future price movements.

Remember that, as a commodity speculator, you are betting against the pros, who are hedging. You can also be sure that those with specialized knowledge have exploited every obvious profit opportunity.

The only thing that the investor has going for him is his ability to forecast the inflation rate. And to beat the pros he must expect a major swing in the inflation rate. If the swing isn't big, the price of any commodity is likely to be more influenced by special factors—weather conditions in the Midwest, rainfall in Nigeria, hoof-and-mouth disease in Argentina, and the like—than by moderate changes in the general inflation rate.

Commodity rule number 3

Diversification applies to commodities just as it applies to everything else. Even with a big and largely unanticipated swing in the inflation rate, specialized factors could still make your commodity investment look very bad.

There is a futures market for shell eggs. A single contract calls for 750 cases of 30 dozen each. Which translates into 22,500 dozens or 270,000 fresh, large white eggs. When you buy those eggs you had better make sure you can sell them.

Suppose the Surgeon General of the United States releases a report that clearly demonstrates a positive and direct link between heart disease and egg consumption. Or that the link between cholesterol in eggs and heart disease is even closer than was indicated by previous research. If your monetary indicators had told you that inflation was about to accelerate and you put all your commodity money in the egg basket, you would get wiped out even though you were 100 percent right about the commodity inflation. Remember, it always pays to diversify. Buy several commodities or a mutual fund that holds a diversified portfolio of contracts.

Commodity rule number 4

Always bear in mind that gold is just another commodity. Gold is not a surefire hedge against inflation. As a matter of fact, now that governments no longer seriously peg the price of gold, and U.S. citizens can buy it, its price has become super-sensitive to changes in the inflation rate. So be supercareful, because there is a huge gold inventory out there. Virtually all the gold ever produced is still in existence. Central bankers alone hold 1.2 billion ounces.

Moreover, gold is useless—it heats no homes, feeds nobody, and earns no income. Central bankers will be highly tempted to sell it in a world faced with big oil-related balance-of-payments deficits. In fact, in late 1974 the U.S. Government decided to auction some of its gold hoard. At some point, other governments will also dump gold.

Commodity rule number 5

Stay away from exotic commodities like wine and art. Specialized knowledge is even more important here than in such prosaic things as cocoa and soybeans. If you are selling a painting, you may not be able to find a buyer without incurring a catastrophic sacrifice in price. Artists move in and out of fashion much more rapidly than do lead and zinc. The art market, moreover, depends very much on the financial conditions of museums, which in turn depend on gift tax laws in a few countries. These can and do change.

Wine is for drinking, not for speculation. While it might be nice to time the wine purchases for your cellar so as to take advantage of lower prices, don't plan on selling out when prices go up. You are likely to miss the peak and incur high middleman charges.

Prices of exotic investments move up as well as down, but there are far better ways to play the inflation cycle.

Commodity rule number 6

Stay away from high-priced coins produced by private "mints." They have flourished by mixing gold with other metals and engraving pictures on the resulting alloy. There has to be a big mark-up over the price of gold. Someone is paying promotion-campaign bills, among other things. Unless the price of gold really soars, the game can only be won by their stockholders.

Stamps and old coins should be collected only by those who actually enjoy this kind of thing—not as an inflation hedge. They may rise in price during the accelerating phase of inflation but, as in the case of wine, there is a big spread between the buying and the selling price.

These rules indicate that commodity plays are a much tougher row to hoe than the more traditional kinds of investment vehicles. You are better off to stay away under most circumstances. To make money in the commodities market you need a big, unanticipated swing in the inflation rate and you have to get in there early. The year 1973 did present such an opportunity to buy commodity contracts, and 1974 was a good time to sell commodity contracts—but opportunities such as these rarely occur.

CHAPTER 9

What Currencies Should You Hold?

Currencies float these days, and this opens up a whole new world for the investor. Prior to the summer of 1971 governments kept the price of their currencies fixed in terms of the dollar, and therefore in terms of all other currencies. Sometimes governments were forced to change the price of their currency but the timing of these changes was spasmodic and highly unpredictable. Furthermore, when the changes finally came they were mammoth. The value of a currency could change by as much as 10 to 20 percent in one day.

But now that currencies are floating, they change in price relative to each other by fairly small amounts every day, much as common stocks and bonds do. There are still extra political risks in investing in currencies but they have become a much more reasonable investment play.

In recent years currencies have become as easy to play as commodities. The International Monetary Market of the Chicago Mercantile Exchange is a place where you can buy a standardized contract for the pound sterling, Canadian dollar, German mark, Dutch guilder, Japanese yen, Mexican peso, and Swiss franc as easily as you can buy 100 shares of General Motors. In fact, your local broker is likely to be dealing in currency futures. Just like stocks, currencies have their own ticker symbols. For example, the British pound has the symbol BP, the Canadian dollar CD, and so on. A standard contract for, say, the British pound is for 25,000 pounds or approximately $60,000. The minimum fluctuation on a sterling contract is approximately .0005, or $30.00.

Like the commodities market, the currencies market is a dangerous play. In 1974 the newspapers were full of stories about banks that got into trouble because a foreign-exchange trader stepped out of line. This was one of the primary reasons the Franklin National Bank had severe problems in the United States, why the Bankhaus Herstatt went bust in Germany, and why the Swiss branch of the prestigious Lloyds Bank of London got into deep trouble.

Anybody who wants to invest for profit must also remember that gold, bonds, short-term money instruments, commodities, and currencies all have their downs as well as their ups.

The Japanese yen provides a graphic example. Thought to be indestructible in 1972, the yen began to tumble in 1973 and fell in 1974. On the average, you would have gotten 265 yen to the dollar in September of 1973, but one year later you would have gotten 300 yen to the dollar. This means that the man who bought 265,000 yen at the average price of the first quarter of 1973 for $1,000, would have gotten $883 for his 265,000 yen at the average price that prevailed during September of 1974. And if, as is more likely, our currency speculator had used his money to buy a forward contract for yen on the Chicago International Monetary Market and had used margin, he probably would have been sold out of his position and had a lot less than $883 per $1,000 to show for it.

What happened to the yen? The oil embargo and the subsequent quadrupling of the oil price did cause special problems for the Japanese. A huge percentage of their oil needs are satisfied by Middle East sources. But the oil price was quadrupled for everybody. And the most general explanation of the sinking yen was a Japanese inflation rate that made United States double-digit inflation look like price stability. At the beginning of 1973 Japanese wholesale price inflation was running at a 9.3 percent annual rate, U.S. wholesale price inflation at an 8.6 percent annual rate. By the first quarter of 1974, Japanese wholesale price inflation was at a 35.5 percent annual rate, that of the U.S. at a 17.4 percent annual rate. A similar comparison made for consumer prices shows that the Japanese inflation rate went from 7.2 percent to 24.2 percent, while the U.S. consumer price inflation went from 4.1 percent to 9.9 percent. The yen sank relative to the dollar mainly because the Japanese inflation rate soared above the U.S. inflation rate.

The countries that have the fastest inflation always see the price of their currency sink compared to the currencies of countries that have relatively little inflation. Opportunities to make money in currencies will therefore occur when anticipated inflation rates, incorporated in the price of foreign exchange, get way out of line with what the investor himself expects. The difficulty is in spotting these situations.

Currency rule number 1

Buy a country's currency in the wake of a sharp deceleration of the country's monetary growth rate; sell a currency in the wake of a sharp acceleration in a country's monetary growth rate.

When a country's monetary growth rate accelerates sharply it is a signal that higher inflation rates are down the road. Faster monetary growth will translate itself into an intensified decline in the purchasing power of that currency, not only with respect to domestic goods, but also with respect to the amount of foreign goods it can command. When money accelerates, prices go up, not only at home but also for goods produced for sale in the world market. Moreover, imports from countries not experiencing so rapid an inflation begin to look cheap. Thus, when money growth moves up, exports are hit on the head and imports soar. In the world money markets, rising inflation for a country dooms its currency to fall. Falling exports reduce the demand for that currency, and rising imports increase the supply.

Currency rule number 2

In world currency markets it is the relative inflation rate that really counts. A country's currency should be bought if you expect that country to experience a lower inflation rate than other countries. It should be sold if you expect it to experience a higher inflation rate than other countries. Remember, if you are to make any money, your expectations have to differ markedly from those of average opinion in the marketplace.

The behavior of the Japanese yen during 1973 and 1974 represented a classic instance where rules one and two could have been put into action to outwit average opinion in the currency market. Early in 1973 opinion that the Japanese yen would rise sharply was widespread. But, the beat-inflation investor would have foreseen a sharp, relative acceleration in the Japanese price level because he would have noticed a sharp acceleration of Japanese monetary growth in 1972. He would then have been led to expect a fall in the yen relative to the currencies of those countries where monetary growth was not accelerating. And fall the yen did. The comparison to the dollar is instructive. The Federal Reserve put on a good show of monetary restraint compared to the Bank of Japan, the Japanese Central Bank. It happened in fits and starts. But the differences in the monetary growth rates did lead to a fall in the yen relative to the dollar. All the classic elements of a profitable currency play were there for the yen versus the dollar. In early 1973 the market expected the yen to stay strong. But the beat-inflation investor knew it was fated to weaken.

One word of warning: Because of institutional differences in the rate at which money turns over, there will always be differences in the size of the monetary growth rates between countries. What really matters in making money in the currency market is the acceleration and deceleration in the country's own monetary growth rate. What was important for the yen versus the dollar was that the Japanese monetary growth rate jumped while the U.S. monetary growth rate declined.

The 1973 Nobel Prize for monetary restraint went to Germany and Switzerland, and their inflation rates fared the best in 1974. To be certain, the currency markets already had great respect for the German mark and Swiss franc. Both countries had a good record in combating inflation. To preserve this good record in the face of the worldwide commodity-price pressures, these countries slammed on the monetary brakes. Observing this, the beat-inflation investor would have expected Swiss and German inflation rates to come down faster than in other countries. He would, therefore, have been able to foresee the rise in the Swiss franc and German mark that took place.

Given the monetary growth rates of Germany, Switzerland, and Japan, the best currency play was to borrow yen and buy Swiss francs and German marks. The safest thing to do is to bet against the currency with the biggest acceleration in its monetary growth rate and to bet in favor of the currency with the smallest acceleration or, even better, biggest deceleration. But beware. Before going for the German mark, Dutch guilder, or the Swiss franc remember that even a sound currency can become overpriced if average opinion is reflecting too sanguine a view of the country's inflation rate compared to inflation rates in other countries.

Currency rule number 3

Currency plays as outlined above should only be made when there is a major shift in the monetary growth rate. Smaller movements can be swamped by other unpredictable factors.

What is true of commodities is also true of currencies. Currency values will depend not only on the inflation rate in a particular country compared to the inflation in other countries but also on special factors. The world of international trade and finance, moreover, is complex. People who spend their lifetime studying it get themselves excited about such concepts as the liquidity balance of payments. But, most important, unlike the commodities market, Central Banks fiddle in the currency markets and can upset or delay the workings of the fundamentals. Thus, if a knowledge of the beat-inflation strategy is to prove helpful in currency trading, the swing in the monetary growth rate must be big enough so that it provides strong odds that other factors will be swamped.

Currency rule number 4

Don't ignore weak currencies; they may offer excellent opportunities to make money.

When a currency falls into disfavor the market tends to be too pessimistic about its outlook. Moreover, economic difficulties push even the most recalcitrant governments into some action to bring their inflation rate under control.

The investor may easily find the best currency plays among countries that are generally considered to be weak sisters. So the investor should keep his eye riveted on historically weak currencies, such as those of Italy and Britain, for the signs of a switch toward restraint in monetary policy.

Currency rule number 5

When you buy the stocks of multinational companies it is desirable to buy companies that have good sales penetration in those countries whose currencies you expect to be strong.

Following this rule will not make you rich but it could give you an extra edge under certain circumstances. When you consider the stock of a multinational company in a certain industry, it is worth observing where its sales are concentrated. Then see what the exchange market is saying about the prospects for that country's currency. Whatever the exchange market is saying will be reflected in the price of the stock. So, if you expect the currency of the country where sales are concentrated to do better than what average opinion believes, the stock will have an element of undervaluation from the beat-inflation point of view. Currency expectations are not important reasons to pick a stock. But if you do make investments in multinational companies, keep them in mind.

Currency rule number 6

You can use the currency-plays rules to increase your return from holding short-term money-market instruments in other countries. The other side of this rule is to use currency plays to reduce your net interest costs when you are borrowing money abroad. Right now this rule is only for the corporate treasurer since the individual will have a tough time borrowing from foreign financial institutions. But this may change.

When you buy money-market instruments abroad, the return you get will depend on the relationship between the price of foreign currency when you buy the instrument and the price of the currency when you sell it. Well-informed investors will be aware of the differences in interest rates between countries, and that these differences will reflect the market's view of how exchange rates will change. For example, Swiss interest rates will be low compared to those in other countries if the market expects the Swiss franc to go up. This is because the total return to the holder of a Swiss money-market instrument will include not only the interest yield but also some foreign exchange profit. To a foreign investor this means that he can expect a relatively low interest rate if he can be reasonably sure that the Swiss francs he gets when the instrument matures will be worth more than when he made his original purchase.

When world money markets are relatively free, the total return to investing in money-market instruments tends toward equality. Those countries with relatively high monetary growth rates will have high interest rates and there will be a general expectation that their currencies will be weak. The countries with relatively low monetary growth rates will have low interest rates, and there will be a general expectation that their currencies will strengthen. To put currency rule number six into practice, you must have markedly different expectations than generally prevail in the exchange markets. If you notice, for example, a sharp deceleration in some country's monetary growth and the exchange market does not reflect it adequately, the time may be at hand.

British Treasury bills were a good investment in the third quarter of 1973. At that time their average yield was 11 percent as against 8.3 percent for U.S. Treasury bills of equivalent maturity. By the third quarter of 1973 it was apparent that Britain had already applied the monetary brakes, and this made it apparent that the pound would improve. At that time this would have been a contrary opinion. As it turned out, the pound did improve in 1974, so the investor would have been able to obtain a juicy current yield plus a neat foreign exchange gain.

In the above transaction, the investor was a lender. It also is possible to increase your total return by borrowing in those countries where you expect the currency to weaken substantially. You do just the opposite of what you did when you were buying money-market instruments. If you see a country's monetary growth rate accelerating sharply, its banks and capital markets are a good place to borrow money. If the market does not reflect the full impact of the monetary spurt going on in a country, its currency will probably be overvalued and its interest rates too low. This will give you an opportunity to keep the total cost of borrowing very low.

The situation in Japan in the first half of 1973 presents a classic example. Borrowers lucky enough to have access to the Japanese market were able to get credit at a little over 6 percent; at the same time the Bank of Japan, the Japanese Central Bank, was running wild, pushing the monetary growth rate up at an annual rate of more than 25 percent. Using our currency rules, the investor should have expected a decline in the yen. This did occur. In September of 1973 a dollar bought 265 yen.

By September of 1974 it bought about 300 yen. Vis-à-vis the dollar, the yen declined by almost 12 percent on a quarterly average basis. Thus, the American who was lucky enough to have borrowed yen would have actually paid no interest. A 6-percent one-year loan means that the man who had borrowed 265 yen would have to pay 281 yen back at the end of one year. Since you could buy 300 yen for a dollar, the borrower would have benefited enough from changes in the exchange rate to more than offset his interest costs.

Over the years, the ability of the ordinary investor to make currency plays has been limited by exchange and capital controls and a predisposition on the part of central banks to fix their exchange rates. But the change to a floating rate system has clearly widened opportunities to benefit from exchange-rate differences between countries. But beware. Central bankers will attempt to prevent the fundamental forces that we have been describing from operating, at least temporarily. This increases the risk in using the foreign exchange markets as a beat-inflation vehicle.

It is therefore prudent to play the foreign exchange markets only when there is a very wide divergence from what market participants generally expect and what the beat-inflation rules say will happen.

Exchange controls still exist around the world, and this limits the extent to which investors can use the currency rules. However, controls are not as tough as they used to be, and more important for the individual investor is the development of a good futures market in currencies on the Chicago Mercantile Exchange.

CHAPTER 10

Indexing: Your Job, Pension, and Social Security

High, volatile and permanent inflation isn't changing only the investment environment; it is also changing every aspect of your economic life: the way you get paid, the way you accrue pension rights and even the way in which the Social Security Administration figures how big a check it is going to send you when you are over sixty-five.

The omnibus name for the kinds of change that permanent inflation is bringing to daily economic life is "indexing." Any time an agreement or contract is concluded and contains provisions tying the size of payments to some measure of the inflation rate, indexing is present. Cost-of-living clauses have been around for a long time in union contracts. Workers demanded and received them during earlier bouts of inflation but they tended to fall into disuse when prices again became stable. But now that inflation is permanent, indexing will become a permanent part of your economic life and a household word.

You should think about when and when not to enter into indexed contracts, what kinds of agreements to index and what kinds of agreements not to index, what kinds of price indexes to use for escalator clauses, and when in the inflation cycle indexing best serves to beat inflation.

Indexing is one of those things that is most easily grasped by taking a look at some escalator contracts in action. For example, the 1973-76 wage agreement between the General Electric Company and the International Union of Electrical, Radio, and Machine Workers includes a cost-of-living adjustment tied to price changes. The formula used to calculate the size of the cost-of-living adjustment is as follows: "one cent (1¢) per hour for hourly employees, forty cents (40¢) per week for salaried employees for each full three tenths of one percent (0.3%) by which the National Consumer Price Index (1967=100), as published by the United States Bureau of Labor Statistics, increases in the applicable measurement period."

This example of a cost-of-living escalator is good from labor's point of view. Even so, the formula allows the worker to capture only 80 percent of the rise in the consumer price index.

This is an extremely generous contract—well above average as a study in the July, 1974, Federal Reserve Bank of New York *Monthly Review* shows. The study points out that the consumer price index rose at a 5.3-percent annual rate between 1968 and 1973. Over the same period the average cost-of-living wage increase came to just 2.7 percent per year; so that even those workers covered by cost-of-living escalator clauses managed only about a 50-percent protection against inflation.

Cost-of-living contracts are still far from universal, even in the labor movement. By the end of 1973, approximately 4 million workers, only about 40 percent of the workers under contract, were covered by escalator clauses, so that the unions which have gone the farthest in getting cost-of-living clauses still have a long way to go in obtaining full inflation protection for their members—at least through cost-of-living clauses.

Actually, inflation makes it necessary to change the way in which you think about your job. No one enjoys a job in which the only reward is the size of the paycheck. And inflation should not change your desire for work that is meaningful and brings nonfinancial rewards. Here are four rules that can help you get the best cost-of-living protection that you can. Everybody recognizes that there is less individual freedom in striking job bargains than in investing. But with imagination and guts you may find that you can make these rules work for you.

Job rule number 1

Get your wage expressed in terms of its purchasing power. Make sure that you don't suffer inflation shock. Keep in mind at all times how fast prices are rising so you know exactly how well you are doing on the wage and salary front. Remember the farmers and their parity index. You want parity too. There are local consumer price indexes as well as one for the whole nation. A call to your local office of the Bureau of Labor Statistics will get you on the mailing list for the monthly press release that tells you about changes in the local consumer price index. This index, with all its faults, is still the best instrument around for measuring the way your cost of living is changing. A deal with your boss that gives you good cost-of-living protection will guarantee that your salary will rise by the same percentage as the change in local cost of living—so that if you succeed in getting it tied to changes in the local cost of living you will have succeeded in expressing your wage in terms of its purchasing power. This is full indexing and is better than the best union contract. Try to get it.

Job rule number 2

Make sure that the cost-of-living adjustments come frequently. The faster the inflation rate, the more frequent the adjustments should be. Time is money. The more frequently you get your cost-of-living adjustment, the better off you are. But price changes are big enough so that those who can get monthly or even quarterly cost-of-living adjustments are materially better off than those who have to wait till the end of the year.

Don't let your wages trail; minimize the wage lag. Consumer prices rose by about 12 percent in 1974. Had your agreement with your boss called for a full cost-of-living adjustment at the end of the year, it would not have done you a bit of good during 1974. Maintaining your car, paying your utility bills and setting food on the family table would have left you strapped. You would have been better able to cope had your wage escalation shown up in your pay check quickly. Suppose, for example, that your initial salary was $20,000 per year or $5,000 per quarter. A 12-percent rate of price increase means 3 percent per quarter, so that if you had a quarterly escalation you would have gotten paid $21,545.68 during the year. That extra $1,545.68 that you would have received during the year would have bought meat and potatoes that you would not otherwise have had.

Job rule number 3

To jack up the amount you earn over the course of your working life, make your job changes during the accelerating phase of the inflation cycle. The odds are that your wage will stand still and your purchasing power decline when prices shoot up in the accelerating phase of the inflation cycle. This is not the only reason why the accelerating phase of the inflation cycle is the right time to change jobs. Usually the early upswing in the inflation cycle will be accompanied by booming business, so that companies will be willing to pay more to get new workers. Employees already on the staff may someday catch up but ordinarily it will take them some time to do so.

Job rule number 4

The decelerating phase of the inflation cycle may be a good time to stay where you are. When price increases start to slow, business conditions are generally soft and unemployment is rising. Sending around résumés is apt to be pointless. A sick job market is no place to generate much in the way of salary increases. At the same time, it is quite possible that things will be changing at the place you are already working in a way that is quite favorable to those able to hang onto their jobs. If there is any wage lag at all in your company it is quite likely that the employees will be catching up with past inflation rates during the decelerating phase of the inflation cycle. When inflation is decelerating your present job may be the best plan to maximize your income.

The rules that will maximize your job income will also tend to maximize your pension benefits. In American industry, pension payments are ordinarily based on some formula that ties them to your average salary in your last five years of employment—so that if you have done the right thing to get your salary up, your pension will follow it up.

But beware. No matter how good a job you do in negotiating for your pension, the chances are that it will provide inadequate benefits. To make things worse, Social Security may not turn out to be the cornucopia it is touted to be, particularly if you are young right now. With benefit increases that have occurred over the past three years, and with the indexing of future payments to changes in the cost of living, Social Security is delivering a lot to those currently in retirement and is likely to continue delivering a lot to those who will enter retirement in the next few years. But problems will start to show in the mid-1980s. And that is not too far away when you are thinking about investing for the future. Remember, the Social Security system is not funded. Whatever the defects of your company's pension plan may be, the new 1974 pension law requires that your pension benefits be fully funded at all times. This means that the money that you put in and the money that the boss puts in on your behalf is sequestered in a trust fund, so that if the firm goes bankrupt, your benefits will receive a measure of protection. The law also requires that the trust fund be big enough at all times to pay all the benefits that you have accumulated. So when you get your quarterly statement of the benefits you have accumulated you can have a fair degree of faith that they will actually be paid. In fact, the government has set up an insurance plan that means Uncle Sam will pay any benefits due you that the company can't pay.

Polls show that Americans have enormous faith in the Social Security system. But unlike your funded pension benefits, the Social Security system is what economists call a tax-transfer system. In any given year the benefits paid to retirees are derived from taxes on those who are working. Benefits have shot up over the past few years since the number of people employed has been going up more rapidly than the number of people retiring.

So it has been easy for the government to raise benefits. But the birth rate has now slumped and is likely to continue to be depressed. This means that there will be a continuous deterioration in the ability of the people who are working to support either their parents or somebody else's parents via Social Security. To many experts, this makes the promises of high future Social Security benefits suspect. To insure a comfortable retirement, everybody must have his own investment program.

11

Choosing a Money Manager

If you decide you don't have the time to manage money yourself, you can use beat inflation to help you pick the right people to manage your money for you.

For any money manager to succeed in beating inflation, he must clearly adapt his investment strategy to taking advantage of the ways in which inflation transfers income and wealth.

Investment managers can't bury their mistakes—but they will do everything they possibly can to avoid paying for their mistakes. And the most obvious thing they do to accomplish this is to make their portfolios look as much like everybody else's portfolio as possible. By definition, this leads to almost everybody's showing the same mistakes as well as the same successes. As a consequence the standard money-management brochures, as well as other standard information sources, will not be of much help in finding the right person to manage your money in a world of high and variable inflation. Therefore, if you need professional money-management advice, you are going to have to do some real digging to find the right person or organization.

Consequently, we have developed five questions that will allow you to separate those investment managers who have a good chance of beating inflation from those who don't.

Management question number 1

Is your money-management organization willing to invest in all assets? Money-management brochures, including those put out by mutual funds, more often than not will say that the organization leaves open the option to invest in any kind of asset deemed suitable for making the investor's capital grow. If you examine what these organizations do, however, the record will show that they stick to one or two investment vehicles. And if respectability is part of the image they seek to project, those vehicles are ordinarily stocks, bonds, and short-term money-market instruments. And even this restricted list of potential investment vehicles projects an image of flexibility that doesn't really exist. The reason is that shifts between, say, cash and stocks tend to be small and occur for the wrong reason. For example, anyone who visited a respectable money manager during the 1973-74 stock market debacle would have been told that the organization had made a big move into cash. Chances are that this was true for bad reasons rather than good reasons. Suppose the organization had come into 1973 with 10 percent of its funds in short-term money-market instruments and 90 percent in common stocks. Further, suppose that all the organization did was roll over its short-term money-market instruments and watch the value of the common stocks go down. By fall of 1974 the value of its common stocks would have been down some 42.5 percent and the value of its cash equivalents would have been unchanged. Therefore, by the fall of 1974, cash would have been 16.2 percent of the assets, and common stocks would have been 83.8 percent.

This kind of "flexibility" is going to be the fate of any investment manager who loves the same asset at all times over the entire inflation cycle. The period during which any vehicle will be a shining star will be brief. Accordingly your investment manager must do more than say he considers all assets. He must actually invest in them at the right time.

Finding a money manager who treats all assets with equal

justice and "fine impartiality" will be extremely difficult, and not only because of a commission structure that is still torqued in favor of common stocks. Cultural lag and the pressure of conventional wisdom continue to make investment managers, the press, and even Congress think of some assets as respectable and some as odious and sinister. During 1973-74, many big bank-trust departments sat around and watched the value of their common-stock pension funds fall by 30 to 40 percent. People were upset with this performance but there were few lawsuits against the banks, no Congressional investigations of what happened, and no serious legislative remedy attempted.

Had the major institutions turned in the same investment performance with a portfolio of gold, Japanese yen, and shell egg futures, heads would have rolled.

An asset is an asset. It will be hard for the investor to do, but he must find a money manager whose attitude toward assets is determined solely by their appropriateness to the specific stage of the inflation cycle in which the economy finds itself.

Management question number 2

Does your money-management organization structure its portfolios to reflect its knowledge of the future inflation rate and its impact on asset prices? The money manager must have a framework for picking the appropriate vehicle for each stage of the inflation cycle. This book has described one method; other methods may be available. Make sure your money manager has a method and that the method makes sense to you.

Management question number 3

How does your organization make its projections of the future inflation rate? The success of any program is importantly dependent on the investor's or the investment manager's success in forecasting changes in the rate of inflation. Disastrous investment performance comes about from having the wrong assets for the particular phase of the inflation cycle. Nothing could be worse than a portfolio optimally designed to take advantage of decelerating inflation in a period when the inflation rate starts accelerating.

Beware of the money manager who says that he knows the investment environment will be inflationary but makes no distinction between periods of accelerating and decelerating inflation. He must have a method for picking the points when inflation will speed up and when it will slow down. Find out what that method is and make sure you understand it.

Management question number 4

How does your organization time its purchases and sales of various assets? There may be an investment genius hidden in a major bank's trust department somewhere in the country who really knows how to beat inflation. But all he may be able to do is chalk up paper profits on a mythical portfolio. Institutions frequently impose restraints on individuals that prevent them from quickly changing their portfolios when economic conditions change. The money manager must have the flexibilty to take advantage of changes in the inflation rate through making major changes in his portfolio very quickly. Therefore he must have an early warning system for spotting changes in the inflation rate and complete freedom to move when he gets his signal. Find out what restraints institutions put on their money managers.

Management question number 5

Will the investment manager who runs your portfolio have the freedom to invest in other countries? When an investment manager spots changes in the inflation rate, he has enough asset options open to him so that he can make money for you even if he confines his investments to one country. But there are times when the most visible and surest plays are abroad. Accordingly, an investment manager who can invest in all countries or all currencies can be successful more easily than one who can't. Clearly, the more choices an investment adviser has open to him, the better off you'll be.

The fatal mistake in dealing with investment managers is to be overwhelmed by them and their surroundings. The stock market has been sick since 1968 even though, and maybe because, it has been dominated by professional investment managers.

If the money is in somebody else's hands, constant monitoring of his performance is crucial.

12

Building a Beat-Inflation Portfolio

All the building blocks are now in place. The investor is now ready to assemble a portfolio of bonds, cash, commodities, stocks, and currencies that will profit from inflation.

Before you embark in developing a portfolio you have to get yourself into a postion to benefit from the beat-inflation rules. This requires two steps. Painful as it may be, it is smart to get rid of the cats and dogs in your portfolio. The speed with which you do this will partly depend upon tax considerations. There is a limit to the amount of capital losses that can be used to offset your current income. However, tax considerations should not play a major role. Once you get rid of those cats and dogs, you should put your money in short-term money-market instruments, such as Treasury bills, money-market funds or high-grade commercial paper if you realize at least $25,000 from the sale of your investment portfolio.

The next thing to do is to put yourself into a position to

borrow as much as you can as quickly as you can. This doesn't mean that you have to borrow the money right away. Cultivate your local banker and build up whatever lines of credit you can use when you need to borrow.

Once you have completed these steps, you are liquid and in a position to use leverage. You are ready to pounce on every opportunity and to take advantage of other people's mistakes. The investor knows that those mistakes occur when the price of an asset does not fully reflect the inflation that the investor expects. As you follow the strategy you will be moving into and out of this liquid position. But never give up liquidity unless the odds that a play will work are very high.

One rule of thumb that was followed by "successful" money managers in the 1950s and early 1960s was to stay fully invested. Many people still suffer from this hangover. But our rule of thumb is exactly the opposite—stay liquid, fully liquid, unless you have a very strong reason for doing otherwise. Remember that there is no asset for all seasons and being frozen into the wrong asset for a particular season will cost you dearly.

Short-term interest rates will move up and down with the inflation rate, and therefore your wealth and income will in general keep pace with inflation. There will be periods in which interest rates will move down before the inflation rate moves down and periods when interest rates move up after the inflation rate moves up. But on the average an investor who keeps his assets in a fully liquid portfolio—consisting of money-market instruments—will do better than most investors.

Moreover, the relationship between swings in the price level and swings in interest rates should be even tighter in the future than in the past. There have been periods when short-term rates and inflation did not march in exact step. This was because the money illusion was hard at work. When inflation soared ahead, interest sometimes moved up much more slowly because lenders and borrowers felt that the rate of price increase would soon fall back to its old level. But the money illusion is nearly dead, and people are getting harder to fool about the future rate of inflation.

If you want to beat inflation rather than just keep up with it, you must be prepared to get out of a fully liquid position at the right moment. And that moment comes when your assessment of the future inflation rate differs markedly from what the average assessment is as revealed by interest rates and prices of all other assets. The key to the strategy is therefore to decide where the economy is with respect to the inflation cycle.

Changes in the money-supply growth rate are the single most important factor causing changes in the inflation rate. Therefore, the key to successful investment is understanding what is happening to the money supply and what it will do to the inflation rate and therefore to interest rates, stock prices, commodity prices, and foreign exchange rates. Keeping track of the money supply is a difficult task. But fortunately there will be plenty of help available.

The key source of data is a maverick regional member of the Federal Reserve system, the Federal Reserve Bank of Saint Louis. Over the years this bank has led the way in compiling data on monetary growth rates, not only in the United States but around the world. A letter or postcard addressed to the Federal Reserve Bank of Saint Louis, P.O. Box 442, Saint Louis, Missouri 63166, will bring you a mountain of data organized in a way that will tell you everything you need to know about domestic and world money-supply growth rates. Furthermore, it all comes free.

When you write your postcard ask for the following publications:

Monetary Trends comes to you monthly and will help you determine the trend rate of monetary growth as well as the current rate. Remember that the rate of monetary growth that prevails for about two years is the trend rate of monetary growth.

But, as always, the most important question is whether the inflation rate is about to accelerate or decelerate. And here *Monetary Trends* also proves invaluable.

U.S. Financial Data tells you what is happening to the U.S. monetary growth rate every week. It therefore can be used as a basis for updating monetary growth between issues of *Monetary Trends*. It also provides a convenient weekly source on both short-term and long-term interest rates. The weekly data are useful and should be kept readily at hand. But beware of reading too much into week-to-week movements in the money supply. These data jump around quite a bit on a week-to-week basis and are often subject to substantial revisions.

Rates of Change in Economic Data for Ten Industrial Countries comes out quarterly and gives you information on the monetary growth rates in each country as well as the inflation

rate and the growth in output. It will enable you to continuously update data on monetary growth rates in other countries.

These publications are the minimum tool kit for the investor. You probably also ought to get the Saint Louis Federal
Reserve to send you its *Review*, which often contains articles
on how money impacts inflation, interest rates, and asset
prices around the world. It might also be helpful to get from
them a publication entitled *Annual U.S. Economic Data*,
which will give data going back some twenty years on money
supply, prices, and output. This will enable you to put everything into long historical perspective—long enough to pick out
changes in the trend rate of inflation and to see how the inflation cycle has behaved in the past.

To find out what the current rate of inflation is, another
Federal Reserve Bank of Saint Louis publication, the monthly
National Economic Trends, will prove useful.

The reported money supply usually gives reliable investment signals. But be careful. The money-supply figures reported by the Federal Reserve are subject to major revisions.
These revisions are made infrequently and therefore the reported money-supply numbers can give off false signals.

Therefore, the beat-inflation investor must have some check
on what the money-growth-rate figures themselves are showing. Fortunately, the Federal Reserve Bank of Saint Louis itself
provides such a check. In its basic publication, *Monetary
Trends*, growth rates are presented on the monetary base, the
raw material out of which money is created.

The relationship between the money supply and the monetary base is complex. Ordinarily, however, their growth rates
are within 1 percent of each other. Because the monetary base
is not subject to large and frequent revision, its movements
provide a check for movements in the money supply. If the
money-supply growth rates differ from the monetary-base
growth rate by more than 1 percent, be careful. The money-
supply figure should be suspect—don't make investment
decisions on the money-supply number itself. Adjust the
money-supply figure upward or downward to reflect what is
going on with the monetary base: upward if the monetary base
is rising faster than the money supply, downward if the monetary base is rising more slowly. If the signals are still clear after
this is done, go ahead and make the investment decision that
your reading of the monetary situation suggests.

Once the investor gets a grip on the inflation rate he expects, he faces the problem of adapting his portfolio. The general rule is now simple and apparent: You are always heavily invested in those instruments whose prices are out of line with your view of the inflation prospects. This can occur at any time. But there are times when under- and overvaluation are more likely than others. Under- or overvaluation is likely to be greatest when the monetary growth cycle forecasts a turn in the inflation cycle that has not yet actually occurred. This is because the general market will not see the impending turn in the inflation rate. Consequently, asset prices will be determined based on views of the inflation rate that are doomed to be incorrect.

The longer the accelerating phase or the decelerating phase of an inflation cycle remains in force, the more likely it is that other investors will be acting in a way to change asset prices to conform with the beat-inflation investor's view. This suggests that the rewards are great for those who can move quickly at turning points and stick to their guns through a couple of weeks or months of adverse experience.

We are now in a position to summarize.

Decelerations in the rate of growth of the money supply give way to accelerations when the Federal Reserve begins to shift its concern from fighting inflation to worrying about falling output and rising unemployment. The swing toward faster monetary growth may well occur before inflation shows signs of a material de-escalation. This is because the men who run the Federal Reserve know, just as you do, that it takes time for faster monetary growth to affect the economy. Typically, faster monetary growth leads to higher output and employment within six months, but it takes at least eighteen months for it to show up in more inflation.

Stocks are ideal when monetary growth is in the initial stages of accelerating and inflation is still decelerating. The Graham-Dodd equation will look super. A fall in interest rates has a tonic effect on stock prices because it reduces the attractiveness of alternative forms of investment. Interest rates fall just as the money growth rate is turning around, not only because the increase in money nudges them down but also because inflation will be decelerating and price expectations will be reduced. Moreover, although profits will decline, security analysts will be saying that "the quality" of profits is improving as so-called inventory profits get smaller. In addition, since the re-acceleration in the monetary growth rate will stimulate output, the profits performance of most companies will be much better than people expected. Clearly when you anticipate that the monetary growth rate will turn around, it is an ideal time to buy stocks.

It is also an ideal time to buy bonds. The key to a good performance by bonds is decelerating inflation, which will continue for some time even after the monetary growth rate turns around. With decelerating inflation, price expectations are lowered and long-term interest rates come down some. Therefore bond prices will normally go up, even though monetary growth has already turned around.

Moving through the inflation cycle, the next question that the investor faces is when to start thinking about switching out of stocks and bonds and into other assets. The signals for getting out of bonds and stocks will be most clearly visible in the bond market. But the bond market signal should also be used for the stock market. Be prepared to move out of bonds and stocks when the inflation premium built into bond yields falls down to the trend rate of inflation that is imbedded in your mind as well as in the trend rate of monetary growth. Although bond yields may fall further, the risk/reward ratio of investing in them no longer warrants including bonds in your portfolio. The same will be true of stocks. When the inflation premium in bonds is equal to the trend rate of inflation, the inflation premium in stocks will probably also equal the trend rate of inflation. Like bonds, stocks may continue to rise beyond this point, but again like bonds, the risk/reward ratio of holding them begins to rise.

When the inflation rate drops back down to the trend rate, chances are that the economy will start giving off signals that suggest that the time has come to pull in your horns on stocks and bonds. Unemployment will probably stop rising and the amount of general slack in the economy will stop growing. Since money has been growing fast for quite a while, many investors will begin to expect the inflation rate to turn around.

The point at which interest rates reflect the trend of inflation that you believe will persist is the time to begin getting out of stocks and bonds. It is also the time to start thinking about commodities—gold, as well as real estate and short-term liquid assets. Accelerating inflation is around the corner.

Remember that when monetary growth first turns upward it results in higher employment and higher output, while inflation continues to decelerate for a while. It is during this period that stocks and bonds are the great play. It is after inflation begins to accelerate that hard assets are the great play. Remember what is happening in the economy. Output has responded to the turn in monetary policy with a lag of three to six months. After output and employment expand, the pressures on prices increase and the economy moves into the early stages of accelerating inflation. This is the season for commodities, including gold. But hard assets are to be played very carefully—only under the conditions that make you sure their price embodies a far different inflation rate than you yourself think is likely.

The time when hard assets become dangerous to hold is when the Federal Reserve is about to step on the monetary brakes. At this point, the economy will be pushing capacity to the limit, inventory accumulation will be excessive and there will be a general shortage mentality. Once the Federal Reserve steps on the brakes a reduction in the rate of monetary growth is not far away. This is a good point at which to become liquid, because nothing very good is going to happen for a while. But the investor can be very comfortable indeed. Short-term interest rates on securities where there is minimal chance of capital loss will be sky high. The investor can get his portfolio into a fully liquid position in anticipation of a swing from monetary deceleration to monetary acceleration sometime in the future.

All this sounds relatively simple, and for a good reason. It is relatively simple. Once we realized that inflation would never end, but that there would be a steady progression of inflation cycles, we were able to formulate a way of looking at investment vehicles in which all the component parts fell into place. A major tenet—perhaps *the* major tenet—of the beat-inflation approach is that the prices of hard assets, such as gold and commodities, rise when the prices of financial assets, such as stocks and bonds, fall, and vice versa. When commodity prices are rising, stock prices are falling and when commodity prices are falling, stock prices are rising. That is the way it has been since the birth of the inflation cycle and that is the way it will continue.

How to Open a
SWISS BANK
ACCOUNT

CHAPTER 1

An
Introduction

This is a book about Swiss banks, but it is also a book for our times—times of inflation and recession and doubts about the future of the American economy.

It is intended for the average American, who stands to lose the most in the era of economic turmoil and social confusion that has just begun. The emphasis is on personal accounts, to help middle-class people protect their savings, the results of a lifetime of hard work.

Americans have long known about the existence of Swiss bank accounts. Until recently, though, they have never considered them pertinent to their investment plans. Now, however, the uncertainties of our economy have turned a financial topic of importance only to specialists into a subject of wide and urgent interest.

For years, Swiss bank accounts have fascinated Americans. Numbered accounts are a cliché of popular adventure fiction.

Misconceptions abound: that Swiss accounts are illegal for U.S. citizens, that $100,000 is the minimum for an account. In the popular imagination, Swiss banks are linked with the Mafia, tax evasion, and international intrigue.

The truth is more prosaic—and far more interesting. Many of Switzerland's most respected banks will open an account for $100 or less. American depositors are welcomed by most Swiss banks. Swiss accounts are as legal for Americans as accounts in their hometown bank.

You may be reading this book out of curiosity, because Swiss banks are associated with international finance, with oil sheiks and dictators, with mercenaries and heroin smugglers. If you are, read on. You'll find out how Swiss banks really operate and who their actual customers are. You'll realize why dictators keep their retirement funds in Swiss banks. Numbered accounts, and their true function, will be explained in detail. You'll also be briefed on the formation of Liechtenstein trusts, an even more sophisticated method of hiding the true ownership of a Swiss bank account.

You may have bought this book out of fear—fear of what inflation is doing to your money, your savings. You will learn how a Swiss bank account can act as a buffer between you and the worries of inflation. You'll soon appreciate the usefulness of a Swiss account in protecting your assets when the world financial future is uncertain, as it is now.

Traditionally, Americans have shown little interest in having Swiss bank accounts of their own. In the past few years, though, many foresighted Americans have opted for Swiss accounts, and many more are considering placing at least part of their savings in Switzerland. Raging inflation has been the main reason for these new converts. Accounts in Swiss francs or in other hard currencies have proven to be excellent hedges against loss of purchasing power of the dollar.

There are other motivations, too, behind the flow of money to Switzerland. America is definitely changing. Confidence in our political leaders, and in their ability to successfully manage the change, is low. Many of the individuals opening Swiss accounts are seeking a haven for their money beyond the reach of an unpredictable government. They are using Swiss accounts as insurance, to help maintain their personal freedom of action no matter what the future may bring.

The American dollar has had no gold backing at all since

August 1971. The dollar is now fiat money, paper currency backed only by faith, faith in the U.S. government and its policies. And this faith has been eroding rapidly.

More than faith has been eroding. The annual rate of inflation for 1974 was officially 12.2 percent. A savings account with an interest rate of 4½ percent, compounded, just doesn't keep up with a 12 percent inflation rate, also compounded. A long-term certificate of deposit at 7 percent isn't much better. Your money is worth less when it's withdrawn from the bank than when it was originally deposited.

Inflation has become very personal. In the 1970s, most Americans are well aware that the dollar is worth much less than it used to be. They are painfully reminded of this fact every time they shop for groceries, for a new car, or for a new anything. Before Watergate, before the Vietnamese fiasco, before the Arab oil embargo, we had inflation, too. The rate was perhaps 3 percent, just enough to make things interesting. A little inflation gave us a feeling of progress as prices went up.

Before our economy started to change in the early 1970s, few law-abiding Americans had Swiss bank accounts. They felt no need for the extra margin of privacy, security, and flexibility offered by such accounts. The traditional "inflation hedges" served them well.

Time-honored hedges against inflation, especially common stocks and real estate, worked well as long as the inflation rate remained low, at 3 percent or less. In the past few years, however, as inflation began to rage, it has become apparent that standard investments are inadequate protection.

The stock market in particular has been a disappointment to those who counted on rising stock values to keep pace with inflation. For decades, common stock ownership, either directly or through mutual funds, had been a sensible inflation hedge. Advancing stock prices and dividends were expected to offset the gradual loss of the dollar's value through inflation. When the crunch of double-digit inflation came, though, there was little protection in owning common stocks. Stock prices had already collapsed.

In the great bear market of the last few years, investors have been left sitting numbly on the sidelines, wondering what happened to their money. Collectively, in only two years, 1973 and 1974, they suffered an estimated $389 billion loss of stock value on the New York Stock Exchange alone.

Ownership of real estate has proven a somewhat better investment. Property values have kept pace with inflation, at least on paper. But the main drawback has been a lack of liquidity in the marketplace—it has become difficult to convert real estate investments into cash. There are few buyers, and mortgage money has been difficult to obtain. When it has been available, required down payments and high annual interest rates have discouraged many potential buyers.

In the first part of 1975, as indications appeared that the downturn in the economy would soon "bottom out," the stock market showed signs of life. New records for total daily and weekly volume were set on the Big Board. Market indicators, such as the Dow Jones Industrial Average, rebounded significantly from the lows of late 1974. But later in 1975, when it became apparent that recovery from the recession was not going to be either quick or painless, hope for a new bull market faded and stock prices eased back to more realistic levels.

Regardless of the state of the economy and of the stock market, people need investment advice. Managing one's small share of the nation's wealth is a complex problem, if only because of the bewildering choice of investments available.

This book limits itself to a narrow field of discussion. One specific investment and survival technique, opening and using a Swiss bank account, is explored in depth. To help in choosing a bank for your account, this book provides a unique feature— chapter 10 contains a listing of over 100 Swiss banks that accept accounts from overseas, the results of a survey conducted especially for this book. Correct addresses of the banks, the types of accounts they offer, and other data are given to simplify the selection process.

Swiss bank secrecy, one of the major differences between Swiss and American banks, is discussed. You will discover that privacy in banking matters is an obsession with the Swiss, and protected both by custom and by law. The limitations of secrecy, and its practical uses for Americans, are also explained.

Swiss banks are unique in this world; to use them successfully, you should know something about this uniqueness.

In an attempt to explain the utility of Swiss accounts, this book touches on many subjects. Regardless of the reasons for your interest in Swiss banks, you should become much more knowledgeable about a fascinating subject.

2

Why an American Needs a Swiss Account

Until about 1970, Swiss bank secrecy was the feature that attracted private money to Switzerland from the United States. Naturally, strict banking privacy still has a definite appeal and its own uses. But lately, protecting the purchasing power of their savings from the ravages of inflation has become the primary motivation of most American account holders.

America's dollar is no longer a hard currency. Inflation has destroyed its reputation and much of its value. Once the most favored world currency, the dollar's worth and acceptability have declined markedly. Because of inflation, the dollar will no longer buy what it once would in the marketplaces of the world. As a result, the conversion rate of the dollar into stronger currencies has slipped drastically.,

There is every indication that inflation will be with us indefinitely, recurring in waves. On each cycle, higher levels of inflation will be reached and the dollar will slip farther in value.

The dollar can also be expected to decline in relation to more favored currencies. It will take more and more dollars to buy a given amount of any of the harder currencies. The corollary of this, of course, is that a fixed amount of hard currency will gradually buy larger and larger quantities of the ever-cheaper dollars.

The worst effects of inflation can be avoided by practicing a sort of monetary judo, utilizing the dollar's weakening position in the foreign exchange market to offset its loss of domestic purchasing power. With a Swiss account, dollars can be converted to deposits in a hard currency. When needed at a later date, these deposits can be used to buy dollars again. If the exchange value of the dollar in relation to the hard currency has fallen in the interim, the hard currency deposits should then buy enough extra dollars to compensate for the lost purchasing power of the dollar.

What happened to the dollar

The downgrading of the dollar began in 1934, at the beginning of Franklin Roosevelt's long administration. The right of gold ownership was denied U.S. citizens, except for gold jewelry and certain collectible coins; gold certificates were withdrawn from circulation. Gold's official price was raised from $20.67 to $35 a troy ounce, a 40.9 percent devaluation of the dollar. However, Roosevelt allowed the dollar to remain convertible into gold on an intergovernmental basis at the new $35 rate.

After World War II, the American dollar emerged preeminent, the equal of gold. The currency most in demand, it became the great international money. Dollars and gold together formed the reserves that backed most national currencies. For a while, it seemed that the world would never get enough dollars.

By the late 1960s, though, there were more than enough dollars overseas. Foreign central banks were becoming reluctant to retain dollars in their reserves. They started to exercise their privilege to exchange these dollars for American gold. As early as 1968, the United States was redeeming dollars only begrudgingly. In that year, to remove some of the redemption pressure, an international two-tier gold market was established. The American Treasury still maintained a fixed $35-per-ounce rate for central banks, but the price of gold was allowed to float freely on the private market. Expectations were that the price of gold would drop on the private side of the market, thereby making foreign governments less anxious to redeem their dollars at the official rate. Instead, the free market price of gold rose and redemption pressure increased.

The year 1971 was a bad one for the dollar. U.S. gold reserves totaled $10 to $11 billion, but estimates of redeemable dollars in the hands of foreign governments ranged upward to $70 billion. This forced, in August, Nixon's suspension of the redemption of dollars for gold. In December, the dollar was officially devalued by 8 percent, from $35 per troy ounce of gold to $38 an ounce. Although dollars were no longer convertible, even by central banks, devaluations such as this served a purpose. The paper value of the national gold supply was increased, making the Treasury's books look better. Since, in 1971, the world was still on a system of fixed exchange rates, devaluation also lowered the value of the dollar in terms of other currencies, an improvement for trade purposes.

In February 1973, the U.S. government devalued again, for the second time in fourteen months. Gold moved up, and the dollar down, by about 11 percent, to $42.22 per ounce of gold. This was still the official figure in 1975, although the Treasury would not sell gold at this price since gold was trading at about $140 to $150 per ounce on the free market.

As doubts arose abroad on the value of the dollar, other nations acted independently to protect themselves. In May 1971, Switzerland, West Germany, Austria, and the Netherlands cut their currencies loose from a fixed relationship with the dollar and allowed them to float upward. Thus, even before the first official U.S. devaluation, these nations devalued the dollar on their own initiative. In December 1971, the Japanese revalued their yen in relation to the dollar, too. Even after the second official devaluation in 1973, other nations continued to revalue their currencies and devalue the dollar, unilaterally.

Most major currencies are now floating in relation to the dollar. The dollar is worth only what supply and demand dictate in the foreign exchange marketplace. Since the United States has removed the dollar's gold backing, its main supports have been the wisdom and effectiveness of our government. Foreign governments and currency traders have less faith in our politicians than we do. It appears as though the dollar is in for a rough time for the indefinite future.

The U.S. dollar automatically and immediately became a "soft currency" when President Nixon announced its inconvertibility in August 1971. Since then, over fifteen other currencies have increased in value by more than 10 percent in relation to the dollar. Because of inflationary trends in their economies, however, not all of these currencies offer the prospect of continued appreciation.

The most desirable hard currencies in the world today are those of Switzerland, the Netherlands, and Austria. Swiss francs, Dutch guilders, and Austrian schillings all offer Americans protection from the ills of the dollar. All are currencies of smaller, tough-minded, conservatively governed countries that have maintained strong gold backing for their monies. All have the potential and the reasonable expectation of rising further in value against the dollar.

For the last few years, we have been bombarded with economic news and opinion. Inflation has become a staple of the media. Everyone talks glibly about inflation, and we all recognize the pain in the pocketbook. But what is inflation, really? And what are its causes?

Inflation is commonly considered to be a period of rapidly rising prices. This is because frequent price increases are the most obvious symptoms of inflation. However, there are other important components of inflation that, because they are hidden, are more insidious over the long run.

One old and popular explanation of inflation is: too much money chasing too few goods. A more precise, if less picturesque definition would be: Inflation is an economic condition characterized by an excessive increase in the money supply in relation to the supply of goods available, by constant price increases, and by a resultant decrease in the value of the money in use.

Too much money

Individuals seldom have too much money but economies often do, and when they do they suffer from attacks of inflation.

Inflation starts when there is too large a national "money supply," too much money in an economy in relation to the available stock of goods and services. The money supply is the total amount of money available for spending within an economy. It consists of the currency in circulation plus all the demand deposits in banks. Currency in circulation is simply all the paper money and coins in the hands of the public. Demand deposits include both checking account balances and those savings deposits that are freely available, without withdrawal restrictions.

The size of a nation's money supply is critical; both too little or too much money can cause difficulties. There must be enough money in circulation to facilitate normal business transactions, or trade will slow down and the economy will suffer.

Economists generally agree that, as a rule of thumb, the money supply should grow at about the same rate as the economy. If the gross national product increases by 3 percent in a given year, the supply of money should expand by 3 percent too.

Money is commonly considered to be the medium of exchange. We think of it as the paper bills in our wallets, "money in our pocket," or the balance in our bank accounts, "money in the bank." Money is our paycheck, a reward for our work; money is a credit voucher, exchangeable for goods or for the services of our fellow citizens. Money is also a store of value, our claim against the future.

Many things have been used as money. Acceptability as a standard of value is the key thought; money is whatever is commonly accepted as a standard interchange commodity in trade. The desirability of a commodity as a money depends on its characteristics. Whatever is used as money should be relatively scarce, durable, portable, compact, easily stored, divisible into smaller units, and have a use apart from its use as money. If it is scarce enough, and coveted for its other uses, a monetary commodity has an "intrinsic value" quite separate from its monetary value. If its acceptability in its role as money declines, the commodity will retain some value because of its alternate uses.

Gold is the only real money, the only standard of exchange valued as highly and accepted as readily today as it has been throughout the ages. Silver has dropped in status and value compared to gold because of the discovery of large silver deposits in the last century. Paper money is a comparatively recent innovation, with a checkered past of only 200 years or so.

Paper currency is only a "money substitute." Its sole advantage over gold is its lighter weight; paper is certainly not a scarce commodity, and it has little intrinsic value. Paper money is as good as gold only when it is convertible into gold upon demand. It can still be safely used, even if not redeemable for gold, if a fixed and known relationship is maintained between the gold backing and the amount of currency issued on the basis of this gold. Paper currency becomes dangerous when it is not backed by gold; instead of a "gold standard," an economy is then on a "paper standard." Once unhindered by the requirement that its product be issued only in quantities bearing some relationship to its gold supply, the issuing agency, be it bank or government, can then usually find reasons to print and distribute ever-increasing amounts of its paper currency.

Governments and inflation

The relationship between governments and inflation is a simple one: *governments cause inflation.* At least in our modern times they do. Governments have achieved a monopoly on the issuance of money, and when they create too large a money supply, inflation results.

Sooner or later, all governments inflate; paper money makes it easy. The scenario consistently follows the same pattern. In the interest of stability and efficiency, the government takes over as the sole issuer of currency. Gradually, it changes the rules, freeing itself from the constraints of common sense. In the United States, a minimum of 35 percent gold backing was once required for Federal Reserve certificates in circulation; in 1945, this gold reserve requirement was lowered to 25 percent; and finally, in 1968, the legal necessity to back Federal Reserve banknotes with gold was totally eliminated.

Politicians are elected to office on the basis of their promises to the electorate. Basically, they offer increased prosperity and additional government benefits to the masses in exchange for votes. To be elected, they must outdo the promises of their opponents; to be reelected, they must make good their own campaign promises; government programs must be enacted; the government must spend.

The problem is that tax revenues can seldom be stretched far enough to pay for all the projects desired. A government must then resort to deficit financing, spending more than it collects in taxes. Whether or not there is enough money to cover the federal expenditures, the government must pay for its programs. Bureaucrats, contractors, suppliers, subsidy recipients, and elected legislators themselves all want money, not government promises. The ultimate solution is to manufacture money to pay the government's bills.

In developed nations, the process is not that simple, although the consequences are the same. In the United States, most of the economy's money supply exists only as bank deposits; only about 25 percent of our primary money supply is in the form of circulating banknotes or coins. When the American government creates new money, it is pumped into the economy in the form of government checks. This process is handled through the Federal Reserve System, this nation's central bank.

Financing budget deficits

A federal budget deficit can be financed in a variety of ways. Basically, though, the government can borrow the money or it can create the money. Often it does both at the same time.

The Treasury borrows by issuing several types of interest-bearing paper for both short and long terms. Variously called bonds, bills, notes, or certificates, depending on their size and due dates, these obligations are sold to banks and other investors through the Federal Reserve System. Proceeds from these issues are credited to the Treasury's account with the Federal Reserve; checks are then written against these borrowed funds to help pay the government's operating expenses.

When the federal government's budget deficit is relatively low, as in 1970 when the deficit was only $2.8 billion, this financing method suffices. Funds are readily available on the money market to buy the federal paper. When the amount to be raised is huge, as it tends to be, the nation's banks and institutional investors often cannot easily supply the necessary funds. The Treasury, in its quest for money, crowds private business out of the money markets; the deficit financing effort tends to absorb funds needed to support normal business activity. In years such as 1968, when the budget shortfall was $25.2 billion, or fiscal 1976, when preliminary estimates put the expected budget deficit at $68.8 billion, other methods of financing are obviously needed.

Although the need is obvious, the methods used are not. The Treasury does not simply have the Federal Reserve print and issue more paper money. Neither does the Federal Reserve buy the government's securities directly. The problem is handled in a more roundabout manner.

Member banks are required to maintain reserve accounts with the Federal Reserve System. These required reserves are set as a percentage of a bank's average deposits, depending on the type of deposit, the class of bank, and the goals of the Federal Reserve. For example, the Federal Reserve may set the reserve requirement for checking deposits in a bank located in a metropolitan area at anywhere between 10 percent and 22 percent. However, member banks also have the privilege of borrowing additional reserves from the Federal Reserve when needed. As their reserves increase, they may make additional loans based on any excess in their reserve accounts.

When the Treasury goes to market to seek funds to pay for large budget shortfalls, the nation's banking system is stretched to capacity. The banks must continue to service their regular customers with working capital, inventory, and expansion loans, or the economy will suffer. At the same time, there is heavy pressure to buy the Treasury's offerings. At such times, the Federal Reserve often acts to reduce the strain on the banks by increasing the money supply. Banks are allowed, even encouraged, to borrow funds from the Reserve at what amounts to discount prices. Reserve requirements may also be lowered, freeing funds for the banks to use to make more loans, and to buy the government's securities.

The Federal Reserve System not only sells Treasury obligations, it constantly buys them. Treasury paper is issued in many forms; some issues mature in a few weeks or months, while on others the principal is due in ten or twenty years. Matured issues are redeemed by the Federal Reserve, but others are bought and held for the Federal Reserve's own account. Primarily, this is done to support the market for Treasury securities; the Federal Reserve buys when no one else is willing or able, to protect the market for future issues. However, as the Federal Reserve absorbs and pays for surplus Treasury paper, it is also pumping newly created money into the economy. In 1973, the Federal Reserve was holding $80.4 billion in U.S. government obligations, which it counted among its own assets.

In the same year, other agencies of the federal government were holding $125.4 billion in federal securities in their own accounts. The Social Security Old Age and Survivors' Trust Fund, just one of many such funds, was carrying $36.2 billion in U.S. securities on its books. These securities were its major assets; only $291 million was kept in cash deposits. This illustrates yet another way the federal deficit is funded; taxes collected for special purposes such as Social Security are diverted to help meet more immediate general operating deficits.

All of these Treasury securities represent the national debt, which is seldom reduced but only grows and grows. As older series of Treasury obligations reach maturity, they are "rolled over." Their redemption is paid for with the proceeds of newer issues. At the end of fiscal 1973, the public debt had reached $458.1 billion. It has grown since then and will continue to grow by the amount of the annual deficits. All "new money," created through the banking system and the Federal Reserve, not only finances the public debt; it is the major source of inflationary pressure in our economy. The government increases the money supply but the supply of goods and services does not increase proportionately. The "new" money competes with the "old" for what is available. Inflation results from a classic "too much money, too few goods" situation.

Deficit financing and the inflation it causes may be viewed as an extension of the government's taxing power.

Tax collectors and politicians everywhere recognize that there are limits beyond which a government dares not go in extracting money from its subjects. The government that ignores these limits courts trouble for itself, in the form of rebellion, tax revolt, or defeat at the polls. But politicians are shrewd judges of what the public will bear. Rather than push taxes past the resistance point, they resort to budget deficits. Creating money to pay for government expenditures, even though it causes inflation, is much more subtle than collecting additional taxes. Inflation is less direct, its effects are not immediately apparent: elected officials seem to feel that deficit financing is a painless tax.

Every government must have the ability to raise funds if it is to function at all. Taxes are recognized, if only grudgingly, as a fact of life by citizens of all nations. Resentment builds, though, when taxes become a burden on the economy, when too much is taken by the government and too little is left to the taxpayers. Experts on tax administration have noted that tax evasion becomes much more common when tax levels exceed 30 percent. In the United States, taxes are now just past that point; federal, state, and local authorities together tax away about one-third of the gross national product.

Raising taxes to pay for unpopular causes is another source of potential trouble. Governments have always had difficulty paying for wars, even the popular ones, because they instinctively have hesitated to raise taxes to the necessary levels.

Roots of the current inflation

The obvious example of an unpopular cause is the Vietnamese war. The price of both foreign and domestic pacification was more than the federal budget could bear. As early as 1966, the Council of Economic Advisors warned that taxes must be raised. Hesitant in the face of widespread and violent opposition to the undeclared war, Congress and the President stalled. When a 10-percent tax surcharge was finally imposed a year and a half later, in 1968, it was already too late and the tax increase, too small. The seeds of serious inflation had already been planted in the American economy.

What the total bill for Southeast Asia will be, no one yet knows. Almost certainly the cost will at least equal that of our last global war, World War II. The Veterans' Administration alone will be paying Vietnam-era benefits for the next fifty years or more. However, the damage to the economy can be measured. Approximately half of the direct costs of the war were paid for by deficits; between 1965 and 1972, the national debt rose by $110 billion, while the money supply increased by $225 billion, a full 74 percent.

By 1969, inflation was running over 6 percent, up from about 2 percent in 1965. Attempts to control it led to the recession of 1969-1970. After President Johnson left office, Nixon's administration attempted to stimulate the economy, then lost control again. Mismanagement, and off-again, on-again price controls only aggravated the problem. By 1974, the economy was suffering from a previously unobserved economic disease, a deep recession, the worst since the 1930s, coupled with double-digit inflation. The attending economists were forced to coin a new term, *stagflation,* to classify the phenomenon of an inflationary recession.

Recession and depression

Nothing lasts forever, not even prosperity. Since the Industrial Revolution, boom periods have always been followed by depressions.

America's economy has often been called depression-proof.

Maybe, but it depends on what is meant by depression. Formerly, any slackening of business activity or economic growth was termed a depression. The catastrophic slump of the 1930s, however, colored our understanding of the word *depression.* Since then, no American official has dared to use *depression* to describe the periodic low points of the business cycle. Instead, the less menacing word *recession* has become popular. In current usage, a recession is a mild depression, and a depression is a severe recession.

Recession and depression are essentially degrees of the same thing, the natural cure for an overheated economy. Periodically, during an extended period of prosperity, business becomes overconfident and expands too far. In a free market economy, a recession quickly corrects these excesses and the accompanying inflation of an overextended boom. On the whole, after a corrective recession the economy is sounder because of the unhealthy growth, the nonessential and ill-conceived enterprises, that have been excised from it.

The United States, of course, does not have a free market economy. In America today, free enterprise coexists with the welfare state. The government interferes with economic processes to such an extent that the natural corrective forces of a recession are not allowed free play. To cite just one example, minimum-wage laws place a floor under labor costs. Since salaries cannot be adjusted downward to help lower production costs and prices, the labor force must be cut instead, adding to the unemployment rolls. Admittedly some legislation, the unemployment compensation laws being a prominent example, serves to dampen the worst effects of a slump. But such laws also dampen the speed of a rebound from a recession.

A Swiss account protects

There are hard currencies and there are soft currencies. "Hard" and "soft" are only labels, reflecting the accumulated experience of foreign currency traders. The demand for some currencies is soft because they are in excessive supply, with more potential sellers than buyers; the consensus of market opinion is that their future price movement will be downward. Other currencies are hard, by contrast, because the demand for them is usually stronger than the supply; their general price trend is upward. The Swiss franc is hard, and the U.S. dollar, unfortunately, soft.

In this basic difference between the hard franc and the soft dollar lies protection from inflation. Swiss bank accounts are normally denominated in Swiss francs. Liquid assets held as soft dollars are converted to hard currency assets when they are transferred to a Swiss account. Since the value of a hard currency tends to move in the opposite direction to soft currency values, an inflation hedge is created. In the past few years, this hedge has worked well for those Americans prudent enough to maintain a Swiss account. As inflation rose from an annual 3 percent in the mid-1960s to 8.8 percent in 1973 and 12 percent in 1974, the value of Swiss francs climbed too.

From 1949 to 1969, the exchange rate between the Swiss franc and the Yankee dollar was stable, maintained within narrow fixed limits. For years, a Swiss franc cost about $0.2320, and a dollar bought 4.28 to 4.32 francs. After May 1971, when the Swiss allowed their currency to float, this relationship started to change. By mid-1973, the price of the Swiss franc had risen to the $0.35 range; a dollar could be exchanged for 2.85 francs. In February 1975, the franc reached a temporary peak of $0.4185, with the dollar valued at 2.39 Swiss francs.

As an example of just how well Swiss francs have worked as a hedge against inflation, let us consider the following example. Suppose that sometime in late 1970, $10,000 was placed in a Swiss bank account. The dollars, when converted, would have created a deposit of 43,100 Swiss francs, at 4.31 francs to the dollar. During the next four years, the francs were left on deposit as price levels in the United States rose by 30 percent. By the end of December 1974, the exchange price of a franc had floated up to $0.3950, or 2.53 Swiss francs per dollar.

At this point, the 43,100 francs on deposit would buy $17,035 in American money, 70 percent more dollars than were originally transferred to Switzerland, without even considering the interest earned on the account. Typically, the franc deposit would also have earned at least 3½ percent, compounded annually or semiannually, in a "deposit" account. Earned interest, minus a special Swiss withholding tax on interest (explained in chapter 6), would have added another 4,381 francs, or $1,728, to the final account balance. Calculated in francs, this interest increment would be 10 percent. Computed in dollars, though, accumulated interest added another 17.28 percent, because the francs earned as interest also benefited from the increase in exchange values.

Swiss francs were much more than a successful hedge. Disregarding interest, the 70-percent appreciation from changes in the exchange rates would have more than made up for the rise in price levels in our dollar economy. Those Americans who took advantage of the opportunity actually made a profit on their money, the difference between the 70-percent increase in dollar value of the franc and the four-year climb in the U.S. inflation rate. Even those Americans who recognized the advantages of hard currency accounts much later have generally made out very well. The dollar value of a Swiss franc account opened as late as January 1974 would have grown by 13.1 percent by the end of 1974, again without considering interest.

The exchange rate tends to move upward in spurts, and franc prices have sometimes dipped as the dollar temporarily regained lost ground. There were also long periods when the dollar-franc rate remained rather stable. Most of the price movement in 1974 came late in the year; in fact, an account opened in late September would have done almost as well as one opened in early January, managing a 12.2 percent gain for three months against 13.1 percent for the full year.

Although accounts in a Swiss bank are usually denominated in Swiss francs, it is possible to open accounts in just about any convertible currency. Swiss francs have performed well, but holders of other hard currencies have made their gains, too. Dutch guilders have appreciated by over 40 percent in the last four years, and Belgian francs by about 35 percent. The West German deutsche mark has also moved ahead by approximately 50 percent at the expense of the American dollar.

How much to keep

Financial survival is the name of the game, the main reason for a hard currency account in Switzerland. Preserving the purchasing power of current assets takes precedence over attempts to make a profit. Any gains achieved in hard currencies, as the exchange rate of the dollar slips, should not be thought of as a "profit" in the normal sense. Depositors should consider themselves fortunate if their hard currency deposits increase in value fast enough to offset the rate of inflation in this country. Sometimes, of course, as happened over the last few years, the exchange rate will move ahead faster than the rate of inflation, producing a bonus "profit."

It may very well be possible to obtain 9 percent interest on a time deposit in a Mexican bank, or a point or two more interest at a hometown bank. But the Mexican peso is as soft as the U.S. dollar, locked in an unchanging ratio with the dollar, with no possibility of exchange rate gains to offset inflation. The gain in interest becomes insignificant when measured against the loss of purchasing-power dollars, and dollar-pegged currencies will suffer when U.S. inflation runs 10 percent, 15 percent, or more.

A Swiss account should be thought of primarily as a hedging operation. A hedge is an investment made to counterbalance the risk of another investment. With a hedge, an investor is betting both ways; if either investment shows a loss, the other posts an equal gain. As dollars fall, the Swiss franc rises; and, of course, the hedge works in reverse, if dollars rise at the expense of Swiss francs.

To take full advantage of a hedge, both sides of the investment should be balanced. For this reason, a good starting point would be to consider dividing the available liquid assets equally between hard and soft investments, keeping approximately half in dollar-denominated investments and placing the rest in hard currency deposits or related inflation hedges. Liquid assets are those that can be converted quickly to cash or its equivalent, and spent when the need arises. They include cash, checking-and-savings account balances, certificates of deposit, Treasury certificates and savings bonds, and, of course, common stocks and bonds. Gold and silver coins, gold bullion, and gold-mining shares are liquid assets, too, but they are hard investments because their value tends to move in opposition to the dollar's.

It is neither practical nor convenient to put all of one's funds into a Swiss account. In deciding what balance between hard and soft investments to establish, careful consideration must be given to personal circumstances. What are the sources of personal or family income, and how secure are they? What are anticipated needs and plans for the future? How large an investment fund and an emergency reserve have been accumulated over the years?

To function adequately as an inflation hedge, however, a significant portion of total liquid assets must be committed to hard currency or gold-related investments. If only 10 percent of all available liquid assets were allotted to hard investments, perhaps in Swiss franc deposits, only an equivalent amount of the remaining dollar-denominated investments would be covered by the hedge. With only a 10-percent hedge, 80 percent of total assets would be unprotected from a loss of buying power in the event of more inflation. The closer the balance of investments, the more conservative the hedging operation.

But regardless of all other considerations, an individual should distribute his investments in a way that makes him feel comfortable. One depositor might feel secure with 75 percent of his available funds in hard currency deposits, because he believes strongly that the dollar will get progressively weaker. Another might feel exposed if he transferred over 25 percent of his money to Switzerland. Each reader will have to make his own decision.

When to bring your money back

There are two simple answers to the question of when to transfer your money back from Switzerland: (1) when you need it, and (2) when it's safe.

Retirees and others who find it necessary to live off their accumulated capital can arrange to draw upon their Swiss deposits on a regular basis. A Swiss bank can be instructed to send a fixed sum each month for living expenses, while the bulk of the capital remains in Switzerland, its purchasing power protected from the dry rot of dollar inflation. Some types of Swiss accounts have restrictions on the amounts that can be withdrawn without notice; these limitations are discussed in detail in chapter 7. Forewarned, and taking anticipated needs into consideration, a depositor can choose an account type compatible with his access needs.

The second answer, "when it's safe," deserves a fuller explanation. "Safe" means when the American economy and the foreign exchange rate of the dollar have stabilized, when the threat of continued high inflation recedes, and when the dollar's convertibility into gold is restored, at least for foreign central banks. It may be a long time before these conditions come to pass. The world economy is in a period of adjustment that may last until the end of this century. There is little prospect that the U.S. dollar will soon become a hard currency again; the Treasury remains adamantly antigold and anticonvertibility. The U.S. government shows no sign of living within its means, so there will be more heavy budget deficits and more inflation. It will probably take an economic lesson of the proportions of the Great Depression to trigger the necessary reforms.

Future Swiss franc values

How much protection will hard currencies offer against inflation in the future? Over the long term, the ultimate value of the dollar in relation to other currencies will be determined primarily by its gold backing. It is possible to estimate the potential appreciation of another currency against the dollar by comparing the available gold reserves of the two currencies against the amount of the currencies in circulation.

As of August 20, 1975, the United States' gold stock stood at $11.6 billion and its money supply (currency plus demand deposits) at $294.8 billion; thus the dollar's gold backing was 3.93 percent. In contrast, the Swiss franc was backed by gold at slightly over 20 percent, the Austrian schilling and Dutch guilder by about 15 percent, and the German mark by roughly 10 percent.

Based on these figures we can estimate the future potential exchange value of the hard currencies likely to provide the best inflation hedges. In each of the following projections, the August 1975 exchange value is given, then the currency's estimated ultimate value, and finally the appreciation possible against the dollar expressed as a percentage. The West German deutsche mark has the potential of moving from its August 1975 price of $0.3877 to about $0.9960 for a 250-percent gain. Austria's schilling can move from $0.0550 to $0.2440, or about 440 percent; and the Dutch guilder from $0.3793 to $1.65, a possible 435 percent. Switzerland's franc has the greatest estimated upside potential, from $0.3730 to $2.08, for an eventual 550-percent gain.

Although these figures are exciting, it must be emphasized that they are only an estimate of the possible outer limits of these currencies' long-term movement against the dollar. They represent the real reason, though, why the U.S. Treasury officially opposes any proposals to return to a gold standard. Eventually, if some sort of monetary stability is ever to be achieved, it will be necessary to link the dollar to gold again. It can only be hoped that, in the meantime, the federal government does not dissipate its remaining gold reserves; when the time comes, they will be needed to support a new gold-backed dollar.

For a variety of reasons, it is unlikely that foreign exchange prices will approach their potential limits until the world returns to something resembling a gold standard. First of all, a sudden move to currency values at these levels would be very disruptive to world trade; exports of the hard currency nations would simply dry up. For example, a modestly equipped Volkswagen "Rabbit" sedan, now about $3,500 in the United States would jump in price to $8,750 if the mark became worth 99.6 cents; similarly, a gold Rolex wristwatch from Switzerland, that only a few years ago retailed for about $580 and now sells for $1,000, would be a prohibitive $5,500 in American jewelry stores. Secondly, even the hard currency nations are having trouble with their economies in the worldwide recession; Germany, for one, has been running budget deficits in an attempt to stimulate the economy. As these nations increase their money supplies, the percentage of gold backing for their currencies drops, cutting their potential for appreciation against the dollar.

Over the short term, the next few years, the exchange value of the main hedge currencies will probably be influenced primarily by their "relative purchasing power" compared to the dollar's. Basically this means that as inflation cuts the buying power of the dollar, the dollar's foreign exchange value will fall relative to the currencies of nations that have inflation under better control.

The Swiss have decided that they can live with the dollar priced at 2.5 francs and the franc at 40 U.S. cents or less. They are likely to try to keep the franc from rising above this level; this period would seem to be an opportune time to acquire Swiss francs.

Exchange values for Dutch guilders and Austrian schillings are likely to parallel the movement of the Swiss franc, but with slightly lower percentage increases. The Dutch are members of a European "joint float" which will have a dampening effect on guilder price movements; the Austrian schilling is not as widely recognized as the Swiss franc as an inflation hedge. The future of the West German deutsche mark is more problematic; much depends on how successful the Bonn government is at holding the line on inflation. If it succeeds in keeping it below the 1975 rate of 6 percent, the mark stands an excellent chance of advancing against the dollar, too.

Inflation seems likely to be with us for some time to come;

the only sensible course is to try to minimize its effects on our personal lives. Financial survival is the new game, and, whether we like it or not, we are all players. It is likely to be a long game. Because there are risks in using hard currency hedges, and what seems to be even greater risks in remaining with dollar-denominated investments, it is likely to be an interesting game, too.

CHAPTER 3

More Reasons for a Swiss Account

For the majority of Americans, Swiss bank accounts have always been tinged with an aura of illicitness. Generally when the American press has mentioned Swiss accounts it has been in connection with some sort of knavery. Indeed, in the 1950s and early 1960s, the prime reason for an American to have a Swiss account was to take advantage of Swiss bank secrecy. The U.S. economy was ripe with legitimate business opportunities, and the dollar was sound. Some American companies dealing internationally, and expatriates who lived or worked permanently abroad, kept money in Switzerland for convenience. However, Swiss bank public relations aside, probably most Americans who had Swiss accounts in those days were involved in tax evasion, hiding assets from court proceedings, or making an end run around U.S. securities laws.

American authorities, especially the tax authorities, undoubtedly wish that money in Switzerland would simply disappear. Money in Switzerland is effectively outside their control. Their opinion is shared, no doubt, by the tax authorities of many nations, whose citizens have caused their liquid assets to flee to a safer land.

The pattern of capital flight has occurred throughout history. As conditions deteriorate within a given nation, more and more money is sent outside its borders and converted to harder currencies. As the economy continues to sicken, the government enacts additional laws and regulations. This only causes a more rapid demoralization; asset outflow increases. In desperation, severe measures are applied to stop the flight of capital.

Swiss accounts are legal

Because of a bad press, and because the Internal Revenue Service now asks about foreign bank accounts on the annual tax return, a large portion of the public believes that Swiss accounts are illegal for American citizens or residents.

This is a misconception. At the current time, there is no law prohibiting foreign bank accounts for Americans. However, the Treasury Department requires U.S. citizens and residents to disclose overseas accounts on their income tax returns. This explains the box on the back of the IRS Form 1040 which asks: "Did you, at any time during the taxable year, have an interest in or signature or other authority over a bank, securities, or other financial account in a foreign country . . .?" The taxpayer is supposed to check off "yes" or "no."

Foreign accounts are completely legal, but the average taxpayer is being led to conclude that there is something illegitimate about having an account in a foreign bank.

If the taxpayer checks "yes" on his 1040, a copy of Form 4683, "U.S. Information Return on Foreign Bank, Securities, and Other Financial Accounts" must then be completed and filed as part of the tax return.

The same Treasury regulations that require Americans to report foreign accounts also contain provisions that require residents to report transmittal of more than $5,000 overseas. The report of receipt of similar amounts from other countries is also required.

Swiss banks offer a greater measure of privacy, security, and flexibility than American banks. But what does this mean to the average American considering placing some of his money in a Swiss institution?

Basically, it means more freedom, freedom from additional government interference in private affairs. Inflation may be the primary reason for having a Swiss account, but Swiss bank secrecy remains the main defense against future restrictions.

Freedom from additional restrictions is more important than it may seem now. Historically, as a currency has started to decline in value, governments have placed more and more limitations on their citizens' freedom to invest their assets abroad.

Transfer restrictions

A hard currency account may provide shelter against the worst effects of inflation, but only if you can get some money safely to a foreign bank. Once strict exchange controls are instituted, transferring funds will become exceedingly difficult.

The existing regulations are a compromise. In 1969, when the current law was under consideration by Congress, the Treasury pushed for stricter limitations. As originally proposed, the act would have made secret accounts illegal, and would have limited the amount allowed to be taken out in one year to only $10,000.

Strongly opposed to the projected regulations were the major banks. Their argument, that the excessive recordkeeping required of them would constitute "undue hardship," apparently fell upon sympathetic ears in Congress, and the final legislation was only a watered-down version of the original proposal.

As our economy deteriorates further, fewer profitable investments will be available in the United States. The inertia of the people, their natural reluctance to send money overseas, will be overcome. When the money flowing abroad is mainly from the middle class, the government will certainly react with harsher restrictions. The lobby for tighter controls within Treasury and Internal Revenue will then probably prevail.

Substantial portions of Executive Order 7560, dated January 15, 1934, are still effective. Franklin D. Roosevelt, then the President, issued this order under powers granted him by reason of national emergency.

This Executive Order gave broad powers to the Secretary of the Treasury to either tighten or ease the restrictions. Currently, they are quite loose. Some time ago, a general license was granted to everyone, "authorizing any and all transactions in

foreign exchange, transfer of credit, and exports of currency."
But in fine print it states, "The regulations in . . . the general
license granted in this part may be modified or revoked at any
time."

What the government has taken away, it has given back, but
can take away again at any time, in whole or in part. The order
remains on the books, but temporarily inactive. Without further legislative action, it can be activated again by the Secretary of the Treasury. What future restrictions can be expected
on the transfer of funds overseas?

It would depend on the future economic situation, and on
how high a panic level was reached within the government.

The right to travel

As a people, we have long taken the right to travel for
granted. We can envision few restrictions. When and if transfer restrictions are imposed, though, they will undoubtedly be
part of a package that includes limitations on the amount of
money a traveler can take out of the country with him.

As an example of how exchange controls might affect an
American's ability to travel, let us consider an English example. England is the source of our most precious legal rights.
The English are known as champions of personal liberty. Not
so, however, when taking currency abroad is concerned.

In the 1950s, when I was living in England, I knew an
executive who wanted to take his family on a grand tour of
Continental Europe. He felt that the experience should be
part of his two daughters' education. As English residents,
however, each member of the family was allowed to take only
about the equivalent of $15 in currency and a very limited
amount of travelers' checks. They couldn't go far on that,
which was the whole intent.

Fortunately, this gentleman worked for an international
company with branches all over Europe. He arranged his family's vacation with several of his coexecutives on the Continent.
In France, his French colleague paid the family's way; in
Spain, another company representative financed the Spanish
part of the tour; in Italy, similar arrangements prevailed. Within a few months after the family's vacation was over, these
representatives all visited London, where they were reim-
bursed. This individual found a way around the rules, as some
resourceful and well-placed people will always do.

Over twenty years later, the British are still closely limited as to the amount of money they can take out of the country with them. "Exchange control" is still in force. Vacationing Britons are now permitted to leave with only £25 (about $53) in British currency and £300 ($630) in foreign currencies. Many other countries have similar limitations. Japanese tourists, for example, are permitted only about $1,500 in traveling money.

Americans are fortunate in that they can still travel quite freely, even if the dollar doesn't buy quite as much overseas as it once did. To insure their ability to travel, though, prudent people will have funds available outside of the United States.

Economic problems are largely caused by government policies. The burden and the blame, however, always fall upon the people, shifted there by new restrictive regulations. Typically, rather than trim a balance of payments deficit by cutting government spending overseas, an attempt is made to reduce personal spending on travel and on private investments in other nations.

In 1963, to discourage Americans from investing in foreign stocks and bonds, the American government introduced the interest-equalization tax.

This levy, 11.25 percent on the purchase price of foreign stocks, effectively deterred citizens from seeking investment opportunities in other nations. Fortunately, on January 30, 1974, the tax was eliminated. During the ten years it was in force, however, the government continued to spend billions overseas. During these same years, American investors were prevented, by the same government, from profiting in a worldwide investment boom.

As the world economy changes further, there will be recurring opportunities to profit from foreign investments. There is no guarantee that the U.S. government will not repeat its mistakes, and prevent its citizens from participating in a new boom. With a precedent in hand, the probability is high that, sometime in the coming years, similar restrictions will again be slapped on overseas investments.

A Swiss account is the perfect tool to help maintain your right to invest internationally. Not only will your investment funds be beyond the reach of a capricious government, but Swiss banks can handle investments for their customers in just about any publicly traded security in any country in the world.

Plain old privacy

Freedom from unwarranted intrusion into private affairs is another sound reason for a Swiss bank account.

In our society, the relationship between an individual and his physician or lawyer is considered a privileged one. In Switzerland, banking matters are also private and confidential, both by custom and by law. Protecting a depositor's privacy is a specialty of Swiss banks.

In the United States, there are no effective banking secrecy laws. Just about anyone can find out the approximate amount in your bank account, and the government can determine your balance to the penny. If someone walks up to a teller at your bank and inquires about your account balance, they will be told that such information is confidential. But that's about as far as an American bank will go to protect your privacy. There are no real safeguards, especially where the government is concerned. When you write a check, retail stores will often check your balance before letting you take possession of the merchandise.

They call your bank, give the account number and name, and ask if there are sufficient funds to cover the check. In such cases, the caller is often told that the balance runs in the "low three figures," or "the high four figures."

When you apply for credit, you are asked to name the banks where you have your checking and savings accounts. Banks are reluctant to provide information to credit investigators, but such information is sometimes obtained indirectly, with the lender's bank seeking the data from the borrower's bank. Such tactics are often used to explore credit ratings in business deals, and by divorce lawyers, potential employers, or insurance companies.

Federal government investigators can do much more. Most banks cooperate all too fully with the Internal Revenue's investigators. An IRS agent can obtain your exact balance, review the checks drawn on your account, examine just about anything felt necessary.

For years there have been reports that Internal Revenue investigators have conducted "fishing expeditions" into bank records. Tax evaders sometimes open accounts under false names. In pursuit of this hidden money, it is necessary to have a "John Doe" subpoena drawn up, since the name on the suspect account is not known. Such a legal order then allows the

IRS agent to root through all the bank's account records looking for the hidden account. In the process, the confidentiality of all the accounts inspected is violated.

To compound the indignity, this practice recently became legal. On February 19, 1975, the U.S. Supreme Court decided a test case in the government's favor.

The IRS not only has the power to investigate bank accounts, it has the power to seize them. In case of unpaid taxes, or even a controversy over the amount of taxes due, Internal Revenue has the ability to apply a lien to an account. This is a very powerful tool. The taxpayer often has no choice but to settle; any checks drawn against an account covered by an IRS lien must automatically be returned unpaid by the bank.

Internal Revenue is not the only government agency with the power to investigate your financial affairs. The Federal Bureau of Investigation, the Securities and Exchange Commission, and many other federal and local law enforcement agencies can probe your banking and brokerage accounts with very little trouble.

Basically, a Swiss bank account is protection against the future and what the future might bring. The world economy is in a state of change. What our society will be like after a new world pattern evolves is uncertain. There is a high probability that it will feature continued inflation, stricter regulations, and less personal liberty. A Swiss bank account will be a help in maintaining some freedom of action in the face of future restrictions.

There is still time to act. The next negative signal will be renewed inflation or tighter exchange controls. As the situation slips further, transfer restrictions will almost certainly become reality; the only uncertainty is in the timing.

The only sure thing is that the time to open a Swiss account is now, before it becomes extremely difficult to transfer funds out of this economy.

4

Types of
Swiss
Banks

Swiss banks have suffered far less interference in their affairs than the banks of other nations. For years, Swiss banks operated with little federal regulation. Nevertheless, probably as a result of its experience in the 1930s, Switzerland finally codified its banking traditions. The result was the Federal Banking Law of 1935.

This legislation established the Federal Banking Commission, which is charged with overseeing compliance with the law. Basically, all Swiss institutions that accept deposits are subject to the banking law; the banking commission has the right of final decision if a question arises as to whether an institution is a bank or not. To establish a bank requires the permission of the commission. It must satisfy itself that a projected bank has sufficient capital, and that the planned bank will have adequate facilities and systems to cope with the type of business anticipated. The experience and background of intended management personnel are also scrutinized carefully.

In 1971, the banking law was revised somewhat. One of the apparent motives was to give the banking commission tools to help restrict the number of foreign-controlled banks being opened in Switzerland. Under the new rules, permission is granted to form a foreign-controlled Swiss bank only when the other nation allows the establishment of Swiss banks in its jurisdiction. In addition, a Swiss-owned bank opened in the other country must not be required to operate under conditions more stringent than it would in Switzerland itself. Obviously, if these requirements are strictly interpreted and enforced, there will be very few foreign banks opened in Switzerland in the future.

If the money of a bank's depositors seems threatened, the banking commission has the power to send an observer to inquire into all of a bank's management and operational aspects. If necessary, the commission may withdraw a bank's permission to operate and start the liquidation proceedings.

Periodic statements of financial condition, such as balance sheets and profit and loss statements, are required of all banks. Such reports must also be made available to the public, except in the case of private banks. All banks must furnish statistical reports to the Swiss National Bank. However, this information is kept confidential. Details on a particular bank are never published; when studies on the banking industry are issued by the National Bank, the data is provided only in summarized form, consolidated by type of banks.

Swiss bankers believe that maintaining adequate liquidity is more sensible than merely meeting fixed reserve requirements. Banking law reflects this attitude; it specifies minimum ratios of capital and liquid assets to liabilities for the various types of banks. To insure adherence to these rulings, the banking commission supervises the auditing of Swiss banks. Private outside auditors are used; they must also meet certain net worth and experience requirements set by the commission. These auditors submit their findings to the inspected bank's board of directors. Only when serious financial problems or violations of the banking laws are uncovered are the auditors required to report the audit results to the banking commission.

Much of the regulation of the Swiss banking industry is carried out by the banks themselves, acting jointly through their trade organizations. The most important of these is the Swiss

Bankers' Association, which acts as the industry's main liaison with the Swiss government. Its membership consists of bank officers who represent most of the banks of Switzerland. This association has also sponsored several "conventions," under which most banks have agreed to standardize conditions and fees for the major banking services. There is also a Swiss Private Bankers' Association, an Association of Cantonal Banks, one for Swiss Regional and Savings Banks, and others of more specialized interest. Very few banks do not have a membership in one or more of these trade associations.

Self-regulation extends to areas usually reserved for the government in other nations; for example, interest rate limitations are set by regional bank associations rather than by the Swiss National Bank or the Banking Commission. These interbank agreements would certainly be illegal, "in restraint of trade" in the United States. In Switzerland, however, order in the marketplace is valued more highly than fair play and competition. Such interbank arrangements are considered a normal and sensible way to do business.

Although self-regulation has undoubtedly strengthened the Swiss banking trade and increased its profitability, it is probably best viewed as a typical Swiss solution. It is the Swiss bankers' answer to the problem of avoiding the alternatives, either a banking system in trouble from unbridled competition, or a system saddled with bureaucratic restrictions.

Leslie Waller, in his book *The Swiss Bank Connection,* says that the Swiss banking system "is perhaps a textbook model of what the free and pure-minded pursuit of capital gain will produce if left to form its own structure." Other nations' banking systems, by contrast, could be considered mutants whose natural growth has been warped by the arbitrary interference of their governments. And, on that thought, let us go on to consider the various types of banking houses to be found in Switzerland.

Swiss banks are often described as "universal" banks that offer their customers one-stop financial service. As a generalization, this is accurate. Nevertheless, there are differences between Swiss banks. Not all banks care to engage in all types of banking transactions; their size, their ownership, and their legal structures vary considerably.

Swiss banks are usually classified into seven types: "big" banks, cantonal banks, savings banks, private banks, local banks, loan associations, and "other banks." In addition, the Swiss also have a well-organized postal checking system that supplements the banking system but is not truly a part of it.

The big banks

Only five banking houses, commonly called the "Big Five," are included in this category. They are the Union Bank of Switzerland, the Swiss Bank Corporation, the Swiss Credit Bank, the Swiss People's Bank, and Bank Leu.

The three largest, Union Bank, Swiss Bank Corporation, and Swiss Credit, are the "Big Three." One of their common characteristics is that their branches are to be found everywhere in the Confederation, in almost every decent-sized town. The Big Three are commercial banks par excellence, truly universal banks, providing their Swiss and foreign customers with every required financial service. Because of their size, they tend to dominate most areas of activity in which they participate. The Big Three are the most active foreign exchange dealers in Switzerland, the largest stock brokers and bullion merchants. Since their charters do not restrict them to pure banking, they have subsidiaries active in gold refining, consumer loans, and mortgage lending; they run the largest mutual funds and real estate trusts. Their captive accounting organizations provide auditing services to other banks. All three are publicly owned corporations whose shares are traded on Swiss stock exchanges.

Although these big banks loom large in the Swiss banking world, it must be remembered that Switzerland is a small country. In any international listing of banks by size, all three would fall somewhere about fortieth to fiftieth place. At the end of the first quarter of 1975, the Swiss Credit Bank had admitted assets of over 32 billion Swiss francs. By comparison, the largest bank in the world, California's Bank of America, is about three times this size. Regardless, the Big Three have an international reputation that far outweighs their relatively modest size.

The Union Bank of Switzerland, Schweizerische Bankgesellschaft in German, is the largest of the big banks. It was created in 1912 by a merger of the Bank of Winterthur and the Bank of Toggenberg. Headquarters for the Union Bank is now in Zurich. In the United States, it has a branch in New York and representative offices in Chicago and San Francisco.

The Swiss Bank Corporation has its main offices in Basel. It grew from a loosely organized syndicate of Basel private banks that called itself the *Bankverein,* or bank corporation. In the 1870s, this group formally became a banking house, called the Basler Bankverein, to head off a move to set up a major foreign bank in Basel. It later merged with the Bank Corporation of Zurich and the Swiss Union Bank of St. Gallen. Now called the Schweizerischer Bankverein, it has continued to grow by taking over smaller banks.

After its organization in Zurich in 1856, the Swiss Credit Bank, too, expanded by merger and the takeover of local banks. It now has 112 Swiss branches. Like other members of the Big Three, it is active abroad, with offices in major cities worldwide. In the United States, Crédit Suisse's branches are located in New York and Los Angeles.

The People's Bank of Switzerland, commonly called the Swiss Volksbank or Schweizerische Volksbank, is ranked among the Big Five only because of its Confederation-wide banking network. It has about 106 branches, but only approximately one quarter of the assets of the Swiss Credit Bank. Originally organized as a bank to serve the "common people," the Volksbank grew and gradually evolved into a full-fledged commercial bank.

Like the Volksbank, Bank Leu is much smaller than any of the Big Three. Bank Leu is ranked as a big bank primarily because of its history; it dates its formation to 1755, over a century before any of the Big Three became active. Bank Leu has only fourteen branches; several of the cantonal banks and the newer foreign-controlled banks can claim much larger assets. Originally the semiofficial "interest commission" of Zurich, it became a private mortgage bank in 1822, developing later into a full-service commercial bank.

Cantonal banks

Cantonal banks were formed by the cantonal authorities. Termed a *Kantonalbank* in German, and a *Banque Cantonale* in French, there are now twenty-eight of them. Their assets represent an estimated 20 to 25 percent of the total assets of the Swiss banking system; some of these banks are much larger than the smaller two of the Big Five.

Capital for these cantonal banks was generally furnished by the cantonal governments. In a few cases, notably in the cantons of Zug and Vaud, the banks have private shareholders as well. The cantonal banks were all established in the century between 1816 and 1917. In the years before the Swiss National Bank was opened in 1907, they were banks of issue, a source of the coins and currency used in their respective cantons.

Most of the cantonal banks now operate as general commercial banks, but a few are primarily savings or mortgage institutions. Often cantonal banks maintain branches in the main towns of their cantons. They are heavily involved in mortgage financing, in providing loans for local businesses, and in helping to fund local governments. Most cantonal banks accept accounts from overseas. Indeed, they offer a special advantage; there is no deposit insurance in Switzerland, but the deposits in the majority of cantonal banks are guaranteed by the cantonal governments. When this is the case, their stationery will be marked either *Staatsgarantie* or *Garantie de l'Etat.*

The private banks

Private banks are not incorporated. Under Swiss law, they may be organized only as proprietorships or partnerships. The principals, the partners in a private bank, are not employees, they are the owners. As such, their risk is not limited to the bank's capital and reserves, as is the liability of an incorporated bank. When private bankers make a business decision, they are responsible to the full extent of their personal resources.

All private banks are subject to the Swiss Federal Banking Law. Normal periodic audits are required, but private bankers are not required to make public their statements of financial condition; in return they may not advertise for deposits nor solicit new business in any way. They are not even allowed to post their interest rates in their windows to lure in an occasional customer from the street.

Under Swiss law, private banks must operate under the name of a principal, an unlimited partner. If the family dies out, if no heirs of the same surname come into the business, the bank's business name must be changed or the bank must close its doors. For this reason, and because it is often easier to raise capital as a corporation, the number of private banks has been steadily declining.

Sometimes a private bank just fades away, transferring its customers to another institution. More often, it becomes a joint stock company, or continues under new ownership; sometimes, it does both. Bank von Ernst & Cie., AG, was formerly a private bank in Bern; now it is incorporated, and is a wholly owned subsidiary of an English financial group.

Although the private banks are declining in number, those that remain seem quite vigorous. Because they do not publish statements, and since statistics on the private houses are not included in the National Bank's annual report on the banking system, it is difficult to judge their size. It is generally agreed that the private banks are more of a factor in international finance than in the internal Swiss banking business. Most of their money comes from outside the Confederation and most leaves Switzerland again to be reinvested in other nations. The size of the private banks can be estimated only from their activity on the stock exchanges, the number of their employees, and their participation in large loan syndicates.

In considering the size of any Swiss bank, including those that publish financial statements, the question of "admitted assets" always arises. Swiss bankers do not include managed assets, the investment portfolios they control for their clients, in their reported figures. Since private banks specialize in portfolio management, their true power is probably many times their estimated assets. In Switzerland, the private bankers have an influence in Swiss banking circles much greater than might normally be expected; traditionally, only private bankers are elected as president of the Swiss Bankers' Association (which includes members from all types of banks), as heads of the major stock exchanges, or as president of the Association of Swiss Stock Exchanges.

Savings banks

In Switzerland, all banks invite savings deposits, and savings banks offer checking-type accounts to their customers. The distinguishing mark of a savings bank is that it is organized primarily to promote thrift in its community. Other types of banks seek depositors to generate funds to use in making profitable loans. Savings institutions are less profit minded; their investments are made mainly with the objective of earning enough income to cover the interest due to their depositors.

Although savings banks are generally community oriented, many are quite willing to accept business from overseas. Their primary advantage to an American lies in the greater variety of savings plans they offer.

A savings bank is a *Sparkasse,* or an *Esparnikasse,* in German. In French, it is properly a *Caisse d'Epargne,* although many savings institutions just call themselves a "bank" or "banque." Sometimes a *Kreditanstalt* may be a savings bank, too.

Mortgage and local banks

Mortgage banks and savings banks are basically the same type of savings institution. Savings banks usually have a large portion of their money invested in mortgages, but mortgage banks are considered to be those institutions which hold over 60 percent of their assets in mortgage paper.

A mortgage bank is called a *Hypothekenbank* in German, and a *Caisse Hypothecaire* in French. A *Spar-und Leihkasse* is a savings and loan bank, which is essentially the same thing.

"Local" banks are mostly country banks. They provide a mixture of services: savings accounts, current accounts, loans, and mortgages for the people of their communities. Some maintain only one office, while others have branches in neighboring towns. Many local banks originated as community savings banks and gradually evolved into small-town commercial banks.

The "other" banks

The Swiss National Bank began to issue banking statistics and to classify banks by type as the result of the Federal Banking Act of 1935. "Other" banks are basically banks that do not fit neatly or conveniently into any of the other six categories.

The National Bank, in its breakdown, now distinguishes between two types of "other" banks, those that are Swiss-owned and those that are controlled by foreigners. The Swiss-controlled institutions are largely former private banks that have become corporate, joint-stock banks. Some of the foreign-controlled houses were established as newly created Swiss corporations; others were once Swiss-controlled and have been purchased by non-Swiss interests.

Rapid profusion of foreign-controlled banks has caused much consternation among the Swiss banking fraternity. Giant American banks, led by the First National City Bank of New York, have opened several branches since 1963. Chase Manhattan Bank, the Bank of America, Morgan Guaranty Trust, and the First National Bank of Chicago are among those who have entered the Swiss market. The Dow Banking Corporation is the offspring of the American chemical firm of the same name. Even smaller regional American banks have established footholds in Switzerland; the Bank of Indiana opened Banque Indiana Suisse and the Northern Trust Company became a part owner of the Banque Scandinave en Suisse.

Russia opened the Wozchod Handelsbank. The British expanded their activity, with the Guyerzeller Zurmont Bank and Keyzer Ullman joining such long-established banks as the Société Bancaire Barclays (Suisse). The Bank of Tokyo and Fuji Bank serve the Japanese.

Arab and Israeli banking interests saw Switzerland as the land of opportunity, too. The Arab Bank (Overseas) was established in 1962. Bank Leumi Le-Israel (Schweiz) is part of the Leumi group, which also controls Bank Leumi Trust Company in New York City. The Israeli-controlled Banque pour le Commerce Suisse-Israélien has very rapidly become one of the largest of the new banks, with assets of over a billion Swiss francs.

Swiss bankers have always tried to keep their industry noncompetitive, and as profitable as possible. Needless to say, the large scale intrusion of foreign banking into the Swiss system upset the status quo. Competition increased, as the foreign banks struggled to establish themselves quickly. American-controlled institutions in particular were careful to avoid agreements or situations that might lead to future antitrust problems with U.S. regulatory agencies.

There were manpower problems, too. The Swiss believe in full employment with a vengeance; permission for foreign nationals to work in Switzerland, except as menials, is very difficult to obtain. As a result, foreign banks were unable to utilize many of their own nationals in their Swiss operations. Charges were often made that the new foreign-controlled banks were raiding Swiss banks to obtain qualified people.

Other problems arose, too, because of the shortage of seasoned management. United California Bank in Basel, AG., the Swiss subsidiary of the large Los Angeles bank, collapsed in 1970, primarily because of a lack of internal controls. The bank had lured some Swiss middle management personnel from such established houses as Bank Hoffman, but it apparently did not get all the expertise it needed.

Despite such problems, on balance the influx of foreign banks would seem to have done Swiss banking more good than harm. Although the Swiss do not view competition in the same light as Americans, many Swiss bankers would probably admit that the foreigners have helped to make their industry more progressive. The new banks have also given Zurich and Geneva, where most of them are located, added international importance as banking centers.

The loan associations

The seventh type of Swiss bank is the local loan society, usually called a *Raiffeisen Bank* in German. They resemble the familiar American credit union, and are important in communities too small to support a full-fledged bank.

Individuals become members of their local Raiffeisen cooperative by buying a membership. Secured loans and mortgages are available to members of the cooperative; savings and current accounts as well as certificates of deposit are offered to the local people regardless of whether or not they are members. These cooperatives have no local employees except for a part-time cashier, who keeps office hours in his own home. There are two national associations of these local loan societies, each of whom maintains a headquarters that acts as a central bank for the local units. The dominant association, with its main office in Saint Gallen, has a membership of 1,148 affiliated groups, and total assets of over 1.2 billion Swiss francs.

Because of the community-oriented nature of their business, these loan societies are of no importance to a nonresident. Of course, if a reader is lucky enough to become a full-time Swiss resident, then he might want to join his local Raiffeisen bank.

The giro system

Special checking accounts, designed for the payment of small bills by the average householder, are unknown in Switzerland. Swiss banks offer "current accounts," which are similar to regular checking accounts, but they are intended for larger sums than are involved in the typical family's budget. Instead, the Swiss pay their small bills by means of an unusual, but very efficient, *giro* system that is run by the Swiss postal service.

This postal giro system is not part of the regular banking setup, but instead supplements it. Individuals, companies, stores, and all banks maintain postal giro accounts in their own names. To pay a bill, the account holder fills out a simple giro transfer form which instructs the post office to transfer the sum involved from one giro account to another. The giro system has evolved to such an extent that stores and physicians send special blank giro forms along with their statements. Bank deposits can also be made by means of giro transfers without making a special trip to the bank; a depositor makes his bank deposit at the nearest post office, paying the money directly into his bank's giro account. Most banks with a Swiss clientele print their *Postcheckkonto* number on their letterhead and on their statement forms.

The Swiss National Bank also maintains a parallel giro system that interlocks with the postal giro system. All banks have accounts in this system, too. The National Bank's giro arrangement is utilized to make payments between Swiss banks; it makes it unnecessary for the banks to keep clearing accounts with each other.

CHAPTER 5

Swiss
Bank
Secrecy

The Swiss did not adopt a policy of bank secrecy to attract foreign depositors. Strict secrecy is certainly the best-known feature of Swiss banking, but it is not a promotional scheme; its origins are rooted in the attitudes of the Swiss people toward personal privacy. Banking secrecy is undeniably a lure for foreign money, and not only the Swiss realize this. Other nations have tried, with mixed success, to use bank secrecy to promote business for their banks. Lebanon, for one, has copied many features of the Swiss banking code. Numbered accounts are available in Panama, the Bahamas, Singapore, Uruguay, and Hong Kong. Even Communist Hungary now offers secret, tax-free savings accounts to residents of the Western world.

Secrecy as law

Banking secrecy may have its roots in the attitudes of the Swiss toward personal financial privacy, but banking secrecy is also the law of the land. The traditions of privacy and discretion have been codified and made the primary working rule of Swiss banking.

Switzerland's secrecy laws are defensive, the result of pressure from other governments whose concept of individual liberty does not coincide with that of the Swiss. The secrecy laws are a direct reaction to the attacks on Swiss banking secrecy by Hitler's Third Reich.

When Hitler achieved power in 1933, Germany was in economic turmoil. He rapidly took total control of the economy, placing a moratorium on the transfer of German funds abroad and issuing regulations that forbade German nationals to keep bank accounts outside of Germany. Efforts began to force citizens to repatriate any money they might have abroad.

Much of this money was in Switzerland. The banks of Zurich and Basel, in particular, had long had a substantial German trade. Most of this business was of an ordinary commercial nature, but there were thousands of nervous Germans who maintained secret personal accounts.

It became the task of Reichsführer Heinrich Himmler's Gestapo to seek out information on Swiss accounts that had not been declared by their German owners. Mail and cable communications with Switzerland were monitored; German bank records of years past were carefully examined for leads. Soon Gestapo agents were in Zurich, armed with lists of suspected violators and of the banks where the hot money might possibly be located.

All the Gestapo sought in Switzerland was mere confirmation that an account existed. Inside Germany, it could then easily detain, interrogate, intimidate, and even torture the account holder to extract whatever additional information it needed. Once the account details were known, it became simple to instruct the Swiss bank to return a German depositor's funds to Germany.

In 1934, the Nazis publicly tried and executed three Germans for having secret Swiss accounts. The struggle between Swiss banks and the Gestapo quickly became front page news in Switzerland. Public opinion caused the National Assembly, which was even then considering a new banking code, to react sharply.

The result was article 47 of the *Bundesgesetz über Banken und Sparkassen,* the banking law of 1934. Article 47 made violations of secrecy a criminal offense rather than a civil matter.

In many countries a customer may sue for damages under civil law if his banker violates the confidence of the banking arrangement. Under the new Swiss law, prison terms and heavy fines became the penalty for violators. Bank officers and employees, authorized agents, representatives of the Swiss Banking Commission, and bank auditors are all subject to the law. So is anyone who "tries to induce others to violate professional secrecy." Violators may be punished with jail terms of not more than six months, or fines of up to 50,000 Swiss francs.

Clumsiness is no excuse under the law, either. The regulations provide penalties even when secrecy is broken inadvertently, through negligence. The proscription against breaking professional silence also remains intact even when an individual is no longer connected with the banking profession.

Article 47 is unusual not only because breaking bank secrecy is considered a criminal offense; perhaps its most unique feature is that Swiss government agencies enjoy no special exemption under the law. Several nations have some sort of legal provision for banking secrecy, but none, except Switzerland, go so far as to provide protection from their own government. In Switzerland, a banker would actually be in violation of the law if he discussed a customer's account with the head of the Swiss National Bank. A government employee could be prosecuted if he even asked for information. It is interesting to note that article 47 does not specifically define banking secrecy. There are cantonal banking laws, though, that predate the federal laws of 1934. Article 47 basically reinforces and strengthens the local laws, without superseding them.

There have been several court decisions which have served to clarify and broaden the interpretation of bank secrecy; several accepted rules have emerged. Unless he has specific permission from a depositor, a banker violates the law even if he simply acknowledges that there is an account. If a bank officer has any question as to the correct course of action under the law, he has the duty to refuse to give any information at all. Secrecy covers more than such routine matters as bank accounts and securities purchases; the umbrella of banking secrecy protects the privacy of all discussions and business meetings held in the bank. This is why Swiss banks are normally insistent that all matters pertaining to the formation of corporations or trusts be transacted on the bank's premises.

In Switzerland, taxes are considered to be a routine matter best handled between a taxpayer and his local tax collector. Authorities expect that every Swiss will pay his taxes and by and large the Swiss do. Tax problems are not normally pursued through the courts. Income tax is not even withheld from salary checks. Swiss governments have never claimed the authority to vigorously pursue tax violators, and certainly not the right to inspect bank records.

Banking secrecy also enjoys the protection of article 273 of the Swiss Criminal Code. This provision makes it illegal for anyone to make "trade secrets" available to foreign governments or organizations; banking secrets are considered trade secrets under the law. This section of the criminal code is used mainly to prevent industrial and business espionage.

Numbered accounts

Numbered accounts are the best known and most copied feature of Swiss bank secrecy. Actually, they are more of a special arrangement than a distinct category of account. Savings accounts, checking-type accounts, or investment management accounts can all be set up as numbered accounts.

A numbered account is simply any type of account where the routine bank records are maintained under a code number rather than under a customer's name. This system is used to prevent clerical workers or bank auditors who routinely have access to account records from learning the identity of an account owner. This does not mean that the account is completely anonymous; no bank will ever open a numbered account without knowing the name, address, and something about the depositor's background. However, information linking the account code number with the customer's true identity is kept locked in a vault. Access to this data is restricted to two or three senior bank officers.

Obviously, normal signatures are not practical under a numbered arrangement. When a written authorization is needed to instruct the bank, the customer signs the account number in script. For cabled communications, an alternate code phrase is often substituted.

In the days before banking secrecy was written into the banking law, numbered accounts were an added security measure against the indiscretion or subversion of bank employees. A clerk could not match a number and a name because such information was kept beyond his reach. Nowadays, some banks feel that article 47 has made numbered accounts an unnecessary precaution. Nevertheless, they are popular with the Swiss themselves. Since most communities are quite small, it is common for the Swiss to have relatives or acquaintances working in the banks that they must patronize. For the sake of discretion, to prevent such people from knowing their true financial situation, many Swiss prefer to use a numbered arrangement.

Although numbered accounts are intriguing, they are really not needed by the average depositor with only a modest-sized bank balance, honestly acquired. Many banks, in fact, discourage the frivolous use of numbered accounts by foreigners, by requiring larger minimum balances for such arrangements.

The limits of secrecy

Both numbered accounts and regular accounts enjoy the routine protection of Swiss bank secrecy, but banking privacy does have its limits. Federal and cantonal laws clearly allow access to bank records in certain specified instances. A Swiss bank may be required to provide account records to the courts, in bankruptcy or inheritance proceedings, and in criminal cases.

Cantonal courts may obtain information to assist in settling bankruptcy cases, both domestic and foreign. However, the account details are kept secret by the court. The material provided by the bank is seen only by the judges, not by lawyers for either side nor by other individuals who may be involved in the litigation.

Inheritance cases are a problem area. The law requires that a bank must provide information on an account belonging to a deceased depositor, if requested by all the heirs. But the law also requires a banker to maintain his usual silence if even one heir objects to the information being made available to the others. Since normally there is a great deal of jealousy between claimants, and since it is often difficult to determine the rightful heirs, there have been many inheritance cases filed in Swiss cantonal courts.

A complicating factor is that Swiss banks may not allow depositors to designate beneficiaries in case of death. Instead, they usually require a power of attorney that grants someone else alternate signature power over an account. Such a power of attorney, under Swiss law, remains effective even after the death of the account holder and has the same practical effect as naming a beneficiary. Often, before relatives arrive to claim what they consider rightfully theirs, the money in an account maintained by the deceased has already gone to the person holding such signature power.

Swiss courts have the legal right to obtain pertinent information from Swiss banks to aid in the prosecution of criminal cases. The courts will also cooperate with foreign authorities in such matters, if a treaty of mutual assistance exists. Aid may not be given foreign governments in obtaining information in cases that involve political, foreign exchange, or tax violations. There are no Swiss laws restricting foreign exchange transactions, and taxes are administrative rather than legal matters in Switzerland. In refusing assistance in these cases, the Swiss are only denying foreign regimes the powers they already deny their own government.

Swiss authorities will only assist foreign governments if the alleged criminal act is also a violation of Swiss law. Counterfeiting, fraud, forgery, bank robbery, and embezzlement are among the types of crimes that the Swiss are very happy to help solve. Since banks are sacred to the Swiss, they find crimes against banks particularly abhorrent.

Uncle Sam versus the Swiss

As World War II began, the Allies adopted a policy of economic warfare against the Germans. In April 1940, although the United States was not formally at war with the Axis powers, President Franklin D. Roosevelt signed Executive Order 8389. This gave the U.S. Treasury Department authority over German property in the United States and the power to restrain the business activities of German citizens and others who might be fronting for them. To implement this order, the Treasury began to compile a blacklist of firms suspected of or known to be doing business with Germany. Because of Switzerland's normally heavy trade with Germany, eventually 1,300 Swiss firms were blacklisted.

As the world headed toward total war, capital from many nations began to flow into the United States. Switzerland's federal government sent its gold reserves to New York as a precaution, in case the Germans invaded the Confederation. Swiss banks packed off their dollar reserves, their securities portfolios, and their gold stocks to the New York branches of the

Swiss big banks for the duration. By 1941, Swiss assets in the United States were estimated at $1 billion.

In the eyes of the U.S. Treasury, this Swiss money was suspect. They believed that a large portion of it was actually German money, hiding behind the neutral Swiss flag, and perhaps some of it was. Since Swiss banks in New York operated under American banking laws, Treasury agents could and did force them to open their records for inspection. However, New York account records revealed little. The Treasury agents found, as they should have expected if they had been more knowledgeable about Swiss banking practices, that every Swiss asset in New York was carried in the name of a Swiss bank.

In June 1941 the American government froze all Swiss assets in the United States. Even the Swiss federal gold holdings were frozen, although they obviously did not belong to the Nazis. Throughout the war, the Americans continued their efforts to get the Swiss to reveal the true owners of the frozen accounts and securities kept in New York.

In December 1944, as the war in Europe approached its conclusion, a delegation of Swiss bankers came to the United States to discuss a solution to the stalemate. Treasury officials refused to meet with them on the grounds that they were not Swiss government officials. The Americans stubbornly ignored the fact that, under Swiss secrecy laws, the Swiss government was forbidden to even seek information on the banks' customers. Only the bankers, of course, had any information about German accounts in Swiss banks.

Confidential talks continued in Switzerland between special representatives of President Roosevelt and the Bern government. In early 1945, a compromise was finally reached. The Swiss government would freeze all known German assets, cut off the remaining trade with Germany, and ask the Swiss banks to determine by themselves which of the assets in New York were actually German-owned. Before the banks could complete their survey, though, Germany surrendered and U.S. Treasury agents followed the Allied troops into Germany. The Treasury men seized German bank and corporate records and interrogated bankers and accountants.

In late 1945, the Swiss announced the results of their bank-conducted hunt for Swiss-held German assets; they identified holdings worth only a quarter of a billion dollars. In contrast, the U.S. Treasury claimed, based on its probing of German domestic records, that the total should be a full billion dollars, four times the Swiss estimates. To compare with the tally, the Swiss authorities requested access to the material gathered by the Americans. The Treasury rejected this approach and instead pushed for permission to examine Swiss bank records. The Swiss refused, and the standoff continued.

In October 1945, the Four Power Control Council, the de facto supreme government of conquered Germany, promulgated Public Law No. 5. This edict claimed for the Allies ownership of all German government property and control over all private German assets, both inside and outside of Germany. The Swiss became indignant. They considered the Allied edict arbitrary; to them, it was a threat to their status as a sovereign nation, and illegal under international law, at least as far as private German property was concerned.

After the war, the Swiss quickly moved to locate and return property that had been stolen by the Nazis. Theft is a crime in Switzerland, and the proceeds of theft are not protected by bank secrecy.

After Franklin Roosevelt's death in April 1945, the power of the New Deal in Washington began to wane. When President Harry Truman replaced Roosevelt's Secretary of the Treasury, Henry Morganthau, Jr., with his own appointee, prospects for a settlement with the Swiss brightened. As Roosevelt's cabinet member, Morganthau had been one of the prime movers behind the "Morganthau Plan." Fortunately for the Germans, this plan was never implemented by the Allies; it called for reducing postwar Germany to an agricultural state by destroying German industrial and financial power.

Truman's officials were more pragmatic than the New Dealers they replaced; they had less fervor for an antitrust, cartel-busting approach to German business.

Nevertheless, the U.S. Treasury still waged a crusade against Swiss bank secrecy. Washington in 1945 and 1946 was in a better position to bring pressure against the Swiss government than it had been in 1941. American military administrators controlled southern Germany and the parts of Austria that bordered Switzerland.

The Swiss were only partially able to resist American pressure. Swiss diplomats met in Washington with a team of American, British, and French negotiators. In the end, a compromise was reached that still kept Swiss banks safe from foreign inspectors but relinquished German assets in Switzerland to the Allies.

All German property in Switzerland was to be identified and seized, but only by the Swiss themselves. The Allies and the Swiss were to divide the proceeds of the seizure, the Allies agreeing to use their share to help pay for rehabilitation efforts in Europe, and not for reparations as originally intended. Finally, with the U.S. State Department pressuring the Treasury to settle the matter, the blacklist was lifted and the frozen Swiss assets released.

The Swiss held that the Allied seizure of German private property was ethically wrong. They felt a moral obligation to those Germans who lost property because of Switzerland's forced cooperation with the Allies. For this reason, the Swiss share of the proceeds of confiscation was used to reimburse private German depositors and the former German owners of property in Switzerland. Swiss bankers pride themselves that eventually all their German customers were paid for the assets the Swiss had given up under American pressure. This repayment did much to restore European confidence in the Swiss banking system; the Germans again quickly became perhaps the heaviest foreign users of Swiss accounts.

Waivers of secrecy

Understandably, Swiss bankers remain cautious about involvement with the American Treasury, and, as a result, quite a few banks seem reluctant to accept Americans as customers.

One way that some Swiss banks use to discourage American depositors is to require a "waiver of secrecy". This waiver usually includes a statement that the customer will satisfy his obligations to the U.S. Treasury on his "own initiative." It also authorizes the bank to give the U.S. tax authorities any information they may request. Some waivers are loosely worded, permitting account details to be given to just about anyone. One bank's release statement allows it to pass data to the IRS or "to any other U.S. government agency or any other U.S. public institution or agency if . . . requested by them."

There seems to be some disagreement among Swiss bankers as to the propriety of requiring such authorizations. Some take the position that no "true" Swiss bank should ever ask for such a waiver, since it denies the customer the benefits of bank secrecy.

Many, but certainly not all, of the American banks operating in Switzerland require signed waivers from U.S. residents. It is understandable why they do; although the branches operate under Swiss law, their home offices are very vulnerable to U.S. government pressures.

There is no real reason to sign this sort of waiver, however. Most banks do not ask for them; those that require waivers offer no special advantages over those that do not.

Banking secrecy cannot be simply disregarded, as unpatriotic or un-American, even by those who see a Swiss account primarily as protection against inflation. If a hard currency hedge is successful, if gains are made that offset the declining value of the dollar, the "profit" is subject to American taxes. It is uncertain whether the IRS will attempt to tax such foreign exchange "profits" at regular rates as ordinary income or will allow taxpayers to classify them as "capital gains" if the currency is held for more than six months. Since such problems have yet to be decided in court, this remains a very gray area.

The future of secrecy

For Americans, the future will probably bring increased pressure against their use of Swiss bank secrecy. Even now it is illegal to maintain a *secret* account, for all foreign bank accounts must be declared to Internal Revenue at tax return time. The future dangers to secrecy lie in the prediction that U.S. residents may be required to give the government a blanket "waiver of secrecy," that additional transfer restrictions might be imposed, or that all foreign accounts may be made illegal for private parties.

The United States for years has pushed the Swiss for access to their bank records. In December 1974, the Swiss Nationalrat ratified a treaty which, if approved by both the U.S. and Swiss upper houses, would provide better procedures for disclosure in criminal cases. Although U.S. officials can be expected to publicize this pact far out of proportion to its real effect, it is an opening wedge. Over the long term, support could develop for greater cooperation.

Although Americans may find it more difficult to utilize, banking secrecy will remain the law in Switzerland. Both the Swiss voters and the Swiss bankers would have it no other way. Swiss banks depend on secrecy to draw a certain portion of their foreign trade, even though secrecy was not planned with that in mind. The Swiss banking system has grown too large to exist solely on the trade of Swiss residents; it can only be hoped that Swiss bankers value their American business enough to resist future moves by the U.S. government.

6

Swiss Regulations Affecting Americans

Regardless of the reasons Americans may have for maintaining Swiss accounts, two Swiss regulations will complicate their banking affairs. Neither ruling was enacted to restrict personal accounts, but they are factors that must be considered.

Limitations on interest

Swiss banks are allowed to pay interest only on the first 50,000 Swiss francs held in an account by foreign depositors. An additional 50,000 francs may be accepted on an interest-free basis. On any balance over 100,000 francs, however, the banks must collect a "negative-interest" tax of 10 percent a quarter (40 percent annually) for the benefit of the Swiss government.

Basically, under the provisions now in effect, Swiss banks are not allowed to pay any interest at all on Swiss franc accounts held by nonresidents. However, the first 50,000 francs in savings accounts or savings books, and in deposit or investment accounts, are exempt from these restrictions. A nonresident is allowed only one Swiss franc interest-earning account.

The negative-interest charge is collected monthly, a prorated one-third of the 10-percent quarterly charge. The tax computation is based on the average daily balance for the month. A temporary surge in the amount of francs in an account does not necessarily create a tax liability; if the daily average balance for the entire month is less than 100,000 francs no tax is deducted for that month.

Foreigners with Swiss franc accounts that were established before October 1974 are fortunate; they can maintain higher balances without being penalized by the interest limitations or the negative-interest tax. The current regulations were imposed on November 20, 1974, retroactive to October 31, 1974; if an account was already in existence on that date, the balance as of October 31 is exempt from these restrictions. Interest limitations and negative-interest charges are based only on increases over the October 31 account balance. For instance, if the balance of a previously established account were 200,000 francs on October 31, 1974, interest could now be paid on all balances up to 250,000 francs (200,000 + 50,000). Negative-interest tax would not be deducted until the average balance in this account exceeded 300,000 francs (200,000 + 100,000).

These restrictions and charges were imposed by the Swiss Bundesrat, the Federal Council, to discourage the inflow of foreign money to be exchanged for Swiss francs. Switzerland is a small country and does not want its money to replace the dollar as the primary international currency. Similar measures have been in effect, almost continually, since 1971. During the monetary crisis of that year, foreign money poured into Switzerland, seeking the safety of the Swiss franc. The Swiss government, in an effort to stem or at least slow the flood, put certain emergency regulations into effect. A limit of 50,000 francs for interest purposes was imposed; for a while, from July 1972 to September 1973, there was also a negative-interest tax of 2 percent a quarter.

The 1971 interest ceiling for foreigners remained in effect until October 21, 1974. Then, in an apparent miscalculation, the Federal Council again allowed Swiss banks to pay interest to nonresident foreigners on the same basis as to the Swiss themselves. The result was another inpouring of foreign money, and a tremendous surge in the demand for Swiss francs. As dollars and other weak currencies were sold for Swiss francs, the exchange value of the franc increased rapidly. In one day alone, on November 14, 1974, the Swiss franc rose by 2.9 percent against the dollar.

This state of affairs lasted only one month, during which there was steady upward pressure on the franc. To protect the franc, in late November, the Federal Council reimposed the interest limitations and added a quarterly 3-percent negative tax. They acted because exports and tourism are two main props of Switzerland's delicately balanced economy. As the foreign exchange value of the Swiss franc rises, Swiss goods cost more and become less competitive on the world market. The tourist industry also suffers as fewer foreign visitors can afford to vacation in Switzerland.

Despite the reimposition of interest limitations, and the addition of a 2-percent negative tax, foreign money continued to flow into Swiss franc accounts. Apparently, there were non-Swiss, with large amounts of money, who were quite willing to pay an annual 12-percent penalty for the privilege of keeping their liquid assets in Swiss francs.

Consequently, the Swiss Federal Council increased the negative-interest penalty to 10 percent quarterly, or 40 percent annually, effective January 27, 1975. This drastically higher rate achieved the desired effect, to stop larger chunks of the weaker currencies from being converted into Swiss franc deposits.

Three loopholes

Three great loopholes exist in the interest limitation regulations, however. The first is deliberate. The regulations are aimed at large depositors, primarily multinational corporations and institutions, who control a huge international pool of liquid capital. A $50-million lump of Arab oil money, moving into Swiss francs, is the equivalent of 10,000 individual accounts of $5,000 each. The Swiss would rather have the 10,000 smaller accounts; they are a more stable type of deposit, considerably easier to reinvest, and far less likely to be withdrawn as a lump sum at a later date. If the amount you wish to tuck away, at interest, in Switzerland is less than 50,000 Swiss francs, or about $20,000, there is no problem at all.

Furthermore, joint accounts of up to 100,000 francs can also be maintained under the basic exemption; or a husband and wife can each open a separate account for the same effect. Current accounts, the equivalent of checking accounts, earn no interest but are exempt from negative-interest tax up to 100,000 francs.

Loophole number two is inherent in the Swiss banking system. Since each foreign depositor is allowed only one interest-bearing account, banks are now required to ask new depositors if they have another exempt account anywhere in Switzerland. Swiss bank secrecy, however, prevents banks from exchanging information on depositors with other banks or with the Swiss government. There is nothing, therefore, to prevent an American overseas depositor from having several interest-bearing accounts, each under 50,000 francs and each in a separate bank.

The third gap in the regulations is that the restrictions on account size apply only to Swiss franc accounts. Unlimited sums may be kept on deposit in other currencies. Almost all Swiss banks offer current accounts, from which withdrawals can be made at any time; these may be denominated in U.S. dollars, Dutch guilders, Canadian dollars, or other major convertible currencies. A few banks offer interest-earning accounts in such currencies as the West German deutsche mark. Swiss banks have also devised a system of placing deposits in other currencies, outside of Switzerland, where the money earns interest that is not subject to the Swiss federal tax.

Swiss withholding tax

A major source of revenue for the Swiss government is the Federal Anticipatory Tax. This is a withholding tax of 30 percent, collected on interest income and on dividends from bonds and stocks. Whenever a Swiss bank credits earned interest to an account, 30 percent of the interest is deducted automatically and paid directly to the Swiss federal authorities.

This tax withholding at the source applies to Swiss account holders as well as to nonresident depositors; a Swiss taxpayer can claim credit for the interest deduction when he pays his cantonal taxes. To avoid the problems of dual taxation, an income tax convention was signed between the United States and Switzerland on May 24, 1951; this agreement set up the necessary procedures for Americans to claim a partial refund on taxes held out by the Swiss. An American taxpayer can obtain a refund of five-sixths (83.3 percent) of the amount withheld, directly from the Swiss Federal Tax Administration.

To obtain a refund, it is necessary to complete Form R-82, "Claim to Refund of Swiss Tax." Copies of this form are obtainable from the Administrative Office of International Relations, Internal Revenue Service, Washington, D.C. 20225.

Since the Swiss banks collect and forward the withholding tax without identifying the account holders, it is necessary to provide the Swiss tax authorities with some details. Form R-82 asks for the name of the depositor's Swiss bank, the account number, and details on the amount of interest earned and the tax collected. The claimant must compute the amount of refund due, and specify whether the refund is to be sent to him by check or paid directly back into his Swiss account.

Proof that the tax was deducted, generally a copy of an account statement from your bank, should accompany the claim, which must be signed before a notary public. The completed refund request is sent to: Federal Tax Administration of Switzerland, Bundesgasse 32, CH-3003 Bern, Switzerland.

Whether or not an American depositor should file a claim for a tax refund depends on several considerations. The amount of the refund will equal 25 percent of the total interest earned on the deposit, which is certainly significant. Six percent interest becomes only 4.2 percent, and 5 percent only 3.5 percent, if a refund is not claimed.

A taxpayer who did not disclose ownership of a foreign account on his U.S. tax return would probably decide not to ask for a refund. Form R-82 is an American IRS form; a copy will undoubtedly be checked against the individual's U.S. tax returns.

An American with several Swiss franc interest-bearing accounts finds himself in an interesting dilemma. The prime reason for opening separate accounts in different banks is to place more than the allowed 50,000 francs at interest. The more money on deposit in Swiss francs, the more interest earned, the more tax withheld. However, to file a claim for a refund on more than one account is to call the attention of the Swiss tax authorities to the fact that the depositor possesses multiple accounts. This individual will probably also decide not to apply for a refund and just to settle for a reduced interest rate.

Regulations breed paperwork, loopholes, and modifications. Sooner or later, if pressure on the Swiss franc slackens, the reader can expect the negative-interest rulings to be eased. At some future date, however, if the influx of foreign funds becomes unmanageable, the Swiss government might conceivably be forced to ban the opening of new Swiss franc accounts by foreigners. Regardless of what the Swiss authorities might do, it is unlikely that they will apply harsher terms to already existing accounts; and this is just another reason why an American should open a Swiss account while he is still able to.

7

Types of Swiss Bank Accounts

Swiss banks offer a wide variety of accounts. To select an account for his purposes, a potential depositor should understand the basic differences between the kinds of available accounts.

Many of the accounts offered by Swiss banks resemble their American counterparts. The major difference is that Swiss banks are universal banks. Commercial banks and savings banks both offer checking-type accounts as well as savings-type accounts.

Depositors' accounts in any bank, in any of the world's banking systems, are divided into two broad categories: demand deposits and time deposits.

Demand deposits are those which may be withdrawn from the bank by the customer at any time, without prior notification. Money on deposit in demand accounts, since it can be removed from the bank suddenly, provides little support for a bank's long-term loans.

Time deposits are those which are committed to the bank for a longer period of time, by means of withdrawal restrictions. The money that can be taken from these accounts is limited to certain amounts during a given time period. Since these deposits are more predictable, they form the basis of a bank's loan-making ability.

Current accounts

Current accounts are the most common type of Swiss demand deposit. This type of account is called *Kontokorrent* in German. Sometimes, a Swiss bank will refer to a current account as "at sight," or as a "sight deposit," after the British usage.

Current accounts are very much like American checking accounts, although a checkbook is not usually issued. These are all-purpose accounts, used to hold funds temporarily. The funds in a current account remain available for use at any time, without restriction.

When making investments through a Swiss bank, a current account is often used as a base account. For example, a depositor dealing in securities must have a current account. The cost of the stock purchased is deducted from his current account; proceeds from a sale of stock are automatically deposited back into the account.

Sometimes a bank customer will have two or more current accounts, denominated in different currencies. An individual's investment program might involve buying short-term certificates of deposit, denominated in U.S. dollars, and stocks listed on the Zurich stock exchange, priced in Swiss francs. Such an investor would probably require two current accounts, one in dollars, the other in francs.

Checkbooks are not normally issued for current accounts, unless they are specially requested. Withdrawals can be made by a letter of instruction to the bank. If so instructed, the bank will send a remittance to the depositor, or to anyone else, anywhere in the world, that he may designate. However, if withdrawal instructions are sent by Telex or by cable, most Swiss banks will only remit a draft to the customer's home address of record, unless specific arrangements are made beforehand.

A checkbook might be useful to an individual who traveled a great deal. With a passport for identification and a letter of introduction from his Swiss banker, he could cash checks at almost any bank in the world. Moreover, the checks could be written in any convertible currency, simply by crossing out the denomination imprinted on the check and writing in the desired currency. In France, a check could be written for French francs; in Hong Kong, for Hong Kong dollars; or, in Israel, for Israeli pounds.

It is not recommended that a Swiss checking account be used to pay routine bills in the United States. The American check-clearing system relies on magnetic numbers imprinted on all checks. A check drawn on a Swiss bank would cause confusion in a typical American bank. Besides, for obvious reasons, it is not a good idea to flaunt ownership of a Swiss account.

As you have learned, the Swiss themselves generally rely on the efficient postal giro system to pay their small bills. As an inducement to use bank checking accounts, a nominal rate of interest is paid on current accounts. Sometimes, when you inquire about accounts from Swiss banks that do not have many foreign depositors, they will send you literature intended for Swiss residents. For example, I have a brochure, in German, from a cantonal bank. It offers 1½ percent interest on Konto-korrent deposits. Unfortunately, though, Swiss federal regulations have not allowed Swiss banks to pay interest on current accounts maintained by foreigners since 1971.

There are sometimes small charges made for servicing current accounts. Some banks will levy a small percentage, based on the amount of activity—the number of withdrawals during a given period. Most banks will also charge the account for such incidentals as foreign postage and the cost of bank drafts or cables.

Time deposits

In this category fall the accounts that are similar to savings accounts in the United States. They should not be confused with "certificates of deposit," or CDs. The CDs issued by Swiss banks are sometimes called "time deposits" in English. As used here, "time deposits" refer only to the general classification of accounts that are not "current accounts."

Interest rates paid and the withdrawal restrictions that apply are the main differences between the several types of accounts in this category. Higher interest rates are paid on those accounts where withdrawals are more limited.

Account terminology will vary slightly from bank to bank. In their English correspondence and literature, the banks will often translate the account names differently. The accounts, however, are essentially the same from bank to bank. For the specifics, there is no substitute for information from a particular bank.

The most common types of time deposits are explained below:

Deposit accounts. Einlagekonto or *Depositenkonto* are the German translations of "deposit account." Some banks call this account a "private account." Regardless of name, it typically pays 3½ percent per annum. Generally, withdrawals can be made up to 10,000 francs monthly, without notice. Three months' advance notice is required for larger withdrawals.

Many banks allow depositors to use deposit accounts as the base accounts for their investment funds. They can buy gold, or stocks, or make other investments from this type of account. When such investments are made through the bank, the normal withdrawal restrictions usually do not apply.

Savings accounts. Savings accounts, or *Sparkontos,* pay more interest but have tighter limitations on withdrawals. This type of account might pay 5 percent interest, with the depositor able to withdraw only SFr 5,000 freely within a thirty-day period. Advance notice required for larger withdrawals might run six months.

In the United States some banks still use savings books to record deposits, withdrawals, and interest. Other banks provide periodic statements rather than passbooks. In Switzerland, too, both systems are used, depending on the bank.

Banks with many foreign depositors often issue deposit memorandums, with occasional statements, for the various types of savings accounts. Banks with a largely local clientele sometimes use passbooks to record account activity. Banks using savings books will hold the passbooks in safekeeping in their vaults for foreign depositors. This prevents loss in the mail and allows the bank to post accrued interest easily. If necessary, the passbook could be sent to you by registered mail. Or, if you were in Switzerland, you could obtain the booklet by identifying yourself.

In its English correspondence, a Swiss bank will usually identify a passbook-style account as a "savings book" account. In German, *Sparkonto* means a savings account, and *Sparheft* generally indicates a savings book is involved.

Investment savings accounts. If a depositor does not anticipate needing to draw upon the money in an account, he can
earn higher interest rates with an investment savings account.
Called *Anlagesparkonto* in German, this type of account
would commonly earn 6 percent interest. However, only 5,000
francs could be withdrawn without notice in a given year. Six
months' notice, again, would typically be required to obtain
larger sums.

Youth savings accounts. Savings banks and cantonal banks
offer a greater variety of savings accounts than commercial-
type banks. One special type of account is the *Jugendsparheft,*
or youth savings book account. One bank quoted 6 percent
interest, up to an account maximum of 10,000 francs, for this
special type of account. Minimum deposit required was only
10 francs with withdrawals limited to 1,000 francs yearly.
Higher amounts require six to twelve months' notice.

As the name implies, these accounts are designed to encour-
age younger savers. Age limits vary a bit from bank to bank,
but twenty years of age is the typical upper limit. Such an
account might be the ideal way to introduce a youngster to
Swiss banks and to the concept of international investment in
general.

Certificates of deposit. As a deposit form, certificates of deposit, or CDs, are much the same the world over. A depositor's
money is accepted by the bank for a definite time period. The
bank pays a higher rate of interest because it knows it will have
the money available, and therefore lendable, until a certain
date. At the end of the agreed-upon period, principal plus
earned interest are returned to the depositor. Often arrangements are made to have the money redeposited automatically
in a new certificate.

Generally, the Swiss usage in English for CDs is "fixed-time
deposit" or "fixed-term deposit." In German, they are *Festgeld,* or *Festgeldkontos. Fest* means fixed or solid, *geld* is
money.

Under the emergency regulations of 1971, Swiss banks are
not permitted to accept Swiss franc fixed-term deposits from
foreigners. Overseas depositors may, though, invest in fixed-
term deposits in other currencies. Some banks offer these certificates denominated in dollars. Direct time deposits with
Swiss banks, however, are liable for the 30-percent Swiss anticipatory tax, or withholding tax, on the interest earned.

Swiss banks are accommodating. To help their foreign clients evade this Swiss tax, Swiss bankers offer fixed-term certificates of deposit issued and guaranteed by other European or American banks. A depositor's money is placed, through the Swiss bank but at the depositor's own risk, with another bank outside of Switzerland. Since the interest earned on these CDs is technically earned outside of Switzerland, withholding taxes do not apply. This type of deposit is most commonly available in dollars, English pounds sterling, German marks, or Dutch guilders. Terms are usually only three, six, or nine months.

Such deposits are carried in the name of the Swiss bank. In other words, the records of the Dutch or German bank issuing the CD show only the name of the Swiss bank arranging the deposits. The account holder's name appears only in the Swiss bank's own records.

These fixed-term deposits are always made in round figures. Minimum amounts for fixed-term deposits vary widely, from $1,000 upward, depending on the practices of the banks involved. A little comparison shopping is necessary, however, to find certificates issued in the smaller amounts. Interest rates vary daily, according to the market for such money and the currency involved.

Since these are indirect deposits, through the Swiss bank rather than with the Swiss bank, the interest is paid in full to the depositor when the term deposit matures. For its services in arranging the certificates, the bank collects a service charge, determined by the amount and currency of the deposit. Again, you must ask a particular bank for its fee schedule. Average charges run $\frac{1}{16}$ to $\frac{1}{2}$ of 1 percent of face value, with a flat minimum per transaction.

Festgeld deposits, or fixed-term deposits, are practical for moderate sums between about $5,000 and $30,000. For larger amounts, there is an even faster track, paying somewhat higher interest rates.

Fiduciary Eurocurrency deposits

Swiss banks will place a depositor's money in the Eurocurrency market under conditions similar to the interbank certificates just described. The major difference is that larger sums are required, and the interest rates are higher.

Some banks, such as the private banks and the Swiss affiliates of the London merchant banks, specialize in Eurocurrency placements. Again, the bank acts as agent, but funds are placed at the depositor's risk. Swiss withholding taxes do not apply.

Terms are short, one month to six months, with some one-year deposits. Minimums depend on the currency.

The precise rates vary daily. The banks that handle these deposits will gladly quote you current rates. By the time their quotes arrive in the mail, however, they will be out of date. Unless you are dealing in such sums that you are in contact with your Swiss bank by Telex, you will have to rely on them to place your money at the going rate.

You will notice that the less stable the currency, the more chance of devaluation, the higher the interest rates. A depositor gets paid for his risks.

Fiduciary deposits are big time. Multinational corporations, Arab finance ministers, and Zurich private bankers are active in this market. Any American private depositor moving into this type of investment should understand foreign currency fluctuations, and the nature of the Eurocurrency market. Subscribing to one or two advisory services would be a good idea.

Bank bonds

Many Swiss banks offer their own bonds directly to the public. These bonds are denominated in Swiss francs, and generally are sold in multiples of 1,000 francs. In German, they are called *Kassenobligationen,* or "cash obligations."

Two or three classes of Kassenobligationen are usually offered, differing in the interest paid by the bank. Terms commonly run from three to eight years. Interest varies from about 6½ percent to 7¾ percent, with the higher rates on the longer-term bonds.

To invest in these bank bonds, your money should not be needed for the term of the bond. The principal will not be available until maturity. Interest on these bonds, since they are denominated in Swiss francs, is also subject to the 30-percent Swiss withholding tax.

Other accounts

Banking is a very competitive business in Switzerland. Naturally, some banks have devised special accounts to attract more customers. Banks without special literature for overseas depositors will sometimes send their regular brochures, describing all their services in French or German.

English	German	French	Italian
Current account	Kontokorrent	Compte courant	Conto corrente
Checking account	Girokonto*		
Sight deposit			
Deposit account	Einlagekonto	Compte de dépôts	Conto di deposito
Private account	Depositenkonto		
Savings account	Sparkonto	Compte d'épargne	Conto di risparmio
Savings book	Sparheft		
Investment savings account	Anlagesparkonto	Compte d'épargne-placement	Conto di risparmio-investimento
Term savings account			
Certificate of deposit	Festgeld Festgeldkonto	Compte à terme fixe	Conto vincolato
Fixed-term deposit			
Fixed-time deposit			
Bank bonds	Kassenobligationen	Obligations de caisse	Obbligazioni di cassa
Cash bonds	Kassenscheine*		
Cash obligations			

*used only occasionally

Some of these special services, such as salary accounts, are useful only to those depositors living and working in Switzerland. Called *Salärkontos* or *Gehaltskontos,* salary accounts are special arrangements by which employers deposit their employees' pay directly into their bank accounts. In some cases, cash withdrawals can be made from automatic machines, occasionally located right on the employer's premises.

Another type of special account, however, might be of interest to Americans over the age of sixty or sixty-five. They are the older depositor's answer to youth savings accounts. Called *Alterssparhefte* in German, these accounts are what an American bank might call a "senior citizen's savings book." Either higher interest or lower withdrawal restrictions are featured. As an example, an Alterssparhefte paying 6 percent interest, comparable to a regular investment savings account, would allow withdrawals up to 5,000 Swiss francs monthly without prior notice. The comparable investment savings account in the same bank would allow free withdrawal of only 5,000 francs annually.

If you are unsure of exactly what type of account is being described, or what type of account to ask for, the German account name can always be used to clear things up.

A list of common account names in English, German, French, and Italian appears on page 185.

CHAPTER 8

How to Open Your Account

The amount of money that a potential depositor has available for deposit is the most important factor in choosing a bank and determining the type of account to be opened. Obviously, an individual with $50,000 or $100,000 in liquid capital has a wide choice of possibilities. The options for someone with only $200 are naturally more limited. However, both can find a safe home for their money in Switzerland.

Anyone considering placing more than $20,000 in a Swiss bank must weigh the interest limitation and negative-interest factors. As noted previously, Swiss banks may not now pay interest on Swiss franc deposits over 50,000 francs, roughly $20,000. In addition, they must charge a forbidding 10-percent quarterly tax on all balances over 100,000 francs, or about $40,000.

These factors merit consideration. Basically, larger amounts could be placed as a lump sum or as several separate deposits.

As a lump sum, one solution would be to open an account in one of the hard currencies other than the Swiss franc. There is no negative tax on German deutsche mark or on Dutch guilder accounts, although interest-bearing accounts in these currencies are not offered by many Swiss banks. Alternatively, the money could be placed in an investment management account in any of the private or other banks specializing in such services. Your Swiss banker would then handle the placing of the money to achieve your investment goals while staying clear of the interest and tax restrictions.

A combination of several accounts could be handled in many ways, depending on the investment goals and the amount of risk felt acceptable. If getting out of dollars and into a hard currency were the prime consideration, one strategy would be to tuck the money into several interest-bearing Swiss franc accounts, each in a different bank. Each account would of course be limited to the maximum of 50,000 Swiss francs. Bank secrecy would nullify the ruling restricting each foreign depositor to only one interest-earning Swiss franc account. A little extra paperwork would be involved in keeping track of the different accounts, but there would be the added advantage of diversification, with the money in different banks.

As is always the case, the more money available, the more options that can be exercised at the same time. An investor might decide to keep part of his resources in conservative, savings-type accounts, earning interest while waiting for better days; and, on the remainder, to accept slightly higher risk to earn a higher return. Such a combination might include: (1) interest-earning deposit or savings accounts in Swiss francs, in one or more banks; (2) a current account in another hard currency used to make high-yield, short-term Eurocurrency deposits. Arrangements could be made with the bank to "roll" the Eurocurrency deposits, placing new ones as earlier deposits matured and were paid back into the base account. The current account should probably be in deutsche marks or guilders to avoid occasional high balances in Swiss francs that are liable for the 10-percent negative-interest tax.

An average depositor with more limited resources has only a slightly smaller choice of banks and account types. Most banks offer accounts tailored to the depositor with a $2,000 to $5,000 stake. The investor can choose from a variety of offerings, including bonds available in 1,000-franc units. The most common choice here, however, will probably be a savings-type account, offering safety, a decent yield, and simplicity.

Withdrawal restrictions on an account demand careful consideration against your plans and future needs. The smaller the sum that can be withdrawn without notice, and the longer the acceptable notice required to take out larger sums, the higher the interest rate will be. Future needs should be balanced against the natural desire to earn a higher rate of interest.

An important note: withdrawal restrictions are taken very seriously by Swiss bankers. Their approach is conservative. They do not make loans based on deposits that can be withdrawn without notice. American banks will allow you to pull out money that is committed on time deposits, adjusting the interest rate downward, and perhaps penalizing you a few months' interest. Not so with Swiss banks. If you deposit your money, and agree to limit withdrawals to a certain amount within a given time period in order to earn a higher rate of interest, that is the way it will be. Keep the restrictions in mind when you pick an account type.

An individual with a small amount of capital, say $100 to $1,000, can still take advantage of a Swiss bank account. Without question, the options in this case are limited to a deposit, savings, or investment savings account in a bank that requires a low minimum deposit.

The smaller size of the account works to the depositor's advantage here. It is possible to choose a bank with a low minimum requirement, and to put the money into the highest yielding deposit account. If the amount of capital deposited is less than the basic withdrawal restriction, the withdrawal restriction can be ignored as a consideration. For example, a 6-percent account might allow withdrawals to 10,000 Swiss francs (or about $4,000) per year. As long as the total amount on deposit were less than 10,000 francs, in an emergency the total amount on deposit could be removed without notice.

In all probability, someone starting an account with a small amount, as a savings reserve, would plan to add to it regularly. As the account grew in size, the withdrawal restrictions would again require consideration.

Initial contact

The most common misconception about Swiss bank accounts is that it is necessary to go to Switzerland to open one. If you were to confide to a close friend that you had a Swiss account, his most likely reaction would be to ask, "When were you in Switzerland?"

Sometimes it is advisable to visit a Swiss bank personally to open an account. Almost always, however, it is more practical for an American to handle the whole procedure by mail. It is also less expensive, quicker, and less involved.

At this stage, the listing of banks included in this book becomes important. Chapter 10 is devoted to a listing of Swiss banks that accept deposits from nonresidents. Their correct names and addresses are given, together with a summary of the types of accounts and interest rates offered.

Please note that the information on interest rates is offered only as a guideline. With time, however, the rates may vary, depending on many factors, most of them unpredictable. The only way to determine the actual rates a bank is now paying is to write and ask. But rates on savings-type accounts are not likely to fluctuate very much. For the near term, the information given will presumably remain reasonably correct.

The first step, then, is to refer to the listing of banks. Bearing in mind the types of accounts you are considering and the amount of money you desire to deposit, check carefully over the listings. Note the names and addresses of about six banks that interest you.

At this point, you have two alternatives. You can either send an initial deposit directly to a selected bank, and complete the necessary paperwork later, or you can write to the banks for information and forms.

Presumably, most readers will prefer the second option, writing for up-to-date information. Opening a Swiss bank account is a new experience. Comparing the materials sent by the different banks gives an opportunity to select a bank, and an account type, at leisure.

To each of the banks on your preliminary list, you should send a short letter requesting information on the types of accounts offered and their current interest rates. You should specifically ask for forms to open an account. Swiss bankers tend to think literally, to take requests verbatim. If you ask for information, they'll send information. If you ask for forms, they'll generally send forms.

In answering queries from prospective customers, the banks follow different procedures. Some banks with a large overseas trade will routinely send a complete information packet. Other banks, more accustomed to walk-in customers than to mail depositors, will answer with a letter of information, explaining that they will send the necessary forms for completion after the initial deposit is received.

If you are interested in services other than current or savings-type accounts, you should ask for data on these services in your first letter. It will save unnecessary extra correspondence.

The use of red-and-blue-trimmed airmail envelopes is suggested. A letter sent airmail, in a plain envelope, stands a good chance of being misdirected and sent by surface (boat) mail. There is also a special "Aerogramme" letter, that requires no envelope, available at the post office. No enclosures are permitted in Aerogrammes, so these forms may be used to write for information, but not to transmit funds.

The bank's reply

About two weeks after sending off your query letters to Switzerland, you will receive the banks' replies. Swiss banks, for reasons of secrecy and economy, generally use plain airmail envelopes. At the most, a box number is given as a return address. Sometimes, a bank employee's home address is handwritten as the return address.

Contents of the plain envelope will vary. Almost always there will be a letter on the bank's stationery, describing various accounts recommended or available to foreign depositors. The larger banks, with a large volume of inquiries, will often use a form letter, typing in your name and address. Many times, these banks will send a complete information packet, with account descriptions and application forms in English.

Private banks, and those dealing on a more limited basis with English-speaking outlanders, will sometimes send a specially composed letter describing their services. Some banks will send a copy of their latest annual report, multilanguage brochures explaining their services, or detailed information on their specialties.

Quite often, in dealing with banks that have few if any dealings with Americans, you will receive a letter written in an English that seems stilted. Bear in mind that your inquiry was probably answered by a Swiss who learned his English in school, and doesn't use it enough to achieve written fluency. Numbers are the same in all languages.

Some banks will describe their services, and explain that they will send the appropriate forms for completion after the initial deposit. Opening an account is very much like sending a deposit without inquiring first, except that your information is up to date and the bank is expecting your money.

Regardless of how elaborate or simple the reply, the banks need basically the same information on each depositor. They may provide a long form, with all the information requested on one sheet, or several separate cards to collect the data. A form package generally consists of an application form or signature card, a designation of a power of attorney, an acknowledgment of general conditions, and a signature-verification form.

Signature cards. Personal accounts may generally be carried in one of three forms. A single name account is an account in one name only. Joint accounts are carried in two names, but only one signature is required to instruct the bank. Another type of joint account requires a collective signature, with two people signing together to effect a withdrawal or other bank action.

On the application form or signature card, you will be required to designate one of the above types of account. Space is always provided for a specimen of each signature. The bank will also want to know your home address, the address to which mail is to be sent, and often your language preference for correspondence.

In Europe, most countries provide their citizens with identity cards which carry a number. Since Europeans cross national borders frequently, they generally also have passports. Many Swiss banks, accustomed to providing accounts for Europeans, ask for a passport number or an identity card number as routinely as American banks ask for a social security number. If you have a passport, by all means provide the bank with the number. If not, you may safely ignore this question. If you feel that you might want to visit your bank someday, it might be desirable to apply for a passport now. When a passport is issued, you can notify the bank of your passport number. But don't delay opening an account just because you don't have a current passport.

Power of attorney. Swiss banks want to know who your beneficiary is. However, under Swiss law the banks are not allowed to accept instructions naming a beneficiary, nor instructions such as a will that becomes valid only after the account holder's death. Instead, they will routinely ask you to open a joint account with the right of survivorship, or to grant a power of attorney.

Under Swiss law a power of attorney remains effective after the death of the principal. Under article 35 of the Swiss Code of Obligations, a power of attorney "shall not cease by reason of loss of principal's capacity to act nor by his death, but shall continue to remain in force." In the United States, when designating an attorney-in-fact, you are naming someone to act in your stead, giving him the power to act for you in your absence. In Switzerland, you are doing the same, but you are also naming your beneficiary, as far as a particular bank account is concerned.

Granting a power of attorney has basically the same effect as establishing a joint account. Under Swiss law, in case of the death of a holder of a joint account, the surviving account holder still controls the account. An attorney-in-fact also retains full power over an account in case of the death of an account holder. Both a joint holder, where one signature is sufficient, and an attorney-in-fact also have full power over the account during the lifetime of the primary account holder.

When granting a power of attorney, several attorneys-in-fact may be appointed at the same time. It can be specified that the individual signature of any one holder of a power of attorney is sufficient. Or, alternatively, you may require that two signatures are necessary to instruct the bank to act, by designating joint powers of attorney.

Power-of-attorney designations remain in effect until revoked by notifying the bank in writing. On the bank's forms, a sample of the specified individual's signature is needed; you cannot designate a person to act for you without providing his signature on the card. Additionally, some identifying data, such as an address, date of birth, nationality, and passport number are usually necessary for each designated attorney-in-fact.

If you are worried about granting a power of attorney to someone, perhaps because you fear that in a future dispute or misunderstanding he might use his signature power to empty the account, there is a simple solution. At the time you provide his specimen signature to the bank, it is not necessary to let the designated person know the name of your bank, its address, or your account number. This information can be sealed in an envelope and left in the care of a third party, perhaps your lawyer or accountant, to be delivered when certain circumstances, such as your demise, occur. Just be sure that if you follow this course of action some provision is made to provide the appointed attorney-in-fact with the necessary information at the time he will need it to act for you.

Signature verification. Since the Swiss banks are dealing with their mail depositors at long distance, most of them will require a verification of a new depositor's signature.

The rules for signature verification are not clear-cut. Each bank has slightly different requirements. Unlike powers of attorney, where the rules of the game are spelled out by Swiss civil law, the banks make their own policy on signatures.

Generally, they require that your signature be witnessed, on the signature card or on a special form, by some sort of official.

If you live in or near a city served by a Swiss consulate, your signature-verification problems are solved. The official verification form costs a few dollars.

Other banks provide no special verification card but ask that the specimen signature on the bank signature card be officially witnessed. If you wish to be discreet, you can have your signature verified on a "neutral" form, one that gives no indication that it is intended for a Swiss bank. Sometimes the Swiss bank provides a suitable form.

A signature verification by another bank is generally acceptable to the Swiss banks. Some banks will specify that the American bank should be one with a Swiss correspondent, but this includes most larger banks. The only problem here is that most Swiss banks do not seem to understand that an American does not really want to hassle with his bank about providing a signature verification for a Swiss bank. It's sort of like asking your current doctor to refer you to another physician because you feel the first doctor is a bit of a quack. Personally, I'd have an American bank verify my signature only as a last resort, and then only on a "neutral" form.

Notaries public are acceptable to many Swiss banks, but, unfortunately, not to all. Schweizerische Bankgesellschaft, the Union Bank of Switzerland, goes so far as to stamp its signature-verification slip with: "Notary Public not accepted." If a bank does not clearly state to the contrary, a notary's verification would be an excellent choice.

Signature verifications are a nuisance, but the Swiss banks want a piece of paper to show that they've made an effort to check a foreign depositor's identity.

A few banks take a practical approach and require no verification paper. They accept your specimen signature at face value, without "official" witnesses. According to the terms of one bank, "The Bank undertakes to check the authenticity of any signature but is not bound to make any further control on their legality. The Bank is not responsible for any damage resulting from undetected forgeries." In other words, the bank will check the signature on an instruction against the specimen.

In the material sent you by the Swiss bank there will usually be a statement of the bank's general business conditions. The conditions cover signatures, powers of attorney, notifications to clients, statements, and overdrafts. You should read them carefully, and understand them. Generally, when signing the signature card, you are affirming that you have received a copy of the "general business conditions," and have read and accepted them. Some banks go a bit further, and send you two copies of the conditions. You are asked to sign one copy and send it back to the bank.

American banks follow a similar practice. Read the fine print on the back of the signature card at an American bank.

Opening an account without forms

Some readers might prefer to open a Swiss account without waiting for a bank to send them an information packet and forms. Whatever the reason, it's a simple procedure.

Some Swiss banks, when they receive money from an overseas depositor on the first contact, hold the deposit in a special escrow-type account. When the proper paperwork is completed and returned to the bank, they then open a regular account and assign an account number. Other banks, especially if they receive adequate information with the deposit, will immediately assign an account number and open a regular account.

Each bank follows its own internal working procedures in handling accounts opened in this way. The key element is information; the banks naturally hesitate to officially open an account until they are certain of exactly what type of account you prefer. It is obvious that in your letter transmitting the deposit you should clearly state what type of account you want, and in what currency you wish it to be denominated.

Transferring funds

Your money can be transferred to Switzerland in one of several ways:

1. Using your personal check, by mail.
2. Using money orders, by mail.
3. Through the foreign department of almost any large bank. The bank will arrange the transfer directly to the Swiss bank of your choice.
4. In person, by flying to Switzerland. Cash, letters of credit, cashiers' checks, bank drafts, or other forms of negotiable instruments can be used to physically handle the transfer of assets.

Using your own personal check is perhaps the simplest and most direct way to transfer funds. Any Swiss bank will accept it. On your first deposit, your account will probably not be credited until your check has cleared. The check will be routinely returned to you through your American bank with your regular monthly statement. A drawback, however, is that the check, in clearing, will go through many hands, including the Federal Reserve System. Your bank, if it's interested, will know that you have a Swiss account. American banks are required to keep a record of all out-of-U.S. transfers, including checks, of over $5,000. American banks also maintain a microfilm record of all checks drawn on their depositors' accounts, available, naturally, for government inspection.

Money orders are perhaps the best way to transfer funds. Every bank sells money orders; so do drug-stores and neighborhood convenience grocery stores.

Unless they are marked to the contrary, bank money orders are good the world over. A major use of money orders of all types is to remit small sums overseas, to dependent relatives, for example. Many tellers, however, will inform you that the money orders issued by their bank are good only in this country. As a matter of policy, some banks would prefer that you use their foreign exchange departments, where they can charge higher fees than the 25 cents or 40 cents commonly charged for personal money orders.

Limits on the amount that money orders can be bought for vary. Money orders from commercial companies, such as American Express, can usually be bought only in smaller denominations. Their common limits are $200 and $250.

Regardless, the amounts of money that can be transferred by

money order are astounding. Buying four to sixteen money orders a day requires only an hour or so, and some extra diligence. Two or three small denomination money orders can be purchased at one outlet without much fuss.

Transferring $4,000 per day regularly for thirty days will put $120,000 in a Swiss account. Several money orders can be mailed in one envelope. Four thousand dollars a day is well under the legal limit of $5,000, at which point you are required to fill out forms.

Although large amounts can be transferred to Switzerland using multiple money orders, money orders leave a trace, too. They eventually come back to the issuing company.

Money orders commonly carry some restriction, such as, "This personal money order is sold upon the following conditions: (1) The purchaser sign, in ink, his/her name and address after filling in a date and the name of the payee."

Of course, when using money orders to transfer funds, it is important to type or clearly print the name of the recipient bank. Whether or not the bank can read the sender's signature is unimportant. Since American-style deposit slips are not used, each mail deposit, on either a new or an established account, must be accompanied by a note telling the bank the name of the account to which the money is to be credited. The amount of the deposit, and, if the account is already established, the account number, should also be mentioned.

When money is withdrawn from a bank account and then used to immediately purchase a bank money order, many banks will routinely note the number of the customer's account on the bank's copy of the money order. A few banks still insist, when selling money orders, on typing in the name of the recipient. Obviously, if privacy is important, people who do not wish to be cross-referenced will purchase their money orders elsewhere.

Money orders are also sold by U.S. post offices. Anyone using a postal money order to transfer money to a Swiss bank is automatically providing the federal government with a full record of the transaction. Money orders are available from so many other sources that a postal money order would be an absolute last choice.

Any U.S. bank with a foreign exchange department can handle the entire transaction, paperwork and all. They can also sell you a draft made out to a Swiss bank, which you can then airmail to Switzerland, or have the bank transmit for you. Many American banks will try to talk you out of opening a Swiss account, however. No one likes to give business to a competitor.

Another objection, and the primary one in my opinion, to transferring money or opening a Swiss account through a U.S. bank is the lack of privacy. While it is not now illegal to have a foreign bank account, in the intermediate to long term, it could very well become so. If you use a bank foreign-exchange department, you'll be on record.

U.S. branches of Swiss banks fall into the same category as American banks. A New York, Chicago, or Los Angeles office of a big Swiss bank necessarily operates under U.S. banking laws. While they can give you good advice, and perhaps verify a signature, they must maintain records that are accessible to Internal Revenue and Treasury agents.

Transferring your funds in person, especially in the form of cash, is not recommended. Since antihijacking measures have become routine at our airports, hand luggage will be searched. While it is not yet illegal to transfer money out of the United States, you are asked to declare any amount over $5,000 that you take out.

It is reasonable, however, to take smaller sums, enough to open an account, to Switzerland in person. A thousand or two thousand dollars, in money orders, tucked in with your airline ticket is okay. That much in additional travelers' checks is risk-free, too. This money could be used as an initial deposit to open an account. Additional deposits could then be made by mail.

The only valid reason I would consider for going to Switzerland to open an account would be to personally discuss investment plans with a Swiss banker.

Special considerations for big money

For those readers who have substantial funds that they desire to deposit, and who wish to avail themselves of the offices of a Swiss private banker, a different approach is involved. Many private bankers answer routine queries with a noncommittal letter, or with an institutional brochure describing their firm in general terms. Few will give specific interest rates by mail. Their answer will be something like this, "Please indicate your wishes about the transactions you intend to handle with us and we shall offer the appropriate conditions." Most will also ask you how you heard about their bank, or who recommended their services.

If the sum involved is over $100,000, a trip to Switzerland should be considered, though it is not absolutely necessary. The cost of a trip to Zurich or Geneva, including a few days' vacation in the process, is $1,000 to $1,500. This is a small price to pay for meeting your banker. The extra service that you will receive as a result of the trip makes it a good investment, too.

If you follow this course of action to discuss investment plans personally with a Swiss banker, it would be prudent to talk with more than one bank before making a final decision. Appointments should probably be made with two or three banks. It would be more convenient if the banks were all in one city, either Geneva or Zurich. However, if enough time were allowed you could handle discussions in both cities easily enough. Distances in Switzerland are short and internal transportation, excellent.

The formalities and procedures for opening an account in the name of a business are basically identical to those for a personal account. A signature card and signature-verification forms must be completed. In addition, proof that the account is an authorized company account will be needed.

The following is a quote from the general business conditions of one of the Big Five: ". . . there must be submitted an extract of . . . a board resolution or other documents as enacted by your local law . . . in order to prove that the persons signing the card on the lower right-hand corner are entitled to represent the company and to confer authorities, as the case may be. Nonregistered entities, such as single proprietorships, have to submit legally signed articles of association or bylaws." Copies of these supporting documents must be certified by a bank or by a Swiss consulate in the same manner as a signature-verification form.

Opening a Swiss bank account is really a simple process. One needs only to decide how much money to deposit, select an account type, write a letter, transmit the money, and fill out some elementary forms. The biggest hurdle is a psychological one. To open a Swiss account of his own, an individual must first overcome his personal inertia. The rest is easy.

9

Communicating With Your Bank

Most American depositors will be astounded at the ease with which they are able to open a Swiss account. Their pride in their new bank account may turn to bewilderment, however, when they receive their first statement from Switzerland.

Like banks everywhere, Swiss banks give special attention to new accounts. The initial paperwork is handled by individuals competent in English; there is little difficulty at this stage.

Once the account is opened, however, records are kept in the prevailing language of the local Swiss canton. In Zurich and most of central and northern Switzerland, German is used. French predominates in Geneva and the western areas along the border with France. Banks in Bern, the national capital, use either German or French. In the Italian-speaking cantons, German, surprisingly, seems to prevail among the banks with an American trade.

English translations of applications and account-information sheets are quite common. It is unusual, however, for English to be used on routine forms, such as statements, which a depositor will receive periodically. The miscellaneous statement forms sent to American customers are identical to those issued to a bank's local Swiss depositors. Despite the fact that these routine forms are different from those commonly used by American banks, they are not that difficult to understand.

Each Swiss bank has its own style of forms. The ones you receive from your bank may differ in detail, but the essential information will be the same.

Swiss banks offer many types of services other than current or savings-type accounts. If you become involved in buying or selling securities, gold, silver, or foreign currency futures, expect to be deluged with miscellaneous slips of paper. If you understand the basic account forms these will present no problem. The key phrases, such as balance, effective date, rate, and commission, are the same regardless of the type of transaction.

Deciphering the exchange rate

One of the minor complications of foreign exchange is that each country quotes the value of other currencies in terms of its own money. In its communications with its customers, a Swiss bank will note the pertinent exchange rate in terms of Swiss francs; for example, "2.49" or 2.49 francs to a U.S. dollar. An American, on the other hand, checking rates in his newspaper, will find the quotations given in dollars, ".4009" or $0.4009 for a Swiss franc.

Do not be disheartened; converting one rate to another is only a matter of intermediate arithmetic. An exchange rate quoted in one currency is just a "reciprocal" of its equivalent in the other money. If the applicable rate noted on the deposit acknowledgement slip is "2.91," or 2.91 Swiss francs to a dollar, to convert, divide 1 by 2.91; 1/2.91 equals .3436, the price in U.S. dollars of a single Swiss franc.

Instructing your bank

Sooner or later, a depositor will want to send additional money to his bank or withdraw funds from his account. Since deposit and withdrawal slips are not used by overseas customers, it is necessary to instruct the bank by letter.

The important thing is to tell the bank clearly and concisely what you want them to do for you. Your letter should obviously

Reference List of Common Terms

For convenience, here is a listing in German, English, and French of the banking terms most likely to appear on communications from your Swiss bank:

English	German	French
Account	Konto	Compte
Account number	Konto-Nummer	No. de compte
Your account	Ihr Konto	Votre compte
Currency	Währung	Monnaie
Amount	Betrag	Montant
Deposit	Einlage	Dépôt
Withdrawal	Rückzug	Retrait
Balance	Saldo	Solde
Net proceeds	Nettobetrag	Montant net
Prior balance	Saldo vor Abschluss	Solde Précédent
New balance	Neuer Saldo	Nouveau solde
In our favor	Zu Ihren Lasten	En notre faveur
In your favor	Zu Ihren Gunsten	En votre faveur
Debit	Soll, Belastung	Débit
Credit	Haben	Crédit
Status per (date)	Abschluss per	Arrêté au
Effective as of	Wert, Valuta	Valeur
Commission	Kommission	Commission
Free of commission	Francoposten	Mouvement franco
Charges	Spesen	Frais
Postage	Porto	Port
Postage stamp	Briefmarke	Timbre-poste
Interest	Zins, Zinsen	Intérêts
Tax	Steuer	Impôt, Timbre
Subject to with- holding tax	Verruchnungssteuer- pflichtiger	Soumis à l'impôt anticipé

English	German	French
Account holder	Kontoinhaber	Titulaire de compte
Place and date	Ort und Datum	Lieu et date
Date	Datum	Date
Signature	Unterschrift	Signature
Day	Tag	Jour
Month	Monat	Mois
Year	Jahr	Année
Bought	Kauften	Acheté
Sold	Verkauft	Vendu
Price, rate	Kurs	Cours
Payment	Zahlung	Paiement
Check	Check	Cheque
Travelers' checks	Reisechecks	Cheques de voyage
Letter of credit	Akkreditive	Crédit documentaire
Payment order	Zahlungssufträge	Ordre de payment
Safe-deposit box	Tresorfäch	Coffre-fort
Portfolio management	Vermögensverwaltung	Gestion de fortunes
Cash bonds	Kassenobligationen	Bons de caisse
Securities	Wertschriften	Titres
Gold bullion	Goldbarren	L'ingot d'or
Bookkeeping	Buchhaltung	Comptabilité
Trust department	Treuhändabteilung	Département fiduciare

include the essentials, such as the account number, the type of account, and the name in which the account is carried. Use a personal letterhead if possible; if not, be sure to include your return address and your name. The signature on the letter should be in the same form as your specimen signature on file with the bank.

Withdrawal instructions are almost as simple. When asking the bank to send you money, it is necessary to specify the currency desired, to whom the draft is to be payable, and where it is to be sent.

Withdrawals can be sent to anyone, anywhere, in any convertible currency.

Instructions to your bank can be as complex, or as personalized, as you desire.

Normally, using airmail to instruct your bank, it will take about two weeks to receive a withdrawal from a Swiss account. If need be, the process can be speeded up somewhat. Instructions can be cabled or Telexed to the bank. However, this type of withdrawal request does not arrive at the bank over the depositor's authorized signature. Consequently, most banks will only send payment directly to the depositor, at his address of record. If the need can be anticipated, arrangements can be made beforehand, by letter, permitting the bank to make payments to third parties or alternate addresses on cabled instructions. Arrangements can also be made to wire money directly to a depositor's account in another bank. Naturally, the other bank should be informed to expect the wired transfer.

There is always the possibility of using the telephone to communicate with your Swiss bank. This is not recommended, though, because of the language barrier. The probability of misunderstanding is too great. If personal contact had previously been established with an English-speaking bank officer, perhaps on a visit to Switzerland, the telephone could be used in special circumstances. For most account holders, this method remains impractical and unnecessary.

General guidelines

To be happy with your Swiss bank, it is important to have a good relationship; this is essentially a matter of maintaining good communications. Both parties, the bank and the depositor, must understand each transaction. Confidence will grow if misunderstandings are avoided from the beginning.

The language barrier is the main hurdle to overcome. Although the letters exchanged by the depositor and the bank are written in English, it should be remembered that correspondence from your Swiss banker will often seem a bit stiff and unnatural. The formal tone does not indicate a lack of interest or an unwillingness to be helpful; it is merely a carry-over from the thought patterns of another language and from a different set of business customs.

An effort should be made to be careful and concise in your letters of instruction to your bank. Know exactly what you want the bank to do before you attempt to ask them to do it. Plan your letter to make sure all the necessary points are included. Whenever possible, use banking terminology, and avoid slang or abbreviations. Clarify the English description with the German or French word if misinterpretation seems possible. For example: "Will you please open an investment savings account (Anlagesparkonto) in my name?" Review your message for clearness and completeness before mailing it.

Each communication from Switzerland should be read carefully to determine exactly what the bank has done. Some of the forms you receive may have English headings, which makes it easier. If there is no English, use the samples and the word list in this book to decipher the message.

Simpler banking arrangements, such as standard savings-type accounts, offer little possibility of confusion. Funds are deposited and eventually withdrawn. When venturing into more complicated transactions, though, a good rule is to *understand exactly what you are doing.*

If uncertain, ask questions before committing yourself. If, for instance, the purchase of Swiss franc bonds were being considered, you should know how the arrangements work. Who issues the bonds? What is their term and the interest rate? How often is interest paid? How much commission does the bank charge on the transaction? Who physically holds the bond certificates and clips coupons to collect the interest? Is there a charge for this service? Are the certificates issued in the buyer's name, the bank's, or in bearer form? Can the bonds be sold before maturity? What sort of resale market exists? Once the answers to such questions are known, a decision can be made. If a bank is instructed to handle such an investment for a depositor, it will presume that the depositor is familiar with the details of such transactions.

Essentially, there is no real problem in communicating with a Swiss bank. Keep everything as simple as possible, try to make your instructions clear, and ask as many sensible questions as necessary.

CHAPTER 10

Listing of Swiss Banks

A potential depositor needs one essential piece of information. To establish a Swiss bank account, he must first know the name and address of a bank that accepts foreign business.

The listing of Swiss banks provided here should allow the reader an adequate choice, and give him the basic details necessary to make initial contact.

The collection of Swiss banks that follows is perhaps the most extensive listing found outside of a bank directory. Many banks are listed to insure that a reader will be able to find a bank suited to his needs. Individual banks may change their policies in response to varying conditions.

As an example, let's review what happened at the Foreign Commerce Bank of Zurich. The bank is oriented toward the American depositor. All its literature and its forms are in intelligible English, and a very wide range of services is offered.

In early 1974, Foreign Commerce asked for moderate minimum deposits of only $1,000 for a deposit account, and $1,500 for a current account. By April 1974, because of a rush of new accounts, their initial deposit requirement was raised to $4,000. By August 1974 their minimum had to be increased to $15,000. Eventually, in mid-1975, Foreign Commerce was able to lower their minimum requirement back to a more reasonable $5,000. An influx of American funds also caused some other banks to make adjustments upward. The Union Bank of Switzerland (Schweizerische Bankgesellschaft), for example, once had a minimum requirement of 100 Swiss francs, or about $33.50, but raised it under pressure to $500.

A longer listing offers a wider choice. Medium-sized and smaller banks that are well-equipped to handle American accounts are included. A longer listing will hopefully remain accurate for a longer time, at least as far as account minimums and willingness to accept new foreign business are concerned.

Every effort has been made to provide as accurate a listing as possible of banks prepared to open accounts and to accept deposits by mail from Americans. It is intended that this list be a guide to selecting a Swiss bank, based on a matching of the reader's needs and the services offered by a particular bank.

Specific interest rates, the types of accounts available, or the minimums required may change. Banks everywhere reserve the right to adjust their conditions without much notice. A Swiss bank association may recommend a change in the interest rates offered. A particular bank may no longer offer a service to new depositors because its facilities are overloaded.

There is no substitute for up-to-date information from a particular bank. However, if the reader keeps the above limitations in mind, this list will serve him well.

One recommended approach to the selection process was outlined earlier. Having determined the type of account most suitable to your needs, select about six banks that provide this service. Two from among the Big Five, and the rest from among the cantonal, commercial, or private banks would be a good mix. Send all six an identical letter requesting information and forms. From the material sent in response to your queries, select the bank you feel most comfortable with.

Using the list

Data are provided in a standardized format for each of the banks listed. First, the name and address of the bank is given.

Then, the type of bank and information on the common account types is provided. Finally, other types of services offered are covered. Sometimes, there is a special note on any unusual facts about the bank that may be pertinent.

A bank's name and address is given in the form that should be used for the first letter. Some banks, especially the big banks, use up to four translations of their name. Schweizerischer Bankverein calls itself the Swiss Bank Corporation in English, and has special stationery that it uses with its English-speaking customers. However, to the Swiss postman it is still "Schweizerischer Bankverein." By using the local language address form, delivery is certainly surer.

Usually, the first address given in each listing, on the left, is the bank's street address. To the right an alternate address is sometimes provided. This is commonly a postal address; *Postfach*, or *Case Postale*, means simply "P. O. Box." In some cases the bank does not use a box number, leaving it to the postal personnel to sort the mail by name. *If no postal box number is given, it is necessary to include the bank's name* when using this short form of address.

Below the addresses, the bank's alternate names in English, French, or Italian are given, if appropriate. In many cases, the bank uses no translation. For other banks, it is not necessary to translate the name. Migros Bank is Migros Bank in German or in English.

In this listing, an indication of the bank type is given for general information. If known, the year the bank was established is also given.

For banks outside the cities of Zurich, Bern, or Geneva, the approximate location of the town is provided. (When two or more banks are listed for a smaller Swiss city the location is given in the first listing for a bank in that town.) Who knows, someday you may want to visit your bank in person.

Account types offered are listed. After each account type, other pertinent data are given, such as minimums and interest rates. If the account is offered in currencies other than Swiss francs, this is noted.

Almost all banks provide other services for their customers. If a bank offers such special services in its initial correspondence, it is presumed that they are interested in new business of this sort. Such services are listed. Any special notes are self-explanatory.

BIG BANKS

In the listings that follow, the banks are grouped into categories for easy reference. Our first category consists of the Big Three, plus Bank Leu.

Each of the Big Three has upward of eighty branches apiece, and does business all over Switzerland. Each of the four banks listed is ideal for American customers, since the banks are used to dealing with foreign depositors.

Schweizerische Bankgesellschaft
Bahnhofstrasse 45
8021 Zurich, Switzerland

Union Bank of Switzerland, Union de Banques Suisses, Unione di Banche Svizzere.
Big Three, commercial bank, est. 1862.

Current accounts: SFr or convertible foreign currencies, small service charge on current accounts other than SFr. Checkbooks available. *Cash deposit accounts:* 3½ percent int., withdrawals to SFr 10,000 monthly. *Savings accounts:* 5 percent int., withdrawals to SFr 5,000 monthly. *Investment savings accounts:* 6 percent int., withdrawals to SFr 3,000 per half-year. Minimums on above accounts: $500. Also offers: fixed-time deposits in foreign currencies, minimum—SFr 50,000; own bonds, multiples of SFr 1,000. Forms and literature in English.

Schweizerische Kreditanstalt
Paradeplatz 8
8021 Zurich, Switzerland

Swiss Credit Bank, Crédit Suisse, Credito Svizzero.
Big Three, commercial bank, est. 1856.

Current accounts: SFr, US$, Canadian $, DM, Dutch guilders, etc. *Private accounts:* 3½ percent int., withdrawals to SFr 10,000 monthly. *Savings books:* 5 percent int., withdrawals to SFr 5,000 monthly. *Investment books:* 6 percent int., withdrawals to SFr 10,000 per year; if holder over sixty, up to SFr 5,000 monthly. No minimums required, but would "appreciate receiving an initial deposit of at least Fr 6,000." Also offers: own bonds at 6½ or 7 percent, multiples of SFr 1,000. As a large bank, all services available.

Special note: Refers queries to branches which answer promptly. Lists 112 branches in Switzerland. One branch at Bülach, about five miles north of Kloten, the Zurich airport, aggressively seeks foreign accounts: Schweizerische Kreditanstalt, Bahnhofstrasse 28, 8180 Bülach, Switzerland. Also branch at Zurich airport: Schweizerische Kreditanstalt, Filiale Flughafen, 8058 Zurich, Switzerland. English literature and forms.

Schweizerischer Bankverein
Aeschenvorstadt 1   or: Paradeplatz 6
CH-4002 Basel, Switzerland   8021 Zurich, Switzerland

Swiss Bank Corporation, Société de Banque Suisse, Società di Banca Svizzera.
Big Three, commercial bank, est. 1872. Home office in Basel, cantonal capital of 235,000, on Rhine where Germany, France, and Switzerland meet.

Current accounts: SFr or foreign currencies. *Deposit accounts:* 3½ percent int., withdrawals to SFr 10,000 monthly. *Savings accounts:* 5 percent int., withdrawals to SFr 5,000 monthly. *Investment savings accounts:* 6 percent int., withdrawals to SFr 5,000 annually. Minimums on all above accounts: $5,000 or SFr 15,000. Also offers: fixed-term deposits, US$ or other currencies; cash bonds. 6½ or 7 percent. Full services, including silver and securities, available. Literature in English; forms sent after initial deposit. Lists 106 branches in Switzerland.

Bank Leu, AG
Bahnhofstrasse 32   or: Postfach 553
8022 Zurich, Switzerland   8022 Zurich, Switzerland

Big Five, commercial bank, est. 1755.

Current accounts: SFr, US$, DM, guilders, other currencies. *Deposit accounts:* 3½ percent int., withdrawals to SFr 10,000 monthly. *Savings accounts:* 5 percent int., withdrawals to SFr 5,000 monthly. *Investment accounts:* 6 percent int., withdrawals to SFr 5,000 semiannually. No minimums stated. *Euromarket placements:* $50,000 minimum. *Bank bonds:* 7¼ percent for three and four years, 7½ percent for five to six years. *Administration of discretionary accounts:* minimum of SFr 250,000. Also offers: securities, precious metals, coin transactions; Swiss franc time deposits available through subsidiary— Bank Leu International, Ltd., P. O. Box N3926, Nassau, Bahamas. *Special note:* Oldest of the Big Five, conscious of tradition, seems to have attitude of large private bank.

CANTONAL BANKS

Every canton has at least one cantonal bank, each with branches throughout the canton. The cantonal banks listed here are those that are able to handle overseas business in English. Other cantonal banks that will accept foreign accounts, but are not set up for English correspondence, are listed in a later category.

Zuger Kantonalbank
Bahnhofstrasse 1
CH-6301 Zug, Switzerland

Cantonal bank, est. 1892. Zug is twenty miles south of Zurich.

Current accounts. SFr or US$. *Savings accounts:* passbook, 4¼ percent int., withdrawals to SFr 5,000 monthly. No minimums stated.

Banque Cantonale du Valais
Case postale 29291
CH-1951 Sion, Switzerland

Walliser Kantonalbank (Wallis is German for Valais).
Cantonal bank, est. 1917. Sion is cantonal capital of 17,000
people, in Valais, 110 miles east of Geneva.

Current accounts. Ordinary savings accounts: 4¾ percent int.,
six months' notice. *Term savings accounts:* 5½ percent int.,
one-year notice, minimum deposit SFr 5,000. *Bank bonds:* 6½
percent for three or four years, 7 percent for five to eight
years. Also offers: gold, silver, securities. *Special note:* interest
rates believed due for increase.

Banque Cantonale Vaudoise
17, place St. François
CH-1002 Lausanne, Switzerland

Cantonal bank, est. 1845. Lausanne, cantonal capital of
140,000; thirty-six miles northeast of Geneva.

Current accounts: checkbook available. *Deposit accounts:* 3
percent int., withdrawals to SFr 10,000 monthly. *Savings accounts "A":* 3¾ percent int., withdrawals to SFr 5,000 monthly. *Savings accounts "B":* 5 percent int., withdrawals to SFr
3,000 monthly.

Bank Cantonale de Berne
place Fédérale
CH-3001 Bern, Switzerland

Kantonalbank von Bern, Cantonal Bank of Berne.
Cantonal bank, est. 1834.

Savings accounts: 5 percent int., minimum deposit SFr 1,000.

Banque Cantonale de Thurgovie
Bankplatz 1
8570 Weinfelden, Switzerland

Thurgauische Kantonalbank.
Cantonal bank, est. 1871. Weinfelden, town in center of Thurgau canton, thirty-four miles northeast of Zurich.

Private accounts: 3½ percent int., no withdrawal restrictions, recommended if security purchases intended. *Savings booklets:* 5 percent int., withdrawals to SFr 5,000 monthly. *Bank bonds:* 6½ percent for three- or four-year terms, 7 percent for five to eight years. Also offers: securities transactions, gold bullion and coins. *Special note:* emphasizes securities transactions, bonds in various European currencies.

Caisse Hypothécaire du
   Canton de Genève
2, place du Molard   or: Case postale 397
1204 Geneva, Switzerland   1211 Geneva 3, Switzerland

Cantonal mortgage and savings bank, est. 1847.

Savings accounts: 5 percent int., withdrawals to SFr 5,000 monthly. *Savings accounts* (second type): 5¾ percent int., withdrawals to SFr 1,500 monthly. Also offers: silver or gold coins and bullion, securities transactions.

Zürcher Kantonalbank
Bahnhofstrasse 9   or: Postfach
8022 Zurich, Switzerland   8022 Zurich, Switzerland

Banque Cantonale de Zürich.
Cantonal bank, est. 1869.

Current accounts: SFr or other currencies. *Deposit accounts:* 4 percent int., withdrawals to SFr 10,000 monthly. Also offers: securities transactions and precious metals.

Basler Kantonalbank
Spiegelgasse 2   or: Postfach
4001 Basel, Switzerland   4001 Basel, Switzerland

Banque Cantonale de Bâle.
Cantonal bank, est. 1899.

Savings books: 5 percent int., withdrawals to SFr 10,000 monthly. Minimum, SFr 5. *Special note:* regulations on savings accounts in five languages; sends forms after first deposit.

Deposito-Cassa der Stadt Bern
Kochergasse 6   or: Postfach 217
3000 Bern 7, Switzerland   3000 Bern 7, Switzerland

Caisse de Dépôts de la Ville de Berne.
Cantonal savings bank, est. 1825.

Savings accounts: 5 percent int., no withdrawal restrictions, minimum deposit SFr 10. *Deposit accounts:* 6 percent int., withdrawals to SFr 1,000 monthly, minimum deposit SFr 500. Also offers: security transactions, gold coins.

Banque Cantonale Lucernoise
Pilatusstrasse 12
CH-6002 Lucerne,   or: Postfach 1043
Switzerland   CH-6002 Lucerne, Switzerland

Cantonal bank, est. 1850. Lucerne, cantonal seat of 75,000 people, thirty miles southwest of Zurich.

Current accounts: SFr or US$. *Savings accounts:* 5 percent int., no withdrawal restrictions, no stipulated minimums.

Banque de l'Etat de Fribourg
place de la Cathédrale
1701 Fribourg, Switzerland

Cantonal bank, est. 1892. Fribourg is cantonal seat, seventeen miles southeast of Bern.

Savings accounts: 5 percent int. *Bank bonds:* 6¼ percent for three- or four-year terms, 7 percent for five or six years. Also offers: bonds issued by foreign companies in SFr, DM, or Dutch guilders.

Obwaldner Kantonalbank
6060 Sarnen, Switzerland

Cantonal bank, est. 1886. Sarnen, cantonal seat of the half-canton of Obwalden, about forty-two miles southwest of Zurich.

Current accounts. Savings accounts: 5 percent int. *Investment accounts:* 6 percent int. *Bank bonds:* three- to eight-year terms, 6½ or 7 percent. Also offers: usual bank services, including securities safekeeping, acting as trustees.

Caisse d'Epargne Genève
1, rue de la Tour-de-l'Ile
1211 Geneva 11, Switzerland

(Full title: Caisse d'Epargne de la République et Canton de Genève. Use short title for mail.)
Cantonal savings bank, est. 1816.

Current accounts: SFr or other currencies. *Savings books "Ordinaire":* 2½ percent int., no withdrawal limitations. *Savings books "TS":* 5 percent int., withdrawals to SFr 5,000 without notice. *Savings books "Jeunesse":* 5½ percent int., to twenty years of age, withdrawals need six months' notice. *Savings books "A":* 5½ percent int., for people over sixty years, withdrawals to SFr 5,000 without notice. Also offers: safe deposit, securities services, precious metals. *Note:* forms in French, information in English.

Basellandschaftliche Kantonalbank
Rheinstrasse 7
CH-4410 Liestal, Switzerland

Banque Cantonale de Bâle-Campagne.
Cantonal bank, est. 1864. Liestal is cantonal seat of the half-canton of "Basel District," eight miles southeast of Basel.

Current accounts. Savings accounts: 5 percent int. Also offers: SFr, DM, guilder bonds of European industries and governments.

COMMERCIAL BANKS

This broad category includes all the general purpose institutions that do not fit into any of the other groupings. No distinction has been made between "other banks" that are foreign-controlled and those with Swiss ownership.

Migros Bank
Seidengasse 12   or: Postfach 2826
8023 Zurich, Switzerland   8023 Zurich, Switzerland

Commercial bank, est. 1958.

Current accounts. Deposit accounts: 5 percent int., withdrawals to SFr 10,000 without notice. Minimum deposit, SFr 200. Offers full range of services, own bonds, investment counseling, trust management, precious metals, coins, securities. *Special note:* Part of Migros Trust, consumer-oriented retail and service group.

Gewerbebank Zürich
Rämistrasse 23   or: Postfach 265
8024 Zurich, Switzerland   8024 Zurich, Switzerland

Commercial bank, est. 1868.

Current accounts. Savings books: 5 percent int., withdrawals to SFr 5,000 monthly. No minimums stated. Forms sent after first deposit.

Bank Leumi Le-Israel (Schweiz)
Claridenstrasse 34   or: 80, rue du Rhône
8022 Zurich, Switzerland   1211 Geneva, Switzerland

Commercial bank, est. 1953.

Current accounts: SFr, US$, DM. *Deposit accounts:* SFr—4¼ percent, DM or US$—4 percent, withdrawals to SFr 4,000 monthly. *Fixed-term accounts:* minimums SFr 5,000, US $1,000, or DM 5,000. Rates at market. No minimums stated on current or deposit accounts. All forms in English. *Special note:* Part of Bank Leumi group. Associate, Bank Leumi Trust Company of New York, has four offices in New York City.

Metropolitan Bank, Ltd.
Bärenplatz 7   or: Postfach 2634
3001 Bern, Switzerland   3001 Bern, Switzerland

Commercial bank. Bern, population 160,000, is national capital.

Current accounts: US$, SFr, DM. Minimum balance, US $5,000 or equivalent. *Regular savings accounts:* 5¼ percent, withdrawals to SFr 10,000 monthly. *Term savings accounts:* 6¼ percent, withdrawals to SFr 1,000 per year, minimum deposit SFr 2,000. *Eurocurrency fiduciary placements:* US$, DM, guilders, French francs, £sterling. Minimum US $50,000. Offers usual commercial services: securities, precious metals, investment advisory, safe-custody services. *Special note:* annual report in German, French, and English.

Finanzbank Luzern, AG
Friedenstrasse 2
6000 Lucerne 6,   or: Postfach
Switzerland   6000 Lucerne 6, Switzerland

Commercial bank, est. 1945.

Current accounts. Deposit accounts: 5½ percent int., three months' notice; or 6½ percent, six months' notice of withdrawal. Also offers: three-year bonds at 6½ percent. German literature.

Cosmos Bank
Dreikönigstrasse 7   or: Postfach
8022 Zurich, Switzerland   8022 Zurich, Switzerland

Commercial bank, est. 1959.

Current accounts: SFr, US$, DM. *Time deposits:* US$ or DM, rate varies according to amount, duration, and market—with Cosmos, with affiliated Bahamian bank ($10,000 minimum), or on Euromarket ($100,000 minimum). Also offers: stock brokerage, metals, advisory services. *Special note:* affiliate is Cosmos Bank (Overseas) Ltd., Nassau, Bahamas.

Foreign Commerce Bank
Bellariastrasse 82   or: Postfach 1006
8038 Zurich, Switzerland   8022 Zurich, Switzerland

Commercial bank, est. 1958.

Current accounts: SFr, US$, other convertible currencies. *Deposit accounts:* SFr and DM—4 percent; guilders—5 percent; US$—6 percent; £sterling—7 percent; minimum deposit US $5,000. *Certificates of deposit:* Issued by other banks, int. rates vary. Offers very complete services: mutual funds, securities, precious metals, fiduciary Eurocurrency deposits, commodity trading. *Special note:* All forms and literature in English.

Deliberately geared to American customers. Affiliated with Deak-Perera International, Inc. Branch in Geneva—Foreign Commerce Bank, 3, rue du Marché, 1211 Genève 3 Rive, Switzerland.

Handelsbank in Zürich
Talstrasse 59   or: Postfach
8022 Zurich, Switzerland   8022 Zurich, Switzerland

Commercial bank, est. 1930.

Current accounts: SFr or US$. *Deposit accounts:* SFr 4 percent int., withdrawals to SFr 10,000 monthly; US$, 3¾ percent int., withdrawals to US $4,000 monthly. *Deposit books:* 5 percent int., withdrawals to SFr 5,000 monthly. *Investment accounts:* 6¼ percent int., withdrawals to SFr 10,000 annually. *Time deposits:* US$, minimum US $20,000, interest rates "upon request."

Handwerkerbank Basel
Aeschenvorstadt 2
4001 Basel, Switzerland

Commercial bank, est. 1860.

Deposit accounts: 5 percent int., withdrawals to SFr 10,000 monthly. Also offers: youth savings accounts at 6 percent to age twenty, cash bonds. *Special note:* Offers many types of savings accounts in German literature. Deposit account above is a special mail account, a *Postdepositenheft.*

Société Bancaire Barclays (Suisse), S.A.
6, place de la Synagogue   or: Case postale 221
1204 Geneva, Switzerland   1211 Geneva 11, Switzerland

Commercial bank, est. 1934.

Deposit passbook accounts: 5 percent int., withdrawals to SFr 1,000 monthly. *Cash bonds:* 6¾ percent for three and four years, 7¼ percent for five to eight years. *Fiduciary Euromarket deposits:* rates vary according to currency and term. Minimums—US $50,000; DM 100,000. *Investment portfolio management:* US $25,000 minimum. Also offers: full commercial services, gold bullion, safe deposit boxes, company formation services. *Special notes:* Offers formation of Liechtenstein trusts. Part of British Barclays group. Cayman Islands subsidiary offers offshore banking services.

Weisscredit
Via Pioda 9   or: Casella postale 428
6901 Lugano, Switzerland   6901 Lugano, Switzerland

Weisscredit Trade and Investment Bank.
Commercial bank, est. 1949. Lugano is lakeside resort town in Ticino, the Italian canton of Switzerland. Near Italian border, only forty miles north of Milan, Italy.

Current accounts: SFr, US$, or other currencies. *Deposit accounts:* 4½ percent int., withdrawals to SFr 5,000 monthly. *Time deposit accounts:* US$ only, six- or twelve-month terms, minimum US $10,000. Interest will vary according to market. Suggests contacting for higher rates on time deposits over US $50,000. Signature cards and business conditions in English. *Special note:* Apparently all accounts are numbered accounts. All forms come with a number and code word already filled in. Requires personal data on card marked "Segretariato." Prospective depositor should ask on first inquiry for bank to indicate which forms require "number" signature and which standard, legal signature.

Bank Hofmann, AG
Talstrasse 27   or: Postfach
8022 Zurich, Switzerland   8022 Zurich, Switzerland

Commercial bank, est. 1897.

Current accounts: SFr, DM, or US$. *Deposit book:* 5½ percent int., withdrawals to SFr 5,000 within thirty days. *Time deposits:* DM or US$ (with bank), three- to twelve-month term, minimum—DM 50,000 or US $25,000. *Euromarket time deposits:* DM, guilders, US$; minimums DM or G 100,000, US $35,000. Business conditions and signature card in English, "order card" for deposit book in German.

Overseas Development Bank
40, rue du Rhône
1204 Geneva 3,   or: Case Postale 462
Switzerland   1200 Geneva, Switzerland

Commercial bank.

Current accounts: SFr, US$, other currencies on request. *Regular deposit accounts:* SFr, US$, 4¾ percent int., withdrawals to SFr 3,000 or US $1,000 monthly, minimums SFr 3,000 or US $1,000. *Special deposit accounts:* US$, 6 percent int., withdrawals to US $500 monthly. Minimum US $5,000. *"Euro" deposit accounts:* US$, DM, French francs, variable int. based on average Euromarket rates during quarter. Withdrawals to US $500 per month. Minimums—US $20,000; DM 50,000. Also offers: investment services, securities safekeeping, gold and silver, full services generally. Forms and information packet completely in English. Branch in England: Overseas Development Bank, Berger House, 36 Berkeley Square, London W1X 5DA.

Bank und Finanz-Institut, AG
Waisenhausplatz 25   or: Postfach 1082
3001 Bern, Switzerland   3001 Bern, Switzerland

Bank & Finance Co., Inc.; Comptoir Bancaire et Financier, S.A.
Commercial bank, est. 1955. Main office in Bern, branches in Basel, Geneva, and Zurich.

Savings books: 5¼ percent int. *Deposit accounts:* 5½ percent int., withdrawal to SFr 10,000 monthly. *Investment accounts:* 6¼ percent int., withdrawals to SFr 3,000 monthly. Full services including current accounts, bonds, securities transactions. Branches directly represented on stock exchanges. *Special notes:* affiliated with General Auditing Co., Ltd., of Switzerland. Requires waiver of secrecy from U.S. residents.

Wirtschaftsbank Zürich
Stauffacherstrasse 45
CH-8004 Zurich,   or: Postfach 3294
Switzerland   8023 Zurich, Switzerland

Commercial bank, est. 1959.

Current accounts: SFr, other currencies. *Deposit accounts:* 5 percent int., withdrawals to SFr 5,000 monthly. *Time deposits:* currencies other than Swiss francs. *Euromarket trust deposits:* currencies other than SFr. Prevailing rates vary. Minimums— US $20,000, DM 100,000. Also offers: international trade transactions; management accounts—US $100,000 minimum; precious metals; stock exchange transactions; formation and administration of companies, trusts, and family foundations; real estate investments.

Arab Bank (Overseas), Ltd.
Talacker 21
CH-8022 Zurich,   or: Postfach 958
Switzerland   CH-8022 Zurich, Switzerland

Commercial bank, est. 1962.

Current accounts: SFr, US$, DM, £sterling. *Deposit accounts:* SFr, 5½ percent int.; US$, 6 percent int.; £sterling, 6½ percent. *Trustee time deposits:* Interest according to Euromarket rates. Minimums—US $20,000, DM 100,000, £10,000. *Special note:* When querying, request forms for type of account interested in.

Banque pour le Commerce Suisse-Israélien
15-17, quai des Bergues
1211 Geneva 1,   or: Case postale 320
Switzerland   1211 Geneva 1, Switzerland

Swiss-Israel Trade Bank, Bank für Schweizer-Israelischen Handel.

Commercial bank, est. 1950.

Current accounts: US$. *Savings accounts:* 4¾ percent int. *Certificates of deposit:* US$, interest varies according to market, minimum US $5,000. CDs are with London branch—Swiss-Israel Trade Bank, Lee House, London Wall, London E.C. 2.

American Express International Banking Corporation
Aeschenvorstadt 48-50   or: Postfach 438
4000 Basel 2, Switzerland   4002 Basel, Switzerland

Commercial bank.

Deposit accounts: 5 percent int., withdrawals to SFr 3,000 monthly. *Special note:* American Express operates as banking business overseas. Only deposit accounts available to U.S. residents. All forms in English.

Banque de Commerce et de Placements, S.A.
3, rue du Marché
1211 Geneva 3, Switzerland

Commercial bank.

Euromarket fiduciary investments: Rates vary per market, short-term for one to six months, minimums—US $25,000, DM 100,000. Also offers: "long-term investments of all kinds according to customers' needs."

Bank in Gossau
Poststrasse 4
CH-9202 Gossau,   or: Postfach 35874
Switzerland   9202 Gossau SG, Switzerland

Commercial and mortgage bank, est. 1881. Gossau is smaller town, six miles west of Sankt Gallen, off Autobahn, fifty miles east of Zurich.

Deposit accounts: 4½ percent int., withdrawals to SFr 10,000 monthly. *Savings books:* 5 percent int., withdrawals to SFr 5,000 monthly. *Investment books (Anlageheft):* 6 percent int., withdrawals to SFr 10,000 per year. *Bank bonds:* 6¾ percent to 7¼ percent, three to eight years. Also offers: youth savings account at 6 percent, other commercial services. Letters in English, other material in German.

Inter Maritime Bank
5, quai du Mont-Blanc
1211 Geneva 1,   or: Postfach 423
Switzerland   1211 Geneva 1, Switzerland

Commercial bank, est. 1959.

Current accounts. Deposit accounts: Rates subject to agreement. *Securities safekeeping accounts. Portfolio management. Special note:* Not a typical retail bank. Specializes in "banking services to ships in ports throughout the world." Rates subject to agreement; when querying, indicate type of account desired, approximate size of deposit, and currency desired.

Banque de Dépôts et de Gestion
14, avenue du Théâtre
1002 Lausanne, Switzerland

Depositen und Verwaltungsbank, Banca di Depositi e di Gestioni.
Commercial bank, est. 1933.

Current accounts. Deposit accounts: 6 percent int., withdrawals to SFr 3,000 monthly. Also offers: all other banking services.

Banque Financière, S.A.
Weggengasse 1
8001 Zurich, Switzerland

Finanzbank, AG
Commercial bank, est. 1924.

Current accounts. Ninety-day notice account: 4½ percent int. Also offers: security transactions, gold and silver bullion.

Nordfinanz-Bank Zürich
Bahnhofstrasse 1   or: Postfach 750
8001 Zurich, Switzerland   8022 Zurich, Switzerland

Commercial bank, est. 1938. (Since 1964, controlled by group of four big Scandinavian banks.)

Current accounts: SFr, US$. *Deposit accounts:* SFr or US$, 5¼ percent int., withdrawals to SFr 5,000 or US $1,000 monthly. *Investment accounts:* 6 percent int., withdrawals to SFr 10,000 per year. *Fixed-time deposit accounts:* US$, other currencies. Rates vary, minimum SFr 50,000. *Cash bonds:* rates vary, three- to eight-year terms. *Euromarket fiduciary deposits:* interest varies according to market, minimums—SFr 100,000, US $25,000. Also offers: full services including safe deposit boxes, gold coins and bars, securities transactions, establishment of companies, all other commercial services. *Special note:* All materials in English. U.S. representative—Mr. Lars T. Radberg, Suite 1609, 1 Rockefeller Plaza, New York, N.Y. 10020.

Bank in Langnau
CH-3550 Langnau, Switzerland

Commercial bank, est. 1885. Langnau, main town in Emmental region, eighteen miles east of Bern.

Savings accounts: 5 percent int., withdrawals to SFr 15,000 per quarter. *Bonds:* 6¾ percent—three years, 7¼ percent—five years. Also offers: all regular banking services. *Special note:* Literature in German offers full description of all commercial bank services.

Compagnie Luxembourgeoise de Banque, S.A.
Färberstrasse 6 (Seehof)
CH-8034 Zurich,   or: Postfach 64
Switzerland   CH-8034 Zurich, Switzerland

Commercial bank, est. 1967. Branch of Luxembourg bank, which in turn is wholly owned subsidiary of Dresdner Bank of Germany. Formed to participate in Euromarket.

Euromarket time deposits: US$, DM, £sterling, guilders, other convertible currencies. Rates vary according to market. Minimum US $100,000 or equivalent. Also offers: private portfolio management, Eurobonds, securities transactions.

Chase Manhattan Bank (Switzerland)
63, rue du Rhône   or: Case Postale 476
1204 Geneva, Switzerland   1211 Geneva 3, Switzerland

Commercial bank.

Current accounts: SFr, other currencies, minimum SFr 5,000. *Checking accounts:* SFr, other major currencies, minimum SFr 10,000. *Time deposits* (with bank): interest varies, minimum US $25,000. *Euromarket fiduciary deposits:* US$, minimum US $25,000 to US $100,000 depending on maturity. Other currencies, minimums US $100,000 equivalent. Also offers: investment management, securities transactions. *Special note:* requires waiver of secrecy for U.S. residents.

Hypothekar-und Handelsbank Winterthur
Stadhausstrasse 14
8401 Winterthur, Switzerland

Commercial and mortgage bank, est. 1865. Winterthur is industrial city of 90,000 people, about twelve miles northeast of Zurich.

Current accounts. Savings books: 5 percent int., withdrawals to SFr 3,000 monthly. *Deposit books:* 5 percent int., withdrawals to SFr 5,000 monthly. *Investment books:* 6½ percent int., withdrawals to SFr 5,000 quarterly. Also offers: full range of banking services, including stock exchange transactions, Euromarket investments, safekeeping services.

Privat Kredit Bank
Tödistrasse 47   or: Postfach
8002 Zurich, Switzerland   8022 Zurich, Switzerland

Commercial bank.

Current accounts. Deposit accounts: 5½ percent int. Also offers: full services including fiduciary time deposits, portfolio management, buying and selling securities, precious metals, safe deposit boxes. Branch in Lugano: Privat Kredit Bank, Contrada di Sassello 2, 6900 Lugano, Switzerland.

First National Bank of Chicago
6, place des Eaux-vives   or: Case postale 102
1207 Geneva, Switzerland   1211 Geneva 6, Switzerland

Commercial bank.

Current accounts: SFr, US$, other currencies. Minimum balance, SFr 5,000. *Investment deposit accounts:* SFr—6 percent int., or US$—7 percent int., three-months' notice required on withdrawals. *Euromarket fixed-time deposits:* SFr, US$, or other currencies. Rates according to market. Minimums, US $100,000. Also offers: securities transactions, gold coins, gold and silver bullion, portfolio management, safe-deposit boxes.

Banque de Dépôts
94, rue du Rhône
1211 Geneva 3,   or: Case Rive 550
Switzerland   1211 Geneva, Switzerland

The Deposit Bank, Banco de Depositos.
Commercial bank, est. 1921.

Current accounts: minimum deposit, SFr 5,000. *Savings accounts:* 5 percent int., withdrawals to SFr 5,000 without notice; minimum, SFr 50. *Three months' notice savings accounts (Livret de placement):* 6 percent int., withdrawals to SFr 1,000 monthly, minimum balance, SFr 5,000. *Time deposits:* US$ only, rates vary (was 8 percent), minimum deposit US $10,000. Also offers: full banking services. *Special note:* Number accounts available, SFr 10,000 minimum.

Banque Commercial de Sion, S.A.
15, rue de Lausanne   or: Case postale 28947
1950 Sion, Switzerland   1951 Sion, Switzerland

Commercial bank, est. 1874.

Ordinary savings passbooks: 5 percent int. *Savings deposit accounts:* 6 percent int., withdrawals to SFr 5,000 annually; minimum deposit, SFr 1,000. *Cash bonds:* 7 percent int., five-year term; 7¼ percent int. for six- to eight-year terms. Also offers: youth savings accounts and savings accounts for older persons. *Special note:* forms in French.

Anlagebank Zug, AG
Neugasse 22   or: Postfach 262
6301 Zug, Switzerland   6301 Zug, Switzerland

Banque de Placements Zoug, S.A.; Investment Bank Zug, Ltd.
Commercial bank, est. 1957.

Current accounts. Savings accounts: 5¼ percent int., withdrawals to SFr 2,000 monthly. *Deposit books:* 6 percent int., withdrawals of SFr 5,000 require three months' notice. *Bank bonds:* 6¾ percent for three or four years, 7¼ percent for five to eight years. Also offers: securities transactions, precious metals.

Adler Bank Basel, AG
Aeschenvordstadt 48-50
4001 Basel, Switzerland

Commercial bank, est. 1921.

Current accounts. Private accounts (Einlagekontos): 4 percent int., withdrawals to SFr 10,000 monthly. *Deposit books:* 5¼ percent int., withdrawals to SFr 5,000 monthly. *Investment book accounts:* 6 percent int., withdrawals to SFr 5,000 quarterly. *Bank bonds:* 6¼ percent for three or four years, 7 percent for five to eight years. *Time deposits:* foreign currencies only, rates vary. Also offers: securities transactions, gold purchases.

Dow Banking Corp.
Bahnhofstrasse 24   or: Postfach 931
8022 Zurich, Switzerland   8021 Zurich, Switzerland

Commercial bank, est. 1965.

Current accounts. Deposit accounts: 5 percent int., withdrawals to SFr 10,000 within thirty-day period. *Euromarket fixed-term deposits:* US$, G, £sterling, DM. Rates vary according to market. Minimum—US $50,000. *Bank bonds:* 6½ percent int. for three-year term, 7 percent for four to eight years. *Portfolio management:* minimum—US $50,000. Also offers: securities transactions. *Special note:* requires bank reference and "statement that you will comply with IRS regulations on reporting overseas income."

Bankinvest
Brandschenkestrasse 41   or: Postfach 419
8039 Zurich, Switzerland   8039 Zurich, Switzerland

Bank for Investment & Credit, Ltd.
Commercial bank, est. 1969.

Deposit accounts: "currency of your choice," write for interest rates. *Euromarket time deposits:* minimums—US $25,000 or SFr 50,000. Also offers: securities transactions, gold and silver trading, tax and estate planning advice. *Special note:* has wholly owned subsidiary in Cayman Islands.

Discount Bank (Overseas), Ltd.
3, quai de l'Ile   or: Case postale 357
1204 Geneva, Switzerland   1211 Geneva 11, Switzerland

Commercial bank.

Current accounts: available in US$. *Savings deposit accounts:* 5 percent int., withdrawals to SFr 4,000 monthly. *Fixed-time deposits:* US$; three-, six-, or twelve-month terms. Minimums— US $1,000 or multiples thereof. *Special note:* bank requires "first-class bank references" to open an account. Investment accounts and portfolio management services available, but visit to bank and "detailed discussion" with investment managers necessary.

Gewerbebank Baden
Bahnhofplatz 1
CH-5401 Baden, Switzerland

Commercial bank, est. 1864. Baden, small industrial town with famous spa, thirteen miles northwest of Zurich.

Savings books: 5 percent int., withdrawals to SFr 2,000 without prior notice. *Deposit books:* 6 percent int., withdrawals to SFr 5,000 yearly. *Bank bonds:* 6¾ percent, 7 percent, 7¼ percent, depending on term.

Schweizerische Depositen-und Kreditbank
Löwenstrasse 40   or: Postfach 300
8021 Zurich, Switzerland   8022 Zurich, Switzerland

Banque Suisse de Crédit et de Dépôts.
Commercial bank, est. 1965.

Deposit accounts: 5 percent int., withdrawals to SFr 10,000 monthly. *Savings accounts:* 5¼ percent int., withdrawals to SFr 5,000 monthly.

Gewerbekasse in Bern
Schweizerhoflaube
Bahnhofplatz 7
3001 Bern, Switzerland

Caisse Industrielle à Berne.
Commercial bank, est. 1905.

Savings books: 5 percent int., currently, no withdrawal restrictions. *Deposit books:* 6¼ percent int., withdrawals to SFr 1,000 monthly. *Bank bonds:* 6¾ percent for three and four years, 7¼ percent for 5- or 6-year terms. Also offers: all other bank services.

Banque pour le Commerce International, S.A.
Aeschengraben 25   or: Case postale 1352
4002 Basel, Switzerland   4002 Basel, Switzerland

Bank for International Commerce, Ltd.
Commercial bank, est. 1949.

Current accounts: SFr or other currencies. *Certificates of deposit:* US$, minimum US $15,000; one-, three-, or six-month term. *Investment funds (mutual funds). Special note:* accounts can be name or numbered.

AKO Bank
Talacker 50
8021 Zurich, Switzerland

Commercial bank, est. 1934.

Deposit accounts: 6 percent int., life insurance included. *Cash bonds:* 6¾ percent for three and four years, 7¼ percent for five to eight years. *Special note:* deals mainly in consumer loans.

Banque Scandinave en Suisse
11, Rond-Point de Rive
1211 Geneva 3,   or: Case Postale 490
Switzerland   1211 Geneva 3, Switzerland

Commercial bank, est. 1964.

Current accounts: SFr or US$. *Deposit or savings accounts:* SFr or US$, 5 percent int., withdrawals to SFr 5,000 or US $1,500 per month. *Notice time deposit accounts:* US$, 6 percent int., on an average balance up to US $75,000; 6½ percent int., from US $75,000 to US $150,000. Also offers: securities safekeeping, portfolio management, precious metals, safe deposit boxes, other commercial services. *Special note:* owned by group of seven Scandinavian banks and one American bank, the Northern Trust Company.

Imefbank
6, rue Petitot   or: Case postale 59
1204 Geneva, Switzerland   1211 Geneva 11, Switzerland

Banque d'Investissements Mobiliers et de Financement.
Commercial bank, est. 1957.

Current accounts: SFr or Western European currencies. *Deposit booklets:* 4½ percent int. *Euromarket deposits:* US $50,000 minimum, rates vary. Also offers: all usual banking services, such as securities transactions. *Special note:* numbered accounts offered.

Genossenschaftliche Zentralbank, AG, Basel
Aeschenplatz 3
CH-4002 Basel, Switzerland

Cooperative Central Bank Co., Ltd.; Banque Centrale Coopér-
ative, S.A.
Commercial bank, est. 1927.

Current accounts. Savings accounts: 5 percent int., withdrawals to SFr 5,000 monthly. *Investment accounts:* 6 percent int.,
withdrawals to SFr 10,000 yearly. Also offers: short-term bank
bonds, securities brokerage, portfolio management, full range
of banking facilities.

Neue Bank
Talstrasse 41
8022 Zurich, Switzerland

New Bank, Nouvelle Banque.
Commercial bank, est. 1960.

Current accounts: minimum average balance—SFr 5,000. *Deposit booklets:* 5¼ percent int., withdrawals to SFr 5,000
monthly. *Deposit accounts:* 5¾ percent int., withdrawals to
SFr 5,000 monthly, minimum deposit—SFr 20,000. *Bank
bonds (medium-term notes):* 6½ percent int. for three and four
years, 7 percent for five and six years. Also offers: "all services
of a commercial and investment bank." *Special note:* requires
bank references if customer does not open account personally.

Banco di Roma per la Svizzera
Paizzetta San Carlo   or: Casella postale 6444
6901 Lugano, Switzerland   6901 Lugano, Switzerland

Commercial bank, est. 1947.

Current accounts: SFr, US$, other currencies. *Savings deposit
accounts:* 5 percent int., withdrawals to SFr 5,000 monthly.

Fixed-term deposits: US$, interest rates may vary, for three to twelve months. Minimum US $20,000. *Special note:* banker's reference usually required, numbered accounts available.

Banque de Paris et des Pays-Bas (Suisse), S.A.
6, rue de Hollande
1211 Geneva 11, Switzerland

Parisbas Bank.
Commercial bank, est. 1872.

Current accounts: SFr or other currencies. *Savings accounts:* 4¾ percent int., withdrawals to SFr 3,000 monthly. Also offers: portfolio management, legal and tax services. *Special note:* requires bank references.

SAVINGS BANKS

Banks in this category are devoted primarily to interest-bearing, smaller accounts. Some are community banks, others are privately controlled.

Bank Neumünster
Goethestrasse 14
Stadelhoferplatz
8001 Zurich, Switzerland

Savings bank, est. 1860.

Private account: especially for mail customers, 3½ percent int., compounded quarterly. Withdrawals to SFr 10,000 monthly, minimum SFr 20,000.

Spar-& Leihkasse Schaffhausen
Bahnhofstrasse 2
8201 Schaffhausen, Switzerland

Savings bank, est. 1866. Schaffhausen is cantonal capital of 36,000, on Rhine, thirty miles north of Zurich.

Current accounts. Deposit books: 4 percent int., withdrawals to SFr 10,000 monthly. No minimum deposit. *Savings books:* 5 percent int., withdrawals to SFr 3,000 monthly. No minimum. *Long-term deposit book:* 6 percent int., six-months' notice on withdrawals. Minimum—SFr 2,000. *Bonds:* minimum—SFr 1,000; 6½ percent for three or four years, 7 percent for five to eight years. Also offers: all other services including metals, securities, safe-deposit boxes.

Sparkasse der Gemeinde Schwyz
Herrengasse
6430 Schwyz, Switzerland

Savings bank, est. 1812. Schwyz, 11,500 population, cantonal capital about thirty-five miles south of Zurich.

Savings accounts: 5¼ percent int. No stated minimums. Also offers: securities purchases.

Kreditanstalt Grabs
CH-9472 Grabs, Switzerland

Savings bank, est. 1880. Grabs, small town near Buchs in Sankt Gallen canton, just across Rhine River from Liechtenstein.

Deposit accounts: 4 percent int. *Savings accounts:* 5 percent int. *Investment accounts:* 6 percent int. Also offers: bank bonds.

Spar-und Leihkasse Balgach
CH-9436 Balgach, Switzerland

Savings and loan bank, est. 1868. Balgach, small Rhine valley town in Sankt Gallen canton, near Austrian border.

Current accounts. Savings books: 5 percent int. *Investment books:* 6 percent int. *Cash bonds:* three- to six-year terms, 6¾ percent to 7 percent int. *Note:* correspondence in English, account information in German.

Esparnikasse des Amstbezirks Aarwangen
Jurastrasse 31
4900 Langenthal, Switzerland

Savings bank, est. 1971. Langenthal is town in Aare River valley, thirty miles northeast of Bern.

Deposit books: 3½ percent int., balance freely available. *Savings books (Sparheft):* 5 percent int., withdrawals to SFr 10,000 monthly. *Savings books (Sparbuch):* 5¾ percent int., withdrawals to SFr 20,000, require three months' notice. *Investment savings books:* 6¼ percent int., withdrawals to SFr 3,000 per calendar year, minimum balance SFr 1,000. *Cash bonds:* 6¾ percent for three and four years, 7 percent for five to eight years. *Special note:* offers ten different savings arrangements; accounts described are typical.

Spar-und Leihkasse Steffisburg
Glockentalstrasse 6
3612 Steffisburg,   or: Postfach 11881
Switzerland   3612 Steffisburg, Switzerland

Savings and loan, est. 1863. Steffisburg, small town in Bernese Oberland, outside of Thun, twenty miles south of Bern.

Savings books: 5 percent int., withdrawals to SFr 5,000 quarterly. *Three months' notice savings books:* 5½ percent int. *Six months' notice savings books:* 6 percent int. *Cash bonds:* 6¾ percent for three or four years, 7 percent for five- or six-year terms.

Spar + Leihkasse in Bern
Bundesplatz 4   or: Postfach 2623
3001 Bern 1, Switzerland   3001 Bern 1, Switzerland

Savings and loan, est. 1857.

Savings accounts: 5 percent int. *Deposit accounts:* 6¼ percent int., withdrawals to SFr 1,000 monthly. *Bank bonds:* 6¾ percent int. for three and four years, 7 percent for five and six years.

Schweizerische Bodenkredit-Anstalt
Werdmuhleplatz 1   or: Postfach 921
8021 Zurich, Switzerland   CH-8021 Zurich, Switzerland

Crédit Foncier Suisse
Mortgage bank, est. 1896.

Deposit accounts: 4½ percent int., withdrawals to SFr 10,000 monthly. *Savings accounts:* 5 percent int., withdrawals to SFr 5,000 monthly. *Investment accounts:* 6 percent int., withdrawals to SFr 5,000 per year. No stated minimums on any accounts. Send forms after first deposit. Send full identifying data and type of account desired with first transmittal.

Solothurnische Leihkasse
Westbahnhofstrasse 11
4500 Solothurn, Switzerland

Savings and mortgage bank, est. 1865. Solothurn, cantonal seat, eighteen miles north of Bern.

Savings accounts: 5 percent int., withdrawals to SFr 5,000 monthly. *Savings accounts:* 5¼ percent int., withdrawals to SFr 2,000 monthly. *Savings accounts:* 6 percent int., withdrawals to SFr 10,000 yearly. (Note: bank makes no distinction between types of savings accounts in English translation.) *Bank bonds:* 6¾ percent for three- or four-year terms, 7¼ percent for five to eight years. Also offers: all usual bank services.

Caisse d'Epargne du Valais
place du Midi
1951 Sion, Switzerland

Savings bank, est. 1876.

Current accounts. Deposit accounts: 3½ percent int., withdrawals to SFr 10,000 monthly. *Ordinary savings books:* 5 percent int., withdrawals to SFr 3,000 without notice. *Cash bonds:* three-year term, 6½ percent int., 6¾ percent for four or five years, 7 percent for six to eight years. Also offers: other types of savings accounts, securities transactions. *Special note:* brochures in French.

Esparniskasse Nidwalden
6370 Stans, Switzerland

Savings bank, est. 1827. Stans is cantonal seat of half-canton of Nidwalden, about thirty-seven miles south of Zurich.

Savings books: 5 percent int., no withdrawal limitations. *Deposit accounts:* 6 percent int., withdrawals from SFr 1,000 to SFr 10,000; three months' notice. *Bank bonds:* 6½ percent int. for three-year term, 7 percent for five years. Also offers: all standard services.

Eigenheim Bank Basel
Sankt Jakobstrasse 18   or: Postfach 440
4002 Basel, Switzerland   4002 Basel, Switzerland

Savings bank, est. 1931.

Savings accounts: 5¼ percent int., withdrawals to SFr 5,000 monthly. *Deposit accounts:* 5¾ percent int., withdrawals to SFr 3,000 monthly. *Bank bonds:* three- to eight-year terms, units of SFr 1,000, 5,000, or 10,000. Also offers: securities transactions on Swiss exchanges, gold and silver bullion.

PRIVATE BANKS

Technically, in Switzerland a true private bank is not incorporated. Another type of institution might also be called a private bank, except that it does not fit the legal description. Many were genuine private banks in the past, but have since incorporated, either to increase their capital base or to continue to use a prestigious name. In practice, in character, in style of operations, there is little to distinguish these two types of banking houses.

For simplicity, in this listing both types are grouped together, but under separate categories. Banks in Category I are the "true" private banks; Category II includes banks that describe themselves as "private" banks in bank directories, but that are incorporated and not technically private.

Banks in both categories will generally want to know who referred you to them, or how you came to find out about them.

CATEGORY I

Pictet & Cie.
6, rue Diday
1211 Geneva, Switzerland

Private bank, est. 1805.

Portfolio management: for institutions or individuals, discretionary or per client's instructions. Minimum—US $100,000.

Bordier & Cie.
16, rue de Hollande   or: Case postale 298
1211 Geneva, Switzerland   1211 Geneva 11, Switzerland

Private bank, est. 1844.

Specializes in the management of funds, either on "safekeeping" basis, with client giving instructions, or with general management powers. Offers short-term DM and US$ deposits, minimum US $50,000, rates vary according to market. Prefers to discuss client's objectives and account details in person.

Darier & Cie.
4, rue de Saussure
1211 Geneva 11, Switzerland

Private bank, est. 1837.

Specializes "in international money management for private individuals." Accounts may be either regular or numbered. Provides foreign exchange, gold, checks.

Armand von Ernst & Cie.
Bundesgasse 30   or: Postfach 1081
3001 Bern, Switzerland   3001 Bern, Switzerland

Private bank, est. 1812.

Portfolio management: on discretionary basis or per client's instructions. Minimum securities value—US $100,000. *Deposit accounts:* 2 percent int., withdrawals to SFr 10,000 without prior notice. (Deposit accounts are maintained only for customers who maintain securities management accounts.) *Special notes:* reference from "a bank of good standing" required. Signature verification required from same bank. Remittances should be made through a bank. Waiver of bank secrecy from Americans.

Falck & Cie., Banquiers
Schwanenplatz 2
CH-6002 Lucerne, Switzerland

Private bank, est. 1875.

Current accounts: SFr or "better known Western currencies." *Deposit accounts:* 3¼ percent int. Also offers: negotiable certificates of deposit, minimum—US $25,000; gold and silver; creation of companies. *Special notes:* main concern is asset management. Requires some information on client background.

J. Vontobel & Co.
Banhofstrasse 3
CH-8022 Zurich,   or: Postfach
Switzerland   CH-8022 Zurich, Switzerland

Private bank.

Investment accounts: initial deposit—US $50,000. No interest paid; apparently bank will place funds in other investments, per agreement with client. *Deposit accounts:* 4¼ percent int., initial deposit—SFr 10,000. May only be opened in connection with investment account. *Portfolio management:* minimum—US $100,000. Also offers: formation of companies, trusteeship services. *Special note:* issues English-language booklet describing Swiss banking practices in general.

Sturzenegger & Cie.
Sankt Jakobstrasse 46   or: Postfach
4002 Basel, Switzerland   4002 Basel, Switzerland

Private bank, est. 1920.

Current accounts only. Also offers: securities transactions, administration of customers' securities, "all the usual banking operations." *Special note:* wants to meet new customers, all customers are known personally.

Wegelin & Co.
Bohl 17
9004 Sankt Gallen,   or: Postfach 10
Switzerland   9004 Sankt Gallen, Switzerland

Private bank, est. 1741. Sankt Gallen is cantonal seat of 80,000, forty-seven miles east of Zurich.

Specializes in portfolio management. Can also assist in company formation, many other banking services.

Ferrier, Lullin & Cie.
15, rue Petitot
1211 Geneva, Switzerland

Private bank, est. 1795.

Specializes in "security investment business" and in investment management for clients. Requires waiver of secrecy from U.S. residents and citizens.

Lombard, Odier & Cie.
11, rue de la Corraterie
1211 Geneva 11,   or: Case postale Stand
Switzerland   1211 Geneva 11, Switzerland

Private bank, est. 1798.

Current accounts (cash accounts). Investment accounts: portfolio minimum US $100,000. *Discretionary accounts:* minimum, US $250,000.

CATEGORY II

Von der Muehll & Weyeneth Bankers, Ltd.
Utoquai 37
8011 Zurich, Switzerland

Private bank, est. 1940.

Deposit accounts (time deposits): 6 percent int., withdrawals on ninety days' notice. *Portfolio management* is main activity. Also offers: gold and silver transactions, and safekeeping. *Special note:* policy to require bank or broker's reference from new customers.

Guyerzeller Zurmont Bank, AG
Genferstrasse 6-8
8027 Zurich, Switzerland

Private bank, est. 1939.

Specializes in portfolio management. Minimum for accounts, US $300,000.

Bank Von Ernst & Cie., AG
Marktgasse 63-65
CH-3001 Bern,   or: Postfach 2622
Switzerland   CH3001 Bern 1, Switzerland

Private bank, est. 1869.

Current accounts: SFr or other convertible currencies. *Deposit accounts:* 3½ percent int., freely available. *Savings accounts:* 5¼ percent int. *Investment savings accounts:* 6¼ percent int., withdrawals to SFr 5,000 annually. Minimum deposit, SFr 3,000. *Cash bonds:* SFr 1,000, 5,000, or 10,000 denominations, 6¾ percent for three- and four-year terms, 7¼ percent for five years. Also offers: Euromarket time deposits, investment management. *Special note:* wholly owned subsidiary of Hill Samuel Group, Ltd., London merchant banking and financial group.

Julius Bär & Co.
Bahnhofstrasse 36   or: Postfach 992
8022 Zurich, Switzerland   CH-8022 Zurich, Switzerland

Private bank, est. 1890.

Current accounts: any negotiable currency. *Deposit accounts:* 4½ percent int., withdrawals to SFr 3,000 monthly. *Eurobonds:* various currencies, rates vary, minimum—US $5,000. *Euromarket short-term investments:* rates vary according to currency and term, minimum—US $10,000. *Stock transactions:* minimum—US $5,000. *Silver bullion:* minimum—1,000 oz. *Gold coins:* minimum—US $4,000. *Fully managed accounts:* US $300,000 minimum. Also offers: own investment trusts (mutual funds). *Special note:* wants to know who referred new clients, and would like to know investment goals of customers. Formerly one of the largest private banks, Bär & Co. became a joint-stock bank in January 1975.

Cambio + Valorenbank
Utoquai 55   or: Postfach 535
8021 Zurich, Switzerland   8021 Zurich, Switzerland

Private bank, est. 1959.

Current accounts (regular account): SFr, US$, Canadian $, DM, guilders, £sterling. Minimums—US $1,000. *Deposit accounts:* SFr, 4½ percent int., withdrawals to SFr 5,000 monthly, minimum SFr 1,000. *Eurocurrency fixed-time deposits:* minimum US $50,000. Also offers: securities transactions (also on margin); South African gold-mining stocks; currency futures on margin (minimum trade US $100,000); gold coins, available on margin; silver for delivery in Zurich or in London. Sends forms after receipt of first deposit; requests initial deposit by cashier's check.

Maerki, Baumann & Co., AG
Dreikönigstrasse 8   or: Postfach Fraumünster
8002 Zurich, Switzerland   8022 Zurich, Switzerland

Private bank, est. 1932.

Current accounts: various currencies, name or numbered. Specializes in portfolio management, securities transactions as member of Zurich stock exchange. Also offers: gold, Euromarket transactions.

Banque Galland & Cie., S.A.
8, avenue du Théâtre
1002 Lausanne,   or: Case postale 39960
Switzerland   1002 Lausanne, Switzerland

Private bank, est. 1889.

Current accounts. Also offers: placement of funds in bonds or in time deposits. Portfolio safekeeping.

Banque Pariente
12, rue de Rive
1211 Geneva 3,
Switzerland

Investment bank, est. 1957.

Current accounts. Euromarket time deposits: US$ or DM, rates vary according to market and term. Usual minimum US $25,000, but "amounts as small as US $5,000" from different clients can sometimes be grouped to reach minimums. Also offers: deposit accounts by arrangement for three-month periods, numbered accounts, gold, securities transactions, mutual funds, formation of foreign corporations, and portfolio management. *Special notes:* requires bank references. Minimum balance required is US $3,500.

Banque Pasque, S.A.
10, rue de Hollande
1211 Geneva 11, Switzerland

Private bank, est. 1885.

Portfolio management only: minimum US $35,000. Requires waiver of bank secrecy from U.S. residents.

Banque Courvosier, S.A.
21, faubourg de l'Hôpital
2001 Neuchâtel, Switzerland

Private bank, est. 1926. Neuchâtel, lakeside cantonal capital, about twenty-five miles south of Bern.

Current accounts. Deposit books: type "A"—5½ percent int., withdrawals to SFr 10,000 monthly; type "B"—6 percent int., withdrawals to SFr 2,000 per month. *Cash bonds:* three-year term at 6¾ percent; five years at 7¼ percent.

Banque d'Investissements Privés
7, place de l'Université
1211 Geneva 11,   or: Case Stand 138
Switzerland   1211 Geneva 11, Switzerland

Private bank, est. 1951.

Current accounts: any currency. *Fiduciary time deposit accounts:* interest per Euromarket rates, minimums—US $100,000; DM, guilders, or French francs—100,000; Belgian francs—500,000. *Special notes:* requires waiver of secrecy from U.S. residents. Correspondence in English, all other forms in French.

Privatbank & Verwaltungsgesellschaft
Barengasse 29
8001 Zurich, Switzerland

Private Bank & Trust Company, Société Privée de Banque et de Gérance.
Private bank, est. 1932.

Specializes in trading securities and portfolio management. No savings-type accounts. *Current accounts only:* as base for investment program. Minimums: US $50,000 or equivalent in securities. Also offers: tax-exempt Swiss franc bonds, 7½ to 7¾ percent int.; gold bullion and coins, silver bullion.

Banque Romande
8, boulevard du Théâtre   or: Case postale 180
1204 Geneva, Switzerland   1211 Geneva 11, Switzerland

Private bank, est. 1954.

Current accounts: checkbooks available. *Deposit accounts:* 5½ percent int., no minimums or withdrawal restrictions specified. (Ask when querying.)

Banks that correspond in French or German

Some banks are not equipped to correspond in English. Their replies will be informative and polite, but in German or French. Such banks, however, should present an interesting challenge to many Americans. They are listed here for the use of those readers who have a workable command of French or German.

"French" Banks

Banque A. Tardy & M. Baezner, S.A.
6, place de l'Université   or: Case postale
1211 Geneva, Switzerland   1211 Geneva 4, Switzerland

Private bank, est. 1914.

Only activity is the management of funds, *(la gestion de fortunes)*, operating on instructions of client. Requires waiver of secrecy from U.S. citizens.

Caisse d'Epargne et de Prévoyance de Lausanne
1, galeries Benjamin-Constant or: Case postale 670
1002 Lausanne, Switzerland   1002 Lausanne, Switzerland

Savings bank, est. 1817.

Savings books: 5¼ percent int., name or bearer form, withdrawals to SFr 1,000 monthly.

Banque Cantonale Neuchâteloise
4, place Pury
2001 Neuchâtel, Switzerland

Cantonal bank, est, 1883.

Ordinary savings account: 5 percent int., withdrawals to SFr 5,000 monthly. *Placement savings account:* 6 percent int., to SFr 20,000; 5½ percent int. over SFr 20,000. Withdrawals to SFr 5,000 yearly. *Cash bonds:* 6½ percent for three- and four-year terms, 7 percent for five to eight years.

Piguet & Cie.
14, rue de la Plaine
1400 Yverdon, Vaud, Switzerland

Private bank, est. 1856. Yverdon, industrial town and trading center, forty-five miles southwest of Bern.

Places client's funds to earn interest. Also: brokerage and safe-keeping services, portfolio management, other banking services.

"German" Banks

Volksbank in Schüpfheim
Dorfstrasse 81
CH-6170 Schüpfheim, Switzerland

Commercial bank, est. 1927. Schupfheim is small town near Lucerne, forty-eight miles southwest of Zurich.

Savings deposit accounts: 4 percent int. *Deposit books:* 5¼ percent int., three months' notice. *Investment books:* 6 percent int., one-year notice. *Cash bonds:* 6¾ percent for three to four years, 7 percent for five or six years, 7¼ percent for seven- and eight-year terms.

Bank in Niederuzwil
Ch-9244 Niederuzwil, Switzerland

Savings bank, est. 1858. Niederuzwil, in Sankt Gallen canton, thirty-four miles east of Zurich.

Private accounts: 5 percent int., withdrawals to SFr 20,000 monthly. *Savings books:* 5 percent int., withdrawals to SFr 5,000 monthly. *Investment books:* 6 percent int., withdrawals to SFr 10,000 yearly. *Cash bonds:* 6¾ to 7¼ percent, three-to eight-year terms. Also offers: youth savings accounts.

Basellandschaftliche Hypothekenbank
Rheinstrasse 8
4410 Liestal, Switzerland

Mortgage bank, est 1849.

Savings accounts: 5 percent int., withdrawals to SFr 15,000 per month. *Deposit accounts:* 5½ percent int., withdrawals to SFr 5,000 monthly. *Cash bonds:* 6¾ percent to 7¼ percent, three-to six-year terms. Also offers: *Zinspramien,* under certain conditions; youth savings accounts *(Jugend-Sparheft).*

Kantonalbank Schwyz
Bahnhofstrasse 3
6430 Schwyz, Switzerland

Cantonal bank, est. 1890.

Current accounts. Savings books: 5 percent int., withdrawals to SFr 10,000 monthly. Name and bearer accounts available. Minimums—SFr 10 for name, SFr 500 for bearer. *Youth savings books:* 6 percent int., withdrawals to SFr 1,000 yearly. *Cash bonds:* 6½ percent for three- and four-year terms, 7 percent for five to eight years. SFr 1,000 minimum. Also offers: securities transactions and full gold services. *Special note:* issues informative German-language pamphlets on available securities and gold.

Urner Kantonalbank
Hauptplatz
6460 Altdorf-Uri,   or: Postfach 52556
Switzerland   6460 Altdorf-Uri, Switzerland

Cantonal bank, est. 1915. Altdorf, cantonal seat of Uri, about thirty-seven miles south of Zurich.

Savings accounts: 5 percent int., name or bearer accounts available.

Schaffhauser Kantonalbank
Vorstadt 53
8201 Schaffhausen,   or: Postfach 1843
Switzerland   8201 Schaffhausen, Switzerland

Cantonal bank, est. 1883.

Current accounts. Savings books: 5 percent int., withdrawals to SFr 5,000 monthly. *Investment accounts:* 6 percent int., withdrawals to SFr 5,000 yearly. Also offers: gold and gold coins, securities, Euromarket time deposits, investment advice.

Nidwaldner Kantonalbank
6370 Stans, Switzerland

Cantonal bank, est. 1879.

Current accounts. Savings books: 5 percent int., withdrawals to SFr 3,000 monthly. *Deposit books:* three distinct types, 5¼ percent to 6 percent, depending on restrictions. *Cash bonds:* 6½ percent for eight-year term.

Amtsersparniskasse Burgdorf
Technikumstrasse 2
3400 Burgdorf, Switzerland

Savings bank, est. 1834. Burgdorf, in canton of Bern, thirteen miles northeast of city of Bern.

Savings accounts: 5 percent int., withdrawals to SFr 10,000 monthly. *Savings books:* 6 percent int., withdrawals to SFr 5,000 yearly. *Youth savings accounts:* 6 percent int., withdrawals to SFr 2,000 annually. *Cash bonds:* 6¾ percent for three and four years, 7¼ percent for five and six years.

Esparnisanstalt der Stadt Sankt Gallen
Gallusstrasse 14
9001 Sankt Gallen, Switzerland

Savings bank, est. 1811.

Deposit accounts: 4½ percent int., withdrawals to SFr 10,000 monthly. *Savings accounts:* 5 percent int., withdrawals to SFr 2,000 bimonthly. *Investment accounts:* 6 percent int., withdrawals to SFr 5,000 yearly. Also offers: youth savings accounts and cash bonds.

Spar + Leihkasse Belp
Dorfstrasse 55   or: Postfach Nr. 4
3123 Belp, Switzerland   3123 Belp, Switzerland

Savings and loan bank, est. 1906. Belp is suburb of Bern, five miles south of center of city.

Offers all usual savings accounts and bonds. *Special note:* issues leaflet that describes all accounts; however, when querying ask specifically for interest rates since they are not printed in leaflet.

11

Liechtenstein Trusts and Other Services

Swiss banks are one-stop financial shopping centers. They are able to provide services to their customers that are unusual by American banking standards. To Americans, banks are primarily institutions that accept deposits and make loans. We look to other specialists to set up investment programs, to gain advice on estate and tax matters, or to buy securities. The Swiss expect their bankers to handle most of their financial needs.

The largest banks offer the widest variety of specialized services to their depositors. Nevertheless, smaller Swiss banks provide a wide range of what we might consider "special services" to their local customers. At big banks or small, most of these services are also available to their overseas depositors.

Usually, if a bank is interested in selling certain services, they will be described in the material sent a prospective depositor. If in doubt as to whether your bank is active in areas that interest you, write and ask for a clarification.

Securities brokerage

It usually surprises Americans to learn that Swiss banks handle the purchase and sale of securities for their depositors. In the United States, such activities are the exclusive domain of specialized brokerage firms. Once upon a time, American banks were involved in the securities business, too. But, in 1933, as part of Roosevelt's restructuring of the financial community, commercial banking was separated from investment banking. Investment banks were no longer allowed to accept deposits, and commercial banks gave up their underwriting and brokerage business.

In Switzerland, banks dominate the securities industry. Not only do they buy and sell stocks, but many banks are members of the stock exchange, or *Börse,* in their own right.

There is no federal regulation of stock exchanges in Switzerland. Three exchanges, in Zurich, Basel, and Geneva, are regulated by the cantonal authorities. Zurich's Börse is the largest and most active. Five smaller exchanges, in Saint Gallen, Lausanne, Bern, Chur, and Neuchâtel operate privately.

Swiss banks can easily handle transactions in almost any security regularly traded in the Western world. American, Canadian, and European securities are listed on the Zurich exchange along with Swiss issues. The American issues are primarily those of blue chip companies, whose shares are in international demand; Xerox, IBM, General Electric, AT&T, and Eastman Kodak are typical. Such non-Swiss shares are sponsored on the Swiss exchanges by the Big Three banks, or by an association of Geneva banks, in whose names the shares are registered on the corporations' books. The stock certificates are endorsed in blank, and then traded in bearer form.

Other American and European securities, not listed on Swiss exchanges, are also available through Swiss banks. Many of the larger American brokerage houses maintain branches in Zurich and Geneva whose business consists mainly of executing transactions on behalf of Swiss banking houses. There is also a large internal over-the-counter market in Swiss securities, handled largely by telephone between the banks.

Commissions on Swiss exchanges are low by American standards. As of 1972, a uniform commission schedule allowed charges of ⅝ of 1 percent on shares selling above SFr 150, 1 percent on those below SFr 150, ⅜ of 1 percent on Swiss bonds, and ½ of 1 percent on foreign bonds. There are also

Swiss federal and cantonal transfer taxes and stamps on each transaction; these transfer charges run SFr 0.30 per SFr 1,000 on Swiss securities, and SFr 0.65 per SFr 1,000 on foreign issues.

For foreign securities not listed on a Swiss exchange, the total commissions and charges are somewhat higher. To buy an American stock, for example, the customer must pay charges that include the regular commission to an American brokerage house, and a service charge to the Swiss bank. Buying most American stocks, those not listed on a Swiss exchange, through a Swiss bank will cost one and a half to two times the usual American commission rates. If an American depositor uses a Swiss bank for this purpose, he should have the bank explain all the costs involved.

Swiss banks, because of the strict requirements of secrecy, complete all securities transactions in their own name, not the customer's. Bonds or shares, if registered, will be carried on the issuing company's stockholder register only in the name of the Swiss bank handling the transaction.

Most Swiss securities, however, are not registered in the shareholders' names. The most common type of stock certificate is the "bearer" share, or *Inhaberaktie*. Bearer shares are like cash; possession is presumed ownership. The issuing corporation does not maintain a register of shareholders. Bearer shares can be voted, but the owner/bearer must take the initiative; he will not receive notices of annual meetings and the like because the issuing company doesn't know who its true shareholders are.

Some companies issue registered shares, called *Namensaktien* in German. This is a relatively new custom, dating back to the Second World War. At that time, Swiss companies were under pressure from the belligerent nations to prove that their shareholders were actually Swiss. Registering shareholders was a reluctant solution to this problem. Some companies will only allow Swiss residents to purchase their registered shares.

Partizipationsschein, or participation certificates, are another unique type of security. Dividends are paid, but the holder has no voting rights; foreigners are allowed to own them, since they are usually used to limit outside control.

Some Swiss companies issue two or more types of these securities. The Swiss value anonymity so highly that often the bearer shares sell at a premium over the other available types of shares in a company. Bearer certificates, as issued in Switzerland, resemble bond certificates. Coupons are attached, which must be clipped and presented to collect dividends. On registered shares, dividend payments are usually remitted directly to the registered owner.

One of the difficulties of trading in Swiss securities is in obtaining quotations. Listings of ten to twenty "selected issues" from the Zurich exchange are carried in *The New York Times* and the *Wall Street Journal*. For comprehensive listings it is necessary to see the *Neue Züricher Zeitung*, Zurich's daily newspaper. This is a German-language newspaper, but the stock market quotations should be understandable to anyone with a little effort.

Generally a foreign investor will have to depend on his Swiss bank for quotes, and for execution at the best price. A few Swiss banks provide lists of recommended stocks; *Kantonalbank Schwyz*, for one, periodically issues a pamphlet, entitled "Kursliste und Mitteilungen," which lists popular stocks, *Aktien*, and bonds, *Obligationen*, traded in Switzerland.

Securities may be bought on margin through a Swiss bank; the customary margin requirement is 50 percent. In the past, many American traders have used Swiss banks to avoid the generally higher SEC margin requirements. If your stock drops, the Swiss bank will not issue a call for extra margin, as is American custom, unless special arrangements have been made beforehand. Because the bank has the shares in bearer form, this is time-consuming and unnecessary; the bank will simply sell the stock to avoid further loss.

Most transactions on Swiss exchanges are spot or cash deals; these transactions are similar to American practice, i.e., transfer and payment are completed quickly. A large portion of Swiss stock transactions, however, are "forward" deals. This is basically a sort of option arrangement. The buyer pays a variable premium, called a *dont* by the Swiss, to delay completion of the purchase until "settlement day," four trading days before the end of each month. The buyer can choose between settling at the end of the current month, or at the end of the next month. On settlement day, the purchaser must decide to take the stock or to abandon his claim to it, losing only his premium. His decision, of course, is based on price movement in the interim. A down payment of at least half the total transaction is expected at the start of a forward deal; payment of the balance is made on settlement day, if the stock is taken.

Although Swiss banks can handle almost any sort of securities transactions for a depositor, there are practical limitations. Because of the six-hour difference in time zones between New York and Zurich and because of language and other communications problems, Swiss banks are not geared to the quick in-and-out trader who does not live in Switzerland. Swiss banks are better suited to the individual investing for the long term; they are ideal for the investor who utilizes their expertise to build a diversified international portfolio.

Securities safekeeping

The predominance of bearer certificates and the custom of handling stock transactions in the bank's name causes complications in the storage and administration of securities. Foreign investors find it impractical to take physical possession of their stock certificates. As a result, Swiss banks provide for the safe storage and routine paperwork connected with their customers' securities. This is usually described in their English literature as "safekeeping services" or "portfolio administration." In German it is called *Aufbewährung von Wertschriften* (safekeeping of securities), or *Wertschriften-Verwaltung* (securities administration). Banks in French-speaking areas call the service *Garde de titres.*

Under this type of arrangement, the bank keeps the certificates in its vaults and handles all the detail work. The customer makes his own investment decisions. Bank employees clip coupons, and collect stock dividends or bond interest as they become due. The bank also notifies customers when matters such as rights to new issues arise. Both stock dividends and bond interest payments on Swiss securities are liable to the same 30-percent withholding tax as interest from savings accounts; these taxes are also handled by the bank. Periodic statements of the customer's holding are provided as part of this service.

Customers utilizing a bank's safekeeping services must also maintain a regular bank account with the bank. Dividends, costs of purchases, proceeds from sales, and commissions or fees for services are all run through this base account. Many banks will also handle securities transactions and perform custodial services on a numbered account basis.

Fees charged for securities administration services vary but are always reasonable. One bank quotes a charge of SFr 1.25

per year for administration of SFr 1,000 worth of securities, with a minimum fee of SFr 20 per year. Charges for this service through a numbered-account arrangement run slightly higher, the same bank charging SFr 1.50 per SFr 1,000. Another bank quotes $\frac{2}{10}$ of 1 percent as its charge, with SFr 200 the minimum annual charge. For purposes of determining safekeeping charges, stocks are valued at market, and bonds at face value.

Discretionary accounts

Swiss banks will also undertake full management of a customer's investments. Americans commonly call this service "portfolio management." Swiss banks describe it as *Vermögensverwaltung* in German, or *Gestion de fortunes* in French. Under such an arrangement, the bank makes the investment decisions, buying and selling as it sees fit.

Full portfolio management is a specialty of the private banks, although many other banks offer this service. Substantial minimum funds are usually required for a discretionary account. A few banks will undertake management of sums as small as $25,000, but more typically at least $100,000 is expected.

Some banks charge a separate fee for account management, others do not. One foreign-controlled commercial bank quotes a management fee of $\frac{1}{10}$ of 1 percent over its safekeeping fee of $\frac{1}{10}$ of 1 percent, with a minimum charge of SFr 300 annually for a fully managed account. The banks that do not charge formal management fees generally expect the investment fund to be of sufficient size to generate worthwhile brokerage commissions. Again, a base account is a necessary adjunct; some banks will also handle discretionary accounts on a numbered basis.

Many of the banks, especially the private ones, who specialize in discretionary management of investments like to meet personally with their customers. This makes sense to both parties; investment goals can be agreed upon, the customer can be familiarized with the bank's procedures, and mutual confidence can be established.

A personal meeting to establish rapport is certainly recommended. One reason is that Swiss bankers think differently. Less salesmanship seems to be involved. An investment manager in this country generally makes an effort to explain or at least justify his decisions to his clients. Most Swiss bankers traditionally take a different view; once a customer grants management powers to his bank, they are often reluctant to explain the decisions made under that authority. There are exceptions, of course. Many Swiss bank officers, in private banks and elsewhere, have received part of their business education in an American graduate school, and are more attuned to the psychology of American investors.

Discretionary management accounts are obviously not for everyone. They are probably advantageous only to Americans who lack the time or expertise to manage their own investments, or to those who want large sums handled professionally, conservatively, and, for whatever reason, in complete secrecy.

It is not necessary to open a discretionary account to take advantage of your banker's investment advice. Any bank will generally offer specific recommendations upon request of a depositor. An investor can then make his own decisions, have the bank execute the transactions, and handle the paperwork under a regular safekeeping arrangement.

Mutual funds

Switzerland has mutual funds, although the Swiss usually describe them in English as "investment trusts" or "investment funds." *Anlagefonds* is the German word for "investment funds" and is used to describe all types of mutual funds. Most Swiss funds invest their assets in securities; these are called *Wertschriftenfonds* (securities funds). Real estate investment funds are called *Immobilien-Anlagefonds* in German.

Over one hundred different funds are based in Switzerland and are available through Swiss banks. Some concentrate their investments in Swiss securities or real estate, while others have an international portfolio. All are sponsored by Swiss banks and are managed by the banks or by bank-organized management companies.

As in the United States, the appeal of mutual funds is mainly to investors with limited capital who, nevertheless, seek to diversify their investments. There are Swiss funds designed to generate income, others geared to capital growth. In addition, some Swiss banks offer American mutual funds. Swiss banks can also buy shares for investors in other European funds, such as the Dutch Robeco investment trust, or in the bank-run funds of West Germany.

An investor considering mutual funds will probably have to rely on the advice of his Swiss bank. He should bear in mind that, if the bank sponsors a mutual fund, it will tend to recommend that fund. However, advice can be solicited from two or more banks, if desired, before making a decision.

Liechtenstein trusts

The Principality of Liechtenstein, *Fürstentum Liechtenstein* in German, is a tiny country nestled in the upper Rhine valley between Switzerland and Austria. Liechtenstein has only eleven villages, an area of sixty-five square miles, and some 22,000 inhabitants. Although it is politically independent with its own ruling prince and an elected legislature, Liechtenstein is associated with Switzerland in many ways. Their mutual boundary is open, and the two nations are joined in a customs union. Since 1921, the Swiss franc has been Liechtenstein's official currency.

Liechtenstein's importance to the world lies mainly in its unique "Company Law." This act, the *Personen-und Gessell-schaftsrecht* which dates from 1926, allows many types of companies to be formed. No special government permission is required to organize a Liechtenstein registered company, except to form a bank. Companies based in Liechtenstein and controlled by nonresidents pay no taxes on their earnings from abroad. Bank secrecy is as strict as in Switzerland, and Liechtenstein has no tax agreements with any nation except Austria. Because of these liberal practices, many thousands of companies have been founded and registered in Liechtenstein.

To most Americans, a "Liechtenstein Trust" is even more mysterious than a Swiss numbered account. Any sort of company based in Liechtenstein is generally refered to as a "trust" by our press. In actuality, trusts are only one of the many forms of organizations that can be created under Liechtenstein corporate law. The most important are corporations, establishments, foundations, and trusts, although several sorts of partnerships and cooperative associations are also possible.

An *Aktiengesellschaft*, or company limited by shares, is similar to a corporation as we know it, and is commonly abbreviated to *AG* in German. This form of organization is suitable when large amounts of capital are involved, when there are a number of shareholders, or when public participation is anticipated. At least SFr 50,000 capital is necessary, but an AG can be formed by a single shareholder. Ownership may be kept secret, if so desired; shares can be issued in bearer form or in registered form.

An "Establishment," or *Anstalt* in German, is perhaps the most flexible and interesting form of organization. Establishments are unique to Liechtenstein; they are normally non-share companies, with liability limited to their capital. A minimum capital of SFr 20,000 is required; these funds may be held in Liechtenstein or abroad. An Establishment can be formed by a private person, a legal person, such as a corporation, or a trustee. The legal life of an Establishment is unlimited. At a later date, if desired, an Anstalt can be converted from a nonshare company to a share company or even to a foundation merely by amending its articles of establishment.

Anstalts are often personal holding companies, but they can engage in almost any sort of business. Their objectives, as stated in their articles of establishment, are usually broadly written.

A Liechtenstein Establishment is much more flexible than a plain, numbered account. A numbered account can screen ownership of bank deposits or securities well enough, but becomes awkward when real estate, works of art, or other tangible property is involved.

Anstalts may be formed and controlled through Swiss banks. The first step in organizing a personal Liechtenstein Anstalt is to visit Switzerland and have a private meeting with an officer of a Swiss bank. After this discussion, the Swiss bank arranges with a Liechtenstein bank or lawyer to form and register the Establishment. A name must be chosen that includes the word "Anstalt," "Establishment," or the French "Etablissement." The name selected must be unique, and not duplicate any other firm name in the Public Register of Liechtenstein. The Swiss bank opens an account in the name of the new Establishment, and certifies to the Liechtenstein authorities that the minimum capital has been paid into this account.

The intermediary in Liechtenstein who acts as the official "founder" does not know the name of the real owner of the Establishment. This "founder" then transfers his rights to a "successor" with a "declaration of cession." The name of the successor is usually left blank on this document, which is kept by the Swiss bank in its vault. A board of directors for the Establishment is appointed, one of whom must be a Liechtenstein resident. There is no requirement as to the number of directors, but the Swiss bank will usually appoint one or two of its staff members as directors. This board has the duty of carrying out the instructions of the "successor" who now controls the Establishment.

In practice, only the Swiss bank officer who handled the details knows the identity of the person who controls the Liechtenstein Establishment. The controlling owner communicates his instructions to the bank officer, who handles the necessary transactions through the Swiss bank. With the exception of the confidential papers in the bank's vault, all the bank's records show only the firm-name of the Establishment. All property bought through the bank shows the Establishment as the legal owner. Confidentiality is further protected by the legal restrictions of Swiss bank secrecy.

A foundation, or *Stiftung*, is another common form of legal structure. It is usually used to conserve and administer a family fortune and to provide for members of the family. A Stiftung differs from an Establishment in that it has no owner. Assets are transferred to the foundation for a specific purpose and for certain designated beneficiaries. This type of foundation may be formed during the lifetime of the founder, or after his death by an endowment made in his will. It can be set up to be either irrevocable or revocable by the founder. A foundation board, appointed by the founder, controls the Stiftung. To maintain anonymity, an intermediary can be used to form the foundation. Minimum capital is again SFr 20,000.

There are two basic kinds of "trusts" under Liechtenstein law. One is called a *Treuhänderschaft*, the other a *Treuunternehmen*.

A *Treuhänderschaft* is a trusteeship, or a "trust settlement." Legal title to property is granted to a trustee who has the responsibility of administering the property for the benefit of one or more beneficiaries. The designated trustee may be an individual or a corporate body such as a bank. Under Liechtenstein law, the trust funds remain independent of other assets owned by the trustee. This type of Liechtenstein trust is popular in Europe because in other countries, such as Switzerland or France, trust funds may be endangered by claims against a trustee's other assets. Also, once a trust is established, trust funds are legally beyond the reach of any creditors of the principal who established the trust. A trust settlement can be set up in ways that keep the founder's identity and the financial details secret.

A *Treuunternehmen* is a "trust undertaking." This type of trust is notable because of the various ways it can be organized. Basically, a Treuunternehmen is an independent enterprise, functioning in its own name under the supervision of one or more trustees. Liabilities are limited to its funds. It can function as a business trust, a family trust, or a holding company, depending on how the articles of organization are drafted. Again, it can be anonymously created. Minimum capital for both types of trusts is SFr 20,000.

A Liechtenstein Anstalt, Aktiengesellschaft, Stiftung, or trust can provide a tax-free haven and a secret financial operating base. However, because of the costs involved in creating and administering such a company or trust, over $100,000 is needed to make it worthwhile. While there is no tax on foreign income, there are stamp duties, registration fees, annual capital taxes, and fees to be paid both to the Swiss bank and to its Liechtenstein agent. As an example, an Anstalt must pay a registration fee of SFr 250, and a stamp duty of 2 percent of capital (SFr 400 on the minimum SFr 20,000) when formed. Bank charges vary, but one bank quotes SFr 4,500 as an initial charge. An Anstalt also pays an annual tax of $\frac{1}{10}$ of 1 percent on capital, with a minimum of SFr 1,000. This is paid in advance, on registration, and annually thereafter. The Swiss bank will also collect an annual fee for "representation." It will therefore cost about $2,500 to organize an Anstalt, and about $1,200 each year to maintain one. To be practical, the potential benefits of using Liechtenstein as a secret base must outweigh the costs of administration.

Many Swiss banks provide service in this area, although they seldom advertise it. If a bank offers "trustee services," or "formation of foreign companies" in its literature, this is a definite clue. Companies and trusts can also be organized directly through a Liechtenstein bank, but this approach does not provide the double screen of privacy created by operating a Liechtenstein haven through a Swiss bank.

Liechtenstein corporate law is a specialty unto itself, a legal mirror-maze comprehensible only to the most dedicated student. Forming a Liechtenstein trust is not something to be done by mail. At a bare minimum, a visit to Switzerland and a consultation with a knowledgeable bank officer is essential. Because of the wide variety of possible legal structures, it would seem advisable to have a fairly frank discussion of the planned uses of the projected Liechtenstein entity; only in this way can the most efficient legal setup be arranged.

Booklets in English that describe the various forms of Liechtenstein companies are available from the banks listed below. The material they provide is generally heavy reading, more suitable for a lawyer than a layman, but useful as an introduction to the topic:

Société Bancaire Barclays (Suisse), S.A.
6, place de la Synagogue
1211 Geneva 11, Switzerland

Verwaltungs-und Privat-Bank, AG
Postfach 34672
FL-9490 Vaduz, Liechtenstein

Liechtensteinische Landesbank
Stadtle 44
FL-9490 Vaduz, Liechtenstein

Bank in Liechtenstein, AG
FL-9490 Vaduz, Liechtenstein

A Liechtenstein arrangement is equivalent to being financially "invisible." No one really knows what sort of financial maneuvers are made from behind Liechtenstein screens; the successful strategems remain anonymous forever.

Swiss corporations

Many of the larger Swiss banks are also equipped to help form Swiss corporations. Because of its central location in Europe, its stable government, its free exchange regulations, and the highly developed banking system, Switzerland has become a favored location for holding companies and for European headquarters of firms doing business internationally.

Corporate laws vary from canton to canton. Some cantons, such as Zug and Chur, are noted for their accommodating laws; they are centers for corporate registration in much the same way that Delaware is in the United States. Most commercial banks will be able to help a customer find the best canton for his purposes and to handle the details of corporate creation. If need be, a banker can also introduce a depositor to a Swiss lawyer or accounting firm.

Safe-deposit boxes

Safe-deposit boxes are called *Tresorfächern* in German and *coffres-forts* in French. This service is the same in Switzerland as it is in this country. Normally, safe-deposit facilities are of little interest to a mail depositor. In special situations, however, if periodic visits to Switzerland were made, such a box could be used for long-term storage of valuables. Boxes are normally rented by the year, with a small box renting for perhaps SFr 40 annually. A box may also be taken for shorter terms, perhaps to store important papers temporarily while traveling in Europe.

Gold

In Switzerland, private ownership of gold is not only legal, but respectable. There are no restrictions on owning or trading gold, or on transferring gold in or out of the country.

Such Swiss attitudes have helped to make Zurich one of the most important gold markets in a world where many governments fear gold in the hands of their citizens. One of the major tourist attractions of Zurich is the Bahnhofstrasse, a street where gold bullion and gold coins are displayed in the windows of bank after bank.

Gold coins and gold bars are sold to all comers at Swiss bank counters. The larger banks offer every variety of gold coin imaginable; most banks are able to provide the more common coins. Bullion is usually offered in metric bars, from ten grams to a kilogram. The larger banks with their own gold refineries can provide gold in more exotic measures, such as the *tael* of Southeast Asia, or the *tola* of India.

Many Swiss banks offer special gold accounts to their customers. Under this arrangement, the more popular coins, such as $20 gold pieces, British sovereigns, or Austrian 100 coronas, are available for minimum investments of $1,000 or more. Bullion is also available, in either metric or ounce measures, with ten ounces as a typical minimum buy. For this sort of "gold account," the bank holds the gold in its vaults, charging about $^{15}/_{100}$ of 1 percent annually for insurance and storage. There is also a brokerage fee of about $^{3}/_{8}$ of 1 percent on bullion purchases and sales. Bullion stored by the bank may be resold without an assay charge.

Gold coins can also be bought on margin, generally 50 percent or so. Futures are also available through Swiss banks; a Swiss gold contract is usually for fifty kilograms, or 1,607 ounces. Margin requirement is about 20 percent, with commission ⅜ of 1 percent per contract.

Gold ownership became legal again for Americans at the end of 1974. Before legalization, however, there were apparently many U.S. citizens who owned gold through a Swiss bank. Though gold is now readily available in the United States, there remain certain advantages to Swiss gold. The most important, of course, are privacy and security. Some Americans will always prefer to acquire their gold through a Swiss bank, and to leave it in the bank's safekeeping.

Other services

Established customers will often find Swiss banks willing to serve in ways not normally described in a bank's promotional literature. Introductions and discreet inquiries are examples. A letter of introduction from a Swiss bank to a correspondent bank in another part of the world can be a useful tool. Please note, however, that a Swiss banker's introduction carries weight precisely because such letters are not casually issued. A Swiss bank may also be able to use its international network of contacts to explore commercial possibilities or third-party reputations on behalf of one of its substantial customers.

Swiss banks are not insurance brokers, but they might be willing to refer a depositor to a Swiss insurance agent. Life insurance policies are available from Swiss companies whose proceeds are payable in Swiss francs. A hard-currency policy such as this is a valuable hedge against the future. Arrangements often can be made with the bank for automatic payment from the depositor's Swiss franc account of the premiums on such a policy.

Swiss banks are not real estate brokers either, but they can often assist in overseas realty transactions. Payments for a second home in Ireland or a condominium in Spain could be made through a Swiss account. The bank may be able to help find mortgage money for a foreign property, either through a Swiss mortgage institution or through a source in the country where the property is located.

In general, a Swiss bank is always a good place to start if help in foreign financial matters is needed. Its services are so diverse, and its international connections so broad, that the chances are good it can be of some assistance. If a bank cannot handle the problem directly, it can often act as a source of referrals to other institutions. At the very least, a depositor can expect sound financial advice.